Hermetic Papers of A.E. Waite

By the same author

THE GOLDEN DAWN COMPANION
THE GOLDEN DAWN: TWILIGHT OF THE MAGICIANS
THE TREASURE OF MONTSEGUR (with Walter Birks)

Also in this series

THE ALCHEMIST OF THE GOLDEN DAWN: Letters of W. A. Ayton to F. L. Gardner
Edited by Ellic Howe

THE MAGICAL MASON: Hermetic Writings of W. Wynn Westcott
Edited by R. A. Gilbert

THE ROSICRUCIAN SEER: The Magical Work of Frederick Hockley
Edited by John Hamill

THE SORCERER AND HIS APPRENTICE: Hermetic Writings of S. L. MacGregor Mathers and J. W. Brodie-Innes
Edited by R. A. Gilbert

Hermetic Papers of A.E. Waite
The Unknown Writings of a Modern Mystic
Edited by R.A. Gilbert

THE AQUARIAN PRESS
Wellingborough, Northamptonshire

First published 1987

© THE AQUARIAN PRESS 1987

All rights reserved. No part of this book may be reproduced or utilized in any form or by any means, electronic or mechanical, including photocopying, recording or by information and retrieval system, without permission in writing from the Publisher.

British Library Cataloguing in Publication Data
Waite, Arthur Edward
The hermetic papers of A. E. Waite
  1 Hermetism
 I. Title   II. Gilbert, R. A.
  299'.93   BL820.M5
ISBN 0-85030-437-7

The Aquarian Press is part of the Thorsons Publishing Group
Printed and bound in Great Britain

CONTENTS

	Page
Introduction	7

Chapter

1	What is Alchemy?	13
2	On the Esoteric Literature of the Middle Ages	41
3	Haunts of the English Mystics: Robert Fludd and John Dee	58
4	Thomas Vaughan and his *Lumen de Lumine*	68
5	A Hermetic Apocalypse	91
6	Kabalistic Alchemy	99
7	The Hermetic and Rosicrucian Mystery	120
8	Report to the Convocation of the Independent and Rectified Rite, R.R. et A.C.	137
9	An Address to Neophytes	145
10	The Allocution of the 5=6 Grade	150
11	The Symbol of the Rosy Cross	154
12	The Tarot and the Rosy Cross	161
13	Dionysius and Hierotheos	174
14	On Ceremonial Union	189
15	The Interior Life from the Standpoint of the Mystics	195
16	A Message of Saint-Martin	205
17	On Intimations Concerning the Interior Church in Schools of Christian Mysticism	215
18	The Viaticum of Daily Life	252

INTRODUCTION

EARLY in 1891, at the age of thirty-four years,[1] Arthur Edward Waite entered the Hermetic Order of the Golden Dawn, but Frater Sacramentum Regis, the Order's 99th initiate did not remain a member for long. By April 1892 Waite had attained the 4=7 Grade of Philosophus and also 'began to hear things which, in my several positions at the moment, told me that I should be well out of the whole concern'.[2] He added that 'it was not on the score of morality, seeing that there were *Fratres et Sorores*; for on this ground it is just to say that no breath of scandal ever arose in the G∴D∴ during all that period'. Indeed, so innocuous did the the Order seem that Waite encouraged his wife, Ada Lakeman, to join—although Soror Lumen Christi attended no meetings after her initiation in December 1891, and even then she was 'tempted to hold up the whole galanty-show, in order to win her retreat'. Waite's reason for leaving the Golden Dawn was rather 'a question of things which had an equivocal legal aspect and in which leading Members of the Order should not have been concerned'; more probably he was disenchanted with what he found within the Order for his own knowledge of 'Occult Science and ... the Mysteries of Life and Death, and our Environment'[3] was as great or greater than that of the Order's

---

[1] Waite was born on 2 October 1857 at Brooklyn, New York. At the age of two years his mother brought him, with his sister, to England and the remainder of his life was spent in London and in Kent. He died at Bridge, near Canterbury, on 19 May 1942.
[2] *Shadows of Life and Thought*, p. 126. Waite was wary of financial scandal: he was involved with the Joint Stock Institute and other creations of the dubious financier Horation Bottomley, although in an editorial, not a promotional capacity.
[3] The objects of the Golden Dawns concern, according to the Pledge Form.

founders and of most of his fellow members.

But leaving the Order did not dampen Waite's enthusiasm for its chosen pursuits. Between 1893 (when he 'demitted') and 1896 (when he rejoined the Order) Waite issued eight translations of alchemical texts, published *Azoth: or, The Star in the East*—his first study of alchemy—and edited *The Unknown World*. This 'magazine devoted to the Occult Sciences, Magic, Mystical Philosophy, Alchemy, Hermetic Archaeology, and the Hidden Problems of Science Literature, Speculation, and History' was Waite's brainchild. Designed effectively to appeal to Theosophists concerned with the Western Tradition, and thus to virtually every member of the Golden Dawn, it was launched in August 1894, with Waite acting as editor and providing a fair proportion of the contents of the eleven issues that appeared.

The magazine failed from a lack of financial support and presaged the collapse, in 1896, of the publishing house of James Elliott which Waite had funded. With these troubles looming on his horizon, Waite turned again to the Golden Dawn and was 'readmitted by Ballot on 17 February 1896'. He was probably encouraged to rejoin by Dr Berridge—the homoeopathic physician so detested by Annie Horniman—who had been a regular contributor to *The Unknown World* and who, in his role as 'Resurgam, RR et AC'. had heaped lavish praise upon Waite for his translation of *The Hermetic Museum*. Waite's own account of his readmission is inaccurate; Robert Palmer-Thomas, whom Waite says played a major role in bringing him back within the fold, could have had no part in it as he did not join the Order himself until November 1896, nine months after Waite's readmission.

Whatever the circumstances and whatever his motives for rejoining, Waite immediately emulated Brer Fox and 'lay low and said nuthin' ', concentrating instead on his literary career. In this he earned Westcott's gratitude for his defence of the Societas Rosicruciana in Anglia in *Devil-Worship in France* (his exposé of the Leo Taxil fraud), and the appreciation of the whole Order for his translation of Eliphas Lévi's classic work, as *Transcendental Magic, its Doctrine and Ritual*. He also began work on his first study of Jewish mysticism, *The Doctrine and Literature of the Kabalah*, which was finally published in 1902.

Eventually, in March 1899, he entered the Second Order, and it was this step that Palmer-Thomas probably urged Waite to take (he had himself reached the 5=6 Grade of Adeptus Minor in April 1898), for Waite says that after his readmission 'I got possession of secret scripts which were never shewn to anyone, and I saw that another construction could be placed upon their "cipher" schemes'. This can only refer to Second Order manuscripts.

He adds that 'In the end the scripts themselves had to be abandoned; another gate was opening, for myself alone at the time, into a world of highest *Theosophia*. The gate would in time open for many others, for the doctrine of the Secret Tradition that he was beginning to develop appealed to many within the Golden Dawn, and when in 1903 the 'Third Annual Meeting dissolved in chaos', and Waite proposed 'that those who regarded the Golden Dawn as capable of a mystical instead of an occult construction should and had indeed resolved to work independently, going their own way', a substantial proportion of the Second Order Adepti followed him into the Independent and Rectified Rite.

These were Adepts for whom magic had no appeal and who sought instead that mystical Union with God that was for Waite the final goal of man. It was a goal that could be approached by way of any one of the esoteric practices and traditions studied in the Second Order: correctly understood they were all secret paths to a direct experience of God.

As a result of his own studies Waite had concluded that the symbolism in each of these traditions—whether Alchemy, Kabalah, Freemasonry or Rosicrucianism—had a common root and a common end, and that their correct interpretation would lead to a revelation of concealed ways to spiritual illumination. This theory of a 'Secret Tradition' is implicit in all of Waite's mature works, but it is usually presented in an oblique and diffuse manner. It is, perhaps, expressed most clearly in *The Secret Tradition in Freemasonry*, where Waite says: 'The Secret Tradition contains, firstly, the memorials of a loss which has befallen humanity; and, secondly, the records of a restitution in respect of that which was lost . . . the keepers of the tradition perpetuated it in secret by means of Instituted Mysteries and cryptic literature' (Vol. 1, p. ix). In itself, 'The Secret Tradition is the immemorial knowledge concerning man's way of return whence he came by a method of the inward life' (Vol. 2 p.379). Common to all its forms is the evidence that 'testifies to (a) the aeonian anture of the loss; (b) the certitude of an ultimate restoration; (c) in respect of that which was lost, the perpetuity of its existence somewhere in time and the world, although interned deeply; (d) and more rarely its substantial presence under veils close to the hands of all. '(Vol. 1, p. xi).

His most detailed public exposition of this doctrine is found in his profound study of mystical experience, *The Way of Divine Union* (1915), and in the concluding chapters of his autobiography, *Shadows of Life and Thought* (1938), but it was expressed both more directly and more personally in the dramatic rituals he developed for the Independent and Rectified Rite and, after the final dissolution of the Isis-Urania Temple in 1914, for his Fellowship of the Rosy Cross. He did not, however, intend these rituals to be treated in isolation: the Allocutions that formed a part of the ceremonies, the Addresses to the Grades, and the regular Reports to the Order, all contained expositions of his doctrines both implicitly and explicitly. And while these were necessarily confined to Order members, the historical accounts of the varied strands that make up the Secret Tradition and the critical analyses of the primary texts that were alike essential for a full understanding of Waite's ideas could be, and were, made public.

Much of his published work is well known, but the major works on the Secret Tradition all appeared in their final forms long after the Golden Dawn had ceased to be. More significant for the members of the Order were the papers he contributed to such journals as *The Unknown World, The Occult Review*, and *The Seeker*—all now virtually unobtainable. It is from these, from the private papers of the Independent and Rectified Rite, and from Introductions that he wrote for alchemical, mystical and hermetic tests that the present collection of Waite's papers has been selected.

Although none of these papers can be truly said to lie behind the Golden Dawn—which was founded before even the earliest of them was written—they yet encapsulate the ethos of the Order and illustrate fully the unique contribution that Waite made to it. Seeing in the Adeptus Minor ritual 'the root-matter of a greater scheme than had ever dawned in the consciousness of any maker of Masonic Degrees under any Grand Lodge or Chapter, Conclave or Preceptory, in the whole wide world', Waite took it up and transformed it into something Westcott, Woodman, and Mathers had never dreamed of. He taught the members of his Independent and Rectified Rite to pursue their spiritual quest not by rejecting reason but by retaining it. In this way he raised the Golden Dawn to a level far removed from either the inane credulities of Felkin's *Stella Matutina* or the unbalanced magical obsessions of Mathers's followers. It is this harmony between scholarship and spirituality that gives to Waite's Hermetic Papers their lasting value.

R. A. GILBERT.

1
WHAT IS ALCHEMY?

First Paper

[First printed in the monthly journal *The Unknown World* from August to December 1894 and in April,1895. It was reprinted in *The Alchemical Papers of Arthur Edward Waite*, ed. J. Ray Shute, Monroe, N. C., 1939, a privately printed collection limited to seventy copies.]

In his earlier writings on alchemy Waite maintained that the spiritual interpretation of alchemy was first systematically presented by Mrs Atwood in her *Suggestive Inquiry into the Hermetic Mystery*—a point of view that he was later to reject completely, to the extent of saying that the book 'is not, however, final or satisfactory as a critical study, indeed, in some respects it is a morass rather than a pathway' (*The Secret Tradition in Freemasonry*, 1911, Vol.2, p. 415). For this he was taken to task, in the pages of the *Occult Review*, by Isabelle de Steiger; but he justified himself by stating that 'What I said of the *Suggestive Enquiry* in 1888 and 1893 was in the light of my knowledge at those dates; that which I have recorded since has been under a fuller and clearer light' (*Occult Review*, Vol. 15, No.1. January 1912, p. 50). Nonetheless, his early essays on alchemy retain their value for the obscure information they contain and for their critical comments on Madame Blavatsky's dubious manipulation of her source material on alchemy.

THERE are certain writers at the present day, and there are certain students of the subject, perhaps too wise to write, who would readily, and do, affirm that any answer to the question which heads this paper will involve, if adequate, an answer to those other and seemingly harder problems—What is Mysticism? What is the Transcendental Philosophy? What is Magic? What Occult Science? What the Hermetic Wisdom? For they would affirm that Alchemy includes all these, and so far at least as the world which lies west of Alexandria is concerned, it is the head and crown of all. Now in this statement the central canon of a whole body of esoteric criticism is contained in the proverbial nutshell, and this criticism is in itself so important, and embodies so astounding an interpretation of a literature which is so mysterious, that in any consideration of Hermetic literature it must be reckoned with from the beginning; otherwise the mystic student will at a later period be forced to go over his ground step by step for a second time, and that even from the starting point. It is proposed in the following papers to answer definitely by the help of the evidence which is to be found in the writings of the Alchemists, the question as to what Alchemy actually was and is. As in other subjects, so also in this, *The Unknown World* proposes to itself an investigation which has not been attempted hitherto along similar lines, since at the present day, even among the students of the occult, there are few persons sufficiently instructed for an enquiry which is not only most laborious in itself but is rendered additionally difficult from the necessity of expressing its result in a manner at once readable and intelligible to the reader who is not a specialist. In a word, it is required to popularise the conclusions arrived at by a singularly abstruse erudition. This is difficult—that will be admitted—but it can be done, and it is guaranteed to the readers of these papers that they need know nothing of the matter beforehand. After the little course has been completed it is believed that they will have acquired much, in fact, nothing short of a solution of the whole problem.

In the first place, let any unversed person cast about within himself, or within the miscellaneous circle of his non-mystical acquaintance, and decide what he and they do actually at the present moment understand by Alchemy. It is quite certain that the answer will be fairly representative of all general opinion, and, in effect it will be somewhat as follows: 'Alchemy is a pretended science or art by which the metals ignorantly called base, such as lead and iron, were supposed to be, but were never really, transmuted into the other metals as ignorantly called perfect, namely, gold and silver. The *ignis fatuus* of Alchemy was pursued by many persons—indeed, by thousands—in the past, and though they did not succeed in making gold or silver, they yet chanced in their investigations upon so many useful facts that they actually laid the foundations of chemistry as it is. For this reason it would perhaps be unjust to dishonour them; no doubt many of them were rank imposters, but not all; some were the chemists of their period.' It follows from this answer that this guesswork and these gropings of the past can have nothing but a historical interest in the present advanced state of chemical knowledge. It is, of course, absurd to have recourse to an exploded scientific literature for reliable information of any kind. Goldsmith and Pinnock in history, Joyce and Mangnall in general elementary science, would be preferable to the Alchemists in chemistry. If Alchemy be really included as a branch of occult wisdom, then so much the worse for the wisdom—*ex uno disce omnia*. The question what is Alchemy, is then easily answered from this standpoint—it is the dry bones of chemistry, as the Occult Sciences in general are the debris of ancient knowledge, and the dust from the ancient sanctuaries of long vanished religions—at which point these papers, and *The Unknown World* itself, would perforce come to a conclusion.

There is, however, another point of view, and that is the standpoint of the occultist. It will be pardonable perhaps to state it in an occult magazine. Now, what does the student of the Occult Sciences understand by Alchemy? Of two things, one, and let the second be reserved for the moment in the interests of that simplicity which the Alchemists themselves say is the seal of Nature and art—*sigillum Naturæ et artis simplicitas*. He understands the law of evolution applied by science to the development from a latent into an active condition of the essential properties of metallic and other substances. He does not understand that lead as lead or iron as iron can be transmuted into gold or silver. He affirms that there is a common basis of all the metals, that they are not really elements, and that they are resolvable. In this case, once their component parts are known the metals will be capable of manufacture, though whether by a prohibitively expensive process is another issue. Now, beyond contradiction this is a tolerable standpoint from the standpoint of modern science itself. Chemistry is still occasionally discovering new elements, and it is occasionally resolving old and so-called elements, and indeed, a common basis of all the elements is a thing that has been talked of by men whom no one would suspect of being Mystics, either in matters of physics or philosophy.

There is, however, one obviously vulnerable point about this defensive explanation of Alchemy. It is open to the test question: Can the occultist who propounds it resolve the metallic elements, and can he make gold? If not, he is talking hypothesis alone, tolerable perhaps in the bare field of speculation, but to little real purpose until it can be proved by the event. Now, *The Unknown World* has not been established to descant upon mere speculation or to expound dreams to its readers. It will not ignore speculation, but its chief object is to impart solid knowledge. Above all it desires to deal candidly on every subject. There are occultists at the present day who claim to have made gold. There are other occultists who claim to be in communication with those who possess the secret. About neither class is it necessary to say anything at present; claims which it is impossible to verify may be none the less good claims, but they are necessarily outside evidence. So far as can be known the occultist does not manufacture gold. At the same time his defence of Alchemy is not founded on merely hypothetical considerations. It rests on a solid basis, and that is alchemical literature and history. Here his position, whether unassailable or not, cannot be impugned by his opponents, and this for the plain reason that, so far as it is possible to gather, few of them know anything of the history and all are ignorant of the literature. He has therefore that right to speak which is given only by knowledge, and he has the further presumption in his favour that as regards archaic documents those who can give the sense can most likely explain the meaning. To put the matter as briefly as possible, the occultist finds in the great text-books of Alchemy an instruction which is virtually as old as Alchemy, namely, that the metals are composite substances. This instruction is accompanied by a claim which is, in effect, that the Alchemists had through their investigations become acquainted with a process which demonstrated by their resolution the alleged fact that metals are not of a simple nature. Furthermore, the claim itself is found side by side with a process which pretends to be practical, which is given furthermore in a detailed manner, for accomplishing the disintegration in question. Thus it would seem that in a supposed twilight of chemical science, in an apparently inchoate condition of physics, there were men in possession of a power with which the most advanced applied knowledge of this nineteenth century is not as yet equipped. This is the first point in defence of Alchemy which will be raised by the informed occultist. But, in the second place, there is another instruction to be found in these old text-books, and that is the instruction of development—the absolute recognition that in all natural substances there exist potentialities which can be developed by the art of a skilled physicist, and the method of this education is pretended to be imparted by the text-books, so that here again we find a doctrine, and connected with that doctrine a formal practice, which is not only in advance of the supposed science of the period but is actually a governing doctrine and a palmary source of illumination at the present day. Thirdly, the testimony of Alchemical literature to these two instructions, and to the processes which applied them, is not a casual, isolated, or conflicting testimony, nor again is it read into the literature by a specious method of interpretation; it is upon the face of the literature; amidst an extraordinary variety of formal difference, and amidst protean disguises of terminology, there is found the same radical teaching everywhere. In whatsoever age or country, the adepts on all ultimate matters never disagree—a point upon which they themselves frequently insist, regarding their singular unanimity as a proof of the truth of their art. So much as regards the literature of Alchemy, and from this the occultist would appeal to the history of the secret sciences for convincing evidence that, if evidence be anything, transmutations have taken place. He would appeal to the case of Glauber, to the case of Van Helmont, to the case of Lascaris and his disciples, to that also of Michael Sendivogius, and if his instances were limited to these it is not from a paucity of further testimony, but because the earlier examples, such as Raymond Lully, Nicholas Flamel, Bernard Trevisan, and Denis Zachaire, will be regarded as of less force and value in view of their more remote epoch. Having established these points, the occultist will proceed to affirm that they afford a sufficient warrant for the serious investigation of Alchemical literature with the object of discovering the actual process followed by the old adepts for the attainment of their singular purpose. He will frankly confess that this process still remains to be understood, because it has been veiled by its professors, wrapped up in strange symbols, and disguised by a terminology which offers peculiar difficulties. Why it has been thus wilfully entangled, why it was considered advisable to make it *caviare* to the multitude, and what purpose was served by the writing of an interminable series of books seemingly beyond comprehension, are points which must be held over for consideration in their proper place later on. Those who, for what reason soever, have determined to study occultism, must be content to take its branches as they are, namely, as sciences that have always been kept secret. It follows from what has been advanced that the occultist should not be asked, as a test question, whether he can make gold, but whether he is warranted in taking the Alchemical claim seriously, in other words, whether the literature of Alchemy, amidst all its mystery, does offer some hope for its unravelment, and if on the authority of his acquaintance therewith he can, as he does, assuredly answer yes, then he is entitled to a hearing.

Now, the issue which has been dealt with hitherto in respect of Alchemy is one that is exceedingly simple. Assuming there is strong presumptive evidence that the adepts could and did manufacture the precious metals, and that they enclosed the secret of their method in a symbolic literature, it is a mere question of getting to understand the symbolism, about which it will be well to remember the axiom of Edgar Allan Poe, himself a literary Mystic, that no cryptogram invented by human ingenuity is incapable of solution by the application of human ingenuity. But there is another issue which is not by any means so simple, the existence of which was hinted at in the beginning of the present paper, and this is indeed the subject of the present inquiry. To put it in a manner so elementary as to be almost crude in presentation, there is another school of occult students who believe themselves to have discovered in Alchemy a philosophical experiment which far transcends any physical achievement. At least in its later stages and developments this school by no means denies the fact that the manufacture of material gold and silver was an object with many Alchemists, or that such a work is possible and has taken place. But they affirm that the process in metals is subordinate, and, in a sense, almost accidental, that essentially the Hermetic experiment was a spiritual experiment, and the achievement a spiritual achievement. For the evidence of this interpretation they tax the entire literature, and their citations carry with them, not infrequently an extraordinary, and sometimes an irresistible, force. The exaltation of the base nature in man, by the development of his latent powers; the purification, conversion, and transmutation of man; the achievement of a hypostatic union of man with God; in a word, the accomplishment of what has been elsewhere in this magazine explained to be the true end of universal Mysticism; not only was all this the concealed aim of Alchemy, but the process by which this union was affected, veiled under the symbolism of chemistry, is the process with which the literature is concerned, which process also is alone described by all veritable adepts. The man who by proper study and contemplation, united to an appropriate interior attitude, with a corresponding conduct on the part of the exterior personality, attains a correct interpretation of Hermetic symbolism, will, in doing so, be put in possession of the secret of divine reunion, and will, so far as the requisite knowledge is concerned, be in a position to encompass the great work of the Mystics. From the standpoint of this criticism the power which operates in the transmutation of metals alchemically is, in the main, a psychic power. That is to say, a man who has passed a certain point in his spiritual development, after the mode of the Mystics, has a knowledge and control of physical forces which are not in the possession of ordinary humanity. As to this last point there is nothing inherently unreasonable in the conception that an advancing evolution, whether in the individual or the race, will give a far larger familiarity with the mysteries and the laws of the universe. On the other hand, the grand central doctrine and the supreme hope of Mysticism, that it is possible for 'the divine in man' to be borne back consciously to 'the divine in the universe,' which was the last aspiration of Plotinus, does not need insistence in this place. There is no other object, as there is no other hope, in the whole of Transcendental Philosophy, while the development of this principle and the ministration to this desire are the chief purpose of *The Unknown World*

It is obvious that Alchemy, understood in this larger sense, is mystically of far higher import than a mere secret science of the manufacture of precious metals. And this being incontestible it becomes a matter for serious inquiry which of these occult methods of interpretation is to be regarded as true. A first step towards the settlement of this problem will be a concise history of the spiritual theory. Its first traces are supposed to be found in the writings of Jacob Bohme and about the same time Louis Claude de Saint Martin, the French *illuminé*, is discovered occasionally describing spiritual truths in the language of physical chemistry. These, however, are at best but traces, very meagre and very indefinite. It was not until the year 1850, and in England, that the interpretation was definitely promulgated. In that year there appeared a work entitled *A Suggestive Inquiry into the Hermetic Mystery and Alchemy, being an Attempt to Discover the Ancient Experiment of Nature.* This was a large octavo of considerable bulk; it was the production of an anonymous writer, who is now known to be a woman, whose name also is now well known, at least in certain circles, though it would be bad taste to mention it.[1] For the peculiar character of its research, for the quaint individuality of its style, for the extraordinary wealth of suggestion which more than justifies its title, independently of the new departure which it makes in the interpretation of Hermetic symbolism, truly, this book was remarkable.

Eliphas Lévi affirms that all religions have issued from the Kabalah and return into it; and if the term be intended to include the whole body of esoteric knowledge, no advanced occultist will be likely to dispute the statement. So far as books are concerned, it may, in like manner, be affirmed that all modern mystical literature is referable ultimately to two chief sources: on the one hand, to the wonderful books on Magic which were written by Eliphas Lévi himself, and of which but a faint conception is given in the sole existing translation; and, on the other, to the 'Suggestive Inquiry Concerning the Hermetic Mystery', that singular work to which reference was made above as containing the first promulgation of the spiritual theory of Alchemy. This seems at first sight an extreme statement, and it is scarcely designed to maintain, that, for example, the Oriental doctrine of Karma is traceable in the writings of the French initiate who adopted the Jewish pseudo-

---

[1] [The author was Mary Anne South, later Mrs Atwood. Her book was reissued, with an introduction by W. L. Wilmshurst, in 1918.]

nym of Eliphas Lévi Zahed, nor that the 'recovered Gnosis' of the 'New Gospel of Interpretation' is borrowed from the *Suggestive Inquiry*. But these are the two chief sources of inspiration, in the sense that they have prompted research, and that it is not necessary to go outside them to understand how it is that we have come later on to have Theosophy, Christo-Theosophy, the New Kabbalism of Dr Wynn Westcott, and the illuminations of Mrs Kingsford. Everywhere in *Isis Unveiled* the influence of Eliphas Lévi is distinctly traceable; everywhere in the Recovered Gnosis there is the suggestion of the *Inquiry*. Even the Rosicrucianism of the late Mr Hargrave Jennings, so far as it is anything but confusion, is referable to the last mentioned work. It is doubtful if Eliphas Lévi did not himself owe something to its potent influence, for his course of transcendental philosophy post dates the treatise on the Hermetic Mystery by something like ten years, and he is supposed to have accomplished wide reading in occult literature, and would seem to have known English. As it is to the magical hypotheses of the Frenchman that we are indebted for the doctrines of the astral light and for the explanations of spiritualistic phenomena which are current in theosophical circles, to name only two typical instances, so it is of the English lady that we have derived the transcendental views of alchemy, also everywhere now current, and not among Theosophists only. At the same time, it is theosophical literature chiefly which has multiplied the knowledge concerning it, though it does not always indicate familiarity with the source of the views. It is also to Theosophy that we owe the attempt to effect a compromise between the two schools of alchemical criticism mentioned already, by the supposition that there were several planes of operation in alchemy, of which the metallic region was one.

Later speculations have, however, for the most part, added little to the theory as it originally stood, and the *Suggestive Inquiry* is in this respect still thoroughly representative.

To understand what is advanced in this work is to understand the whole theory, but to an unprepared student its terminology would perhaps offer certain difficulties, and therefore in attempting a brief synopsis, it will be well to present it in the simplest possible manner.

The sole connection, according to the *Suggestive Inquiry*,

which subsists between Alchemy and the modern art of Chemistry is one of terms only. Alchemy is not an art of metals, but it is the Art of Life; the chemical phraseology is a veil only, and a veil which was made use of not with any arbitrary and insufficient desire to conceal for the sake of concealment, or even to ensure safety during ages of intolerance, but because the alchemical experiment is attended with great danger to man in his normal state. What, however, the adepts in their writings have most strenuously sought to conceal is the nature of the Hermetic Vessel, which they admit to be a divine secret, and yet no one can intelligently study these writings without being convinced that the vessel is Man himself. Geber, for example, to quote only one among many, declares that the universal orb of the earth contains not so great mysteries and excellencies as Man re-formed by God into His image, and he that desires the primacy among the students of Nature will no where find a greater or better subject wherein to obtain his desire than in himself, who is able to draw to himself what the alchemists call the Central Salt of Nature, who also in his regenerated wisdom possesses all things, and can unlock the most hidden mysteries. Man is, in fact, with all adepts, the one subject that contains all, and he only need be investigated for the discovery of all. Man is the true laboratory of the Hermetic Art, his life is the subject, the grand distillery, the thing distilling and the thing distilled, and self-knowledge is at the root of all alchemical tradition. To discover then the secret of Alchemy the student must look within and scrutinize true psychical experience, having regard especially to the germ of a higher faculty not commonly exercised but of which he is still in possession, and by which all the forms of things, and all the hidden springs of Nature, become intuitively known. Concerning this faculty the alchemists speak magisterially, as if it had illuminated their understanding so that they had entered into an alliance with the Omniscient Nature, and as if their individual consciousness had become one with Universal Consciousness. The first key of the Hermetic Mystery is in Mesmerism, but it is not Mesmerism working inthe therapeutic sphere, but rather with a theurgic object, such as that after which the ancients aspired, and the attainment of which is believed to have been the result of initiation into the Greater Mysteries of old Greece. Between the process of these

What is Alchemy?

Mysteries and the process of Alchemy there is a distinctly traceable correspondence, and it is submitted that the end was identical in both cases. The danger which was the cause of the secrecy was the same also; it is that which is now connected with the Dwellers on the Threshold, the distortions and deceptions of the astral world, which lead into irrational confusion. Into this world the mesmeric trance commonly transfers its subjects, but the endeavour of Hermetic Art was a right disposition of the subject, not only liberating the spirit from its normal material bonds, but guaranteeing the truth of its experiences in a higher order of subsistence. It sought to supply a purely rational motive which enabled the subject to withstand the temptation of the astral sphere, and to follow the path upwards to the discovery of wisdom and the highest consciousness. There the soul knows herself as a whole, whereas now she is acquainted only with a part of her humanity; there also, proceeding by theurgic assistance, she attains her desired end and participates in Deity. The method of Alchemy is thus an arcane principle of self-knowledge and the narrow way of regeneration into life. Contemplation of the Highest Unity and Conjunction with the Divine Nature, the soul's consummation in the Absolute, lead up to the final stage, when the soul attains 'divine intuition of that high exemplar which is before all things, and the final cause of all, which seeing only is seen, and understanding is understood, by him who penetrating all centres, discovers himself in that finally which is the source of all; and passing from himself to that, transcending, attains the end of his profession. This was the consummation of the mysteries, the ground of the Hermetic philosophy, prolific in super-material increase, transmutations and magical effects.'

It was impossible in the above synopsis, and is indeed immaterial at the moment, to exhibit after what manner the gifted authoress substantiates her theory by the evidences of alchemical literature. It is sufficient for the present purpose to summarize the interpretation of Alchemy which is offered by the *Suggestive Inquiry*.

The work, as many are aware, was immediately withdrawn from circulation; it is supposed that there are now only about twelve copies in existence, but as it is still occasionally met with, though at a very high price, in the book-market, this may be an understatement. Some ten years later, Eliphas Lévi began to issue his course of initiation into 'absolute knowledge', and in the year 1865 [i.e. 1857] an obscure writer in America, working, so far as can be seen, quite independently of both, published anonymously a small volume of *Remarks on Alchemy and the Alchemists*, in which it was attempted to show that the Hermetic adepts were not chemists, but were great masters in the conduct of life. Mr Hitchcock, the reputed author, was not an occultist, though he had previously written on Swedenborg as a Hermetic Philosopher, and no attention seems to have been attracted by his work.

The interpretation of the *Suggestive Inquiry* was spiritual and 'theurgic' in a very highly advanced degree: it was indeed essentially mystical, and proposed the end of Mysticism as that also of the Alchemical adepts. The interpretation of Eliphas Lévi, who was an occultist rather than a Mystic, and does not seem to have ever really understood Mysticism, may be called intellectual, as a single citation will suffice to show.

'Like all magical mysteries, the secrets of the Great Work possess a three-fold significance: they are religious, philosophical, and natural. Philosophical gold is, in religion, the Absolute and Supreme Reason; in philosophy, it is truth; in visible nature, it is the Sun; in the subterranean and mineral world, it is most pure and perfect gold. It is for this cause that the search for the Great Work is called the search after the Absolute, and that the work itself passes as the operation of the Sun. All masters of the science have recognised that material results are impossible till all the analogies of the Universal Medicine and the Philosophical Stone have been found in the two superior degrees. Then is the labour simple, expeditious, and inexpensive; otherwise, it wastes to no purpose the life and fortune of the operator. For the soul, the Universal Medicine is supreme reason and absolute justice; for the mind, it is mathematical and practical truth; for the body, it is the quintessence, which is a combination of gold and light.'

The interpretation of Hitchcock was, on the other hand, purely ethical. Now, as professedly an expositor of Mysticism, *The Unknown World* is concerned here only with the first interpretation, and with the clear issue which is included in the following question: Does the literature of Alchemy belong to Chemistry in the sense that it is concerned with the disintegration of physical elements in the metallic order, with a view to the making of gold and silver, or is it concerned with man and the exaltation of his interior nature from the lowest to the highest condition?

In dealing with this question there is only one way possible to an exoteric inquiry like the present, and that is by a consideration of the literature and history of Alchemy. For this purpose it is necessary to begin, not precisely at the cradle of the science, because, although this was probably China, as will be discussed later on, it is a vexatious and difficult matter to settle on an actual place of origin, but for the subject in hand recourse may be had to the first appearance of Alchemy in the West, as to what is practically a starting-point.

It is much to be deplored that some esoteric writers at this day continue to regard ancient Greece and Rome as centres of alchemical knowledge. It is true that the Abbé Pernety, at the close of the last century, demonstrated to his own satisfaction that all classical mythology was but a vesture and veil of the *Magnum Opus* and the fable of the Golden Fleece is regarded as a triumphant vindication of classical wisdom in the deep things of transmutation. But this is precisely one of those airy methods of allegorical interpretation which, once fairly started will draw the third part of the earth and sea, and the third part of the stars of heaven, in the tail of its symbolism. Neither in Egypt, in Greece, or in Rome, has any trace of Alchemy been discovered by historical research till subsequent to the dawn of the Christian era, and in the face of this fact it is useless to assert that it existed secretly in those countries, because no person is in a position to prove the point. All that is known upon the problem of the origin of Alchemy in the Western Hemisphere is to be found in Berthelot's *Collection des Anciens Alchimistes Grecs*, and the exhaustive erudition which resulted in that work is summed up in the following statement: 'Despite the universal tradition which assigns to Alchemy an Egyptian origin, no hieroglyphic document relative to the science of transmutation has yet been discovered. The Græco-Egyptian Alchemists are our sole source of illumination upon the science of Hermes, and that source is open to suspicion because subject to the tampering of mystic imaginations during several generations of dreamers and scholiasts. In Egypt, notwithstanding, Alchemy first originated; there the dream of transmutation was first cherished;' but this was during and not before the first Christian centuries.

The earliest extant work on Alchemy which is as yet known in the West is the papyrus of Leide, which was discovered at Thebes, and is referable to the third century of this era. It contains seventy-five metallurgical formulæ, for the composition of alloys, the surface colouration of metals, assaying, etc. There are also fifteen processes for the manufacture of gold and silver letters. The compilation, as Berthelot points out, is devoid of order, and is like the note-book of an artisan. It is pervaded by a spirit of perfect sincerity, despite the professional improbity of the recipes. These appear to have been collected from several sources, written or traditional. The operations include tinging into gold, gilding silver, superficial colouring of copper into gold, tincture by a process of varnishing, superficial aureation by the humid way, etc. There are many repetitions and trivial variations of the same recipes. M. Berthelot and his collaborator regard this document as conclusively demonstrating that when Alchemy began to flourish in Egypt it was the art of sophistication or adulteration of metals. The document is absolutely authentic, and 'it bears witness to a science of alloys and metallic tinctures which was very skilful and very much advanced, a science which had for its object the fabrication and falsification of the matters of gold and silver. In this respect it casts new light upon the genesis of the idea of metallic conversion. Not only is the notion analagous, but the practices exposed in this papyrus are the same as those of the oldest Greek alchemists, such as pseudo-Democritus, Zosimus, Olympiodorus, and pseudo-Moses. This demonstration is of the highest importance for the study of the *origines* of Alchemy. It proves it to have been founded on something more than purely chimerical fancies—namely, on positive practices and actual experiences, by help of which imitations of gold and silver were fabricated. Sometimes the fabricator confined himself to the deception of the public, as with the author of Papyrus X (*i.e.*, the Theban Papyrus of Leide), sometimes he added prayers and magical formulæ to his art, and became the dupe of his own industry.' Again: 'The real practices and actual manipulations of the operators are made known to us by the papyrus of Leide under a form the most clear, and in accordance with the recipes of pseudo-Democritus and Olympiodorus. It contains the first form of all these procedures and doctrines. In pseudo-Democritus and still more in Zosimus (the earliest among the Greek alchemists), they are already complicated by mystical fancies; then come the commentators who have amplified still further the mystical part, obscuring or eliminating what was practical, to the exact knowledge of which they were frequently strangers. Thus, the most ancient texts are the clearest.'

Now, there are many points in which the occultist would join issue with the criticism of Mr. Berthelot, but it is quite certain that the Egyptian papyrus is precisely what it is described to be, and there is, therefore, no doubt that the earliest work which is known to archæology, outside China, as dealing with the supposed transmutation of metals is in reality a fraudulent business. This fact has to be faced, together with any consequences which it rigidly entails. But before concluding this paper it will be well to notice

(I) That it is impossible to separate the Leide Papyrus from a close relationship with its context of other papyri; as admitted by Berthelot, who says: 'The history of Magic and Gnosticism is closely bound up with that of the origin of Alchemy, and the alchemical papyrus of Leide connects in every respect with two in the same series which are solely magical and Gnostic.'

(II) That, as Berthelot also admits, or, more correctly, as it follows from his admissions, the mystic element entered very early into alchemical literature, and was introduced by persons who had no interest in the practical part, who therefore made use of the early practical documents for their own purposes.

(III) That the Leide papyrus can scarcely be regarded as alchemical in the sense that Geber, Lully, Arnold, Sendivogius and Philalethes are alchemical writers. It neither is nor pretends to be more than a thesaurus of processes for the falsification and spurious imitation of the precious metals. It has no connection, remote or approximate with their transmutation, and it is devoid of all alchemical terminology. In itself it neither proves nor disproves anything. If we can trace its recipes in avowedly alchemical writers, as M. Berthelot declares is the case, then, and then only, it may be necessary to include alchemists in the category of the compiler of this papyrus.

The next stage of inquiry into the validity of the various answers which have been given to this question will take us by an easy transition from the nature of the Leide papyrus to that of the Byzantine collection of ancient Greek alchemists. It will be recollected that the processes contained in the papyrus are supposed to represent the oldest extant form of the processes tabulated by Zosimus, pseudo-Democritus, and others of the Greek school. The claims of this school now demand some brief consideration for the ultimate settlement of one chief point, namely, whether they are to be regarded as alchemists in the sense that attaches to the term when it is applied as advigoration of men like Arnold, Lully, and Schmurath. It was stated previously that the compiler of the Leide papyrus could not be so regarded, and it will, furthermore, pass without possible challenge that no person could accuse that document of any spiritual significance. The abbreviated formulæ of a common medical prescription are as likely to contain the secret of the tincture or the mystery of the unpronounceable tetrad. In proceeding to an appreciation of the Greek alchemists, our authority will be again M. Berthelot, who offers a signal and, indeed, most illustrious instance of the invariable manner in which a genuine and unbiased archaeologist who is in no sense a mystic can assist a mystic inquiry by his researches. M. Berthelot offers further a very special example of unwearied desire after accuracy, which is not at all common even among French savants, and is quite absent from the literary instinct of that nation as a whole. The fullest confidence may always be reposed in his facts.

The collection of Greek alchemists, as it now exists, was formed during the eighth or ninth century of the Christian era, at Constantinople. Its authors are cited, says Berthelot, by the Arabian writers as the source of their knowledge, and in this manner they are really the fountain-head of Western alchemy as it is found during the middle ages, because the matter was derived from Arabia. The texts admit of being separated into two chief classes, of which one is historical and theoretical, the other technical and covered with special fabrications, as for example, various kinds of glass and artificial gems. It is outside the purpose of an elementary inquiry to enumerate the manuscript codices which were collated for the publication of the text as it was issued by M. Berthelot in 1887. It is sufficient to say that while it does not claim to include the whole of the best alchemists, it omits any author who was judged to be of value either to science or archaeology, and it is thus practically exhaustive. The following synthetic tabulation will be ample for the present purpose:—*a*. General Indications, including a *Lexicon of the best Chrysopeia*, a variety of fragmentary treatises, an instruction of Isis to Horus, &c. *b*. Treatises attributed to Democritus or belonging to the Democritic school, including one addressed to Dioscorus by Synesius, and another of considerable length by Olympiodorus the Alexandrian philosopher. *c*. The works of Zosimus the Panopolite. *d*. A collection of ancient authors, but in this case the attribution is frequently apocryphal, and the writings in some instances are referable even to so late a period as the fifteenth century. Pelagus the philosopher, Ostanes, Iamblichus, Agathodaimon and Moses are included in this section. *e*. Technical treatises on the goldsmith's art, the tincture of copper with gold, the manufacture of various glasses, the sophistic colouring of precious stones, fabrication of silver, incombustible nelphom, &c. *f*. Selections from technical and mystical commentators on the Greek alchemists, including Stephanus, the Christian philosopher, and the Anonymous Philosopher. This section is exceedingly incomplete, but M. Berthelot is essentially a scientist, and from the scientific standpoint the commentators are of minor importance.

The bulk of these documents represent alchemy as it was prior to the Arabian period according to its ancient remains outside Chinese antiquities, and any person who is acquainted with the Hermetic authors of the middle ages who wrote in Latin, or, otherwise, in the vernacular of their country, will most assuredly find in all of them the source of their knowledge, their method, and the terminology of the Latin adepts. For, on examination, the Greek alchemists are not of the same character as the compiler of the Leyden papyrus, though he also wrote in Greek. With the one as with the other the subject is a secret science, a sublime gnosis, the possessor of which is to be regarded as a sovereign master. With the one as with the other it is a divine and sacred art, which is only to be communicated to the worthy, for it participates in the divine power, succeeds only by divine assistance, and invokes a special triumph over matter. The love of God and man, temperance, unselfishness, truthfulness, hatred of all imposture, are the essential preliminary requisites which are laid down closely by both schools. By each indifferently a knowledge of the art is attributed to Hermes, Plato, Aristotle, and other great names of antiquity, and Egypt is regarded as *par excellence* the country of the great work. The similarity in each instance of the true process is made evident many times and special stress is laid upon a moderate and continuous heat as approved to a violent fire. The materials are also the same, but in this connection it is only necessary to speak of the importance attributed to many of the great alchemists in order to place a student of the later literature in possession of a key to the correspondence which exists under this head. Finally, as regards terminology, the Greek texts abound with reference to the egg of the philosophers, the philosophical stone, the same which is not a stone, the blessed water, projection, the time of the work, the matter of the work, the body of Morpresia, and other arbitrary names which make up the bizarre company of the mediæval adepts. This fact therefore must be faced in the present enquiry, and again with all its consequences: that the Greek alchemists so far as can be gathered from their names were alchemists in the true sense of Lully and Arnold: that if Lully and Arnold are entitled to be regarded as adepts of a physical science and not as physical chemists, then Zosimus also is entitled to be so regarded: that if Zosimus and his school were, however, houseminters of metal, it is fair to conclude that men of later generations belong to the same category: that finally, if the Greek alchemists under the cover of a secret and pretended sacred science were in reality fabricators of false sophisticated gold and riches, there is at any rate some presumption that those who reproduced their terminology in like manner followed their objects, and that the science of alchemy ended as it begun, an imposture, which at the same time may have been in many cases 'tempered with superstition', for it is not uncommon to history that those who exploit credulity finish by becoming credulous themselves.

It is obvious that here is the crucial point of the whole inquiry, and it is necessary to proceed with extreme caution. M. Berthelot undertakes to shew that the fraudulent recipes

What is Alchemy?

contained in the Leyden papyrus are met with again in the Byzantine collection, but the judgment which would seem to follow obviously from this fact is arrested by another fact which in relation to the present purpose is of very high importance, namely, that a mystic element had already been imported into alchemy, and that some of those writers who reproduce the mystic processes were not chemists and had no interest in chemistry. Now, on the assumption that alchemy was a great spiritual science, it is quite certain that it veiled itself in the chemistry of its period, and in this case does not stand or fall by the quality of that chemistry, which, as M. Berthelot suggests, may very well have been only imperfectly understood by the mystics who, on such a hypothesis, undertook to adopt it. The mystic side of Greek alchemical literature will, however, be dealt with later on.

When the transcendental interpretation of alchemical literature was first enunciated, the Leyden papyruses had indeed been unrolled, but they had not been published, and so also the Greek literature of transmutation, unprinted and untranslated, was only available to specialists. This same interpretation belongs to a period when it was very generally supposed that Greece and Egypt were sanctuaries of chemical as well as transcendental wisdom. In a word, the *origines* of alchemy were unknown except by legend. Now this paper has already established the character of the Leyden papyrus numbered X. in the series, and it was seen that there was nothing transcendental about it. On the other hand, it was also stated that the Byzantine collection of Greek alchemists uses the same language, much of the same symbolism, and methods that are identical with those of the mediæval Latin adepts, whose writings are the material on which the transcendental hypothesis of alchemy has been exclusively based, plus whatsoever may be literally genuine in the so-called Latin translations of Arabian writers. Does the Byzantine collection tolerate the transcendental hypothesis? Let it be regarded by itself for a moment, putting aside on the one hand what it borrowed from those sources of which the Leyden Papyrus is a survival, and on the other what it lent to the long line of literature which came after it. Let it be taken consecutively as it is found in the most precious publication of

Berthelot. There is a dedication which exalts the sovereign matter, and seems almost to deify those who are acquainted therewith; obviously a spiritual interpretation might be placed upon it; obviously, also, that interpretation might be quite erroneous. It is followed by an alphabetical *Lexicon of Chrysopeia*, which explains the sense of the symbolical and technical terms made use of in the general text. Those explanations are simply chemical. The Seed of Venus is verdegris; Dew, which is a favourite symbol with all alchemists, is explained to be mercury extracted from arsenic, *i.e.*, sublimed arsenic; the Sacred Stone is chrysolite, though it is also the Concealed Mystery; Magnesia, that great secret of all Hermetic philosophy, is defined as white lead, pyrites, crude vinegar, and female antimony, *i.e.*, native sulphur of antimony. The list might be cited indefinitely, but it would be to no purpose here. The *Lexicon* is followed by a variety of short fragmented treatises in which all sorts of substances that are well known to chemists, besides many which cannot now be certainly identified, are mentioned; here again there is much which might be interpreted mystically, and yet such a construction may be only the pardonable misreading of unintelligible documents. In the copious annotations appended to these texts by M. Berthelot, the allusions are, of course, read chemically. Even amidst the mystical profundities of the address of *Isis to Horus*, he distinguishes allusions to recondite processes of physical transmutation. About the fragments on the Fabrication of Asem and of Cinnabar, and many others, there is no doubt of their chemical purpose. Among the more extended treatises, that which is attributed to Democritus, concerning things natural and mystic, seems also unmistakably chemical; although it does term the tincture, the Medicine of the Soul and the deliverance from all evil, there is no great accent of the transcendental. As much may be affirmed of the discourse addressed to Leucippus, under the same pseudonymous attribution. The epistle of Synesius to Dioscorus, which is a commentary on pseudo-Democritus, or, rather, a preamble thereto, exalts that mythical personage, but offers no mystical interpretation of the writings it pretends to explain. On the other hand, it must be frankly admitted the treatise of Olympiodorus contains material which would be as valuable to the transcendental hypothesis as anything that has been cited from mediæval writers—for example, that the ancient philosophers applied philosophy to art *by the way of science*—that Zosimus, the crown of philosophers, preaches union with the Divine, and the contemptuous rejection of matter—that what is stated concerning minera is an allegory, for the philosophers are concerned not with minera but with substance. Yet passages like these must be read with their context, and the context is against the hypothesis. The secret of the Sacred Art, of the Royal Art, is literally explained to be the King's secret, the command of material wealth, and it was secret because it was unbecoming that any except monarchs and priests should be acquainted with it. The philosopher Zosimus, who is exalted by Olympiodorus, clothes much of his instructions in symbolic visions, and the extensive fragments which remain of him are specially rich in that bizarre terminology which characterized the later adepts, while he discusses the same questions which most exercised them, as, for example, the time of the work. He is neither less nor more transcendental than are these others. He speaks often in language mysterious and exalted upon things which are capable of being understood spiritually, but he speaks also of innumerable material substances, and of the methods of chemically operating thereon. In one place he explicitly distinguishes that there are two sciences and two wisdoms, of which one is concerned with the purification of the soul, and the other with the purification of copper into gold. The fragments on furnaces and other appliances seem final as regards the material object of the art in its practical application. The writers who follow Zosimus in the collection, give much the same result. Pelagus uses no expressions capable of transcendental interpretation. Ostanes gives the quantities and names the materials which are supposed to enter into the composition of the all-important Divine Water. Agathodaimon has also technical recipes, and so of the rest, including the processes of the so-called Iamblichus, and the chemical treatise which, by a still more extraordinary attribution, is referred to Moses. The extended fragments on purely practical matters, such as the metallurgy of gold, the tincture of Persian copper, the colouring of precious stones, do not need investigation for the purposes of a spiritual hypothesis, their fraudulent nature being sufficiently transparent, despite their invoking the intervention of the grace of God.

There is one other matter upon which it is needful to insist here. The priceless manuscripts upon which M. Berthelot's collection is based contain illustrations of the chemical vessels employed in the processes which are detailed in the text, and these vessels are the early and rude form of some which are still in use. This is a point to be marked, as it seems to point to the conclusion that the investigation of even merely material substances inevitably had a mystic aspect to the minds which pursued them in the infancy of physical science.

The next point in our inquiry takes us still under the admirable auspices of M. Berthelot, to the early Syriac and the early Arabian alchemists. Not until last year was it possible for anyone unacquainted with Oriental languages to have recourse to these storehouses, and hence it is to be again noted that the transcendental interpretation of Alchemy, historically speaking, seems to have begun at the wrong end. In the attempt to explain a cryptic literature it seems obviously needful to start with its first developments. Now, the Byzantine tradition of Alchemy came down, as it has been seen, to the Latin writers of the middle ages, but the Latin writers did not derive it immediately from the Greek adepts. On the contrary, it was derived to them immediately through the Syriac and Arabian Alchemists. What are the special characteristics of these till now unknown personages? Do they seem to have operated transcendentally or physically, or to have recognised both modes? These points will be briefly cleared up in the present article, but in the first place it is needful to mention that although the evidence collected by Berthelot shews that Syria and Arabia mediated in the transmission of the Hermetic Mystery to the middle age of Europe, they did not alone mediate. 'Latin Alchemy has other foundations even more direct, though till now unappreciated . . . The processes and even the ideas of the ancient Alchemists passed from the Greeks to the Latins, before the time of the Roman Empire, and, up to a certain point, were preserved through the barbarism of the first mediæval centuries by means of the technical traditions of the arts and crafts'. The existence of a purely transcendental application of Alchemical symbolism is evidently neither known nor dreamed by M. Berthelot, and it will be readily seen that the possibility of a technical tradition which reappears in the Latin literature offers at first sight a most serious and seemingly insuperable objection to that application. At the same time the evidence for this fact cannot be really impugned. The glass-makers, the metallurgists, the potters, the dyers, the painters, the jewellers, and the goldsmiths, from the days of the Roman Empire, and throughout the Carlovingian period, and still onward were the preservers of this ancient technical tradition. Unless these crafts had perished this was obviously and necessarily the case. To what extent it was really and integrally connected with the mystical tradition of Latin Alchemical literature is, however, another question. The proofs positive in the matter are contained in certain ancient technical Latin Treatises, such as the *Compositiones ad Tingenda, Mappæ Clavicula, De Artibus Romanorum, Schedula diversarum Artium, Liber diversarum Artium*, and some others. These are not Alchemical writings; they connect with the Leyden papyrus rather than with the Byzantine collection; and they were actually the craft-manuals of their period. Some of them deal largely in the falsification of the precious metals.

The mystical tradition of Alchemy, as already indicated, had to pass through a Syriac and Arabian channel before it came down to Arnold, Lully, and the other mediæval adepts. Here it is needful to distinguish that the Syriac Alchemists derived their science directly from the Greek authors, and the Arabians from the Syriac Alchemists. The Syriac literature belongs in part to a period which was inspired philosophically and scientifically by the School of Alexandria, and in part to a later period when it passed under Arabian influence. They comprise nine books translated from the Greek Pseudo-Democritus and a tenth of later date but belonging to the same school, the text being accompanied by figures of the vessels used in the processes. These nine books are all practical recipes absolutely unsuggestive of any transcendental possibility, though a certain purity of body and a certain piety of mind are considered needful to their success. They comprise further very copious extracts from Zosimus the Panopolite, which are also bare practical recipes, together with a few mystical and magical fragments in a condition too mutilated for satisfactory criticism. The extensive Arabic treatise which completes the Syriac cycle, is written in Syriac characters, and connects closely with the former and also with the Arabian series. It is of later date, and is an ill-digested compilation from a variety of sources. It is essentially practical. The Arabian treatises included in M. Berthelot's collection contain *The Book of Crates, The Book of El-Habib, The Book of Ostanes,* and the genuine works of Geber. With regard to the last the students of Alchemy in England will learn with astonishment that the works which have been attributed for so many centuries to this philosopher, which are quoted as of the highest authority by all later writers, are simply forgeries. M. Berthelot has for the first time translated the true Geber into a Western tongue. Now all these Arabic treatises differ generally from the Syriac cycle; they are verbose, these are terse; they are grandiose, these are simple; they are romantic and visionary, these are unadorned recipes. The book of El-Habib is to a certain extent an exception, but the Arabian Geber is more mysterious than his Latin prototype. El-Habib quotes largely from Greek sources, Geber only occasionally but largely from treatises of his own, and it is significant that in his case M. Berthelot makes no annotations explaining, whether tentatively or not, the chemical significance of the text. As a fact, the Arabian Djarber, otherwise Geber, would make a tolerable point of departure for the transcendental hypothesis, supposing it to be really tenable in the case of the Latin adepts.

Preceding pages have taken the course of inquiry through the Greek, Arabian, and Syrian literatures, and the subject has been brought down to the verge of the period when Latin alchemy began to flourish. Now before touching briefly upon this which is the domain of the spiritual interpretation, it is desirable to look round and to ascertain, if possible, whether there is any country outside Greece and Egypt, to which alchemy can be traced. It must be remembered that the appeal of Latin alchemy is to Arabia, while that of Arabia is to Greece, and that of Greece to Egypt. But upon the subject of the *Magnum Opus* the Sphinx utters nothing, and in the absence of all evidence beyond that of tradition it is open to us to look elsewhere. Now, it should be borne in mind that the first centre of Greek alchemy was Alexandria, and that the first period was in and about the third century of the Christian era. Writing long ago in *La Revue Théasophique,* concerning *Alchemy in the Nineteenth Century,* the late Madame Blavatsky observes that 'ancient China, no less than ancient Egypt, claims to be the land of the alkahest and of physical and transcendental alchemy; and China may very probably be right. A missionary, an old resident of Pekin, William A. P. Martin, calls it the 'cradle of alchemy.' Cradle is hardly the right word perhaps, but it is certain that the celestial empire has the right to class herself amongst the very oldest schools of occult science. In any case alchemy has penetrated into Europe from China as we shall prove.' Madame Blavatsky proceeded at some length to 'compare the Chinese system with that which is called Hermetic Science,' her authority being Mr Martin, and her one reference being to a work entitled *Studies of Alchemy in China* by that gentleman.

When the present writer came across these statements and this reference, he regarded them as an unexpected source of possible light, and at once made inquiry after the book cited by Madame Blavatsky, but no person, no bibliography, and no museum catalogue could give any information concerning a treatise entitled *Studies of Alchemy in China*, so that these papers had perforce to be held over pending the result of still further researches after the missing volume. Mr Carrington Bolton's monumental *Bibliography of Chemistry* was again and again consulted, but while it was clear on the one hand that Mr Martin was not himself a myth, it seemed probable, as time went on, that a mythical treatise had been attributed to him. Finally, when all resources had failed, and again in an unexpected manner, the mystery was resolved, and Mr W. Emmett Coleman will no doubt be pleased to learn—if he be not aware of it already—that here, as in so many instances which he has been at the pains to trace, Madame Blavatsky seems to have derived her authority second-hand. The work which she quoted was not, as she evidently thought, a book separately published, but is an article in *The China Review*, published at Hong Kong. From this article Madame Blavatsky has borrowed her information almost verbatim, and indeed where she has varied from the original, it has been to introduce statements which are not in accordance with Mr Martin's, and would have been obviously rejected by him.

Mr Martin states (1) that the study of alchemy 'did not make its appearance in Europe until it had been in full vigour in China for at least six centuries,' or *circa* BC 300. (2) That it entered Europe by way of Byzantium and Alexandria, the chief points of intercourse between East and West. Concerning the first point Madame Blavatsky, on an authority which she vaguely terms history, converts the six centuries before AD 300, with which Mr Martin is contented, into sixteen centuries before the Christian era, and with regard to the second she reproduces his point literally. Indeed, it is very curious to see how her article which does not treat in the smallest possible degree of alchemy in the nineteenth century, is almost entirely made up by the expansion of hints and references in the little treatise of the missionary, even in those parts where China is not concerned. Mr Martin, himself more honourable, acknowledges a predecessor in opinion, and observes that the Revd Dr Edkins, some twenty years previously, was the first, as he believes to 'suggest a Chinese origin for the alchemy of Europe'. Mr Martin, and still less Dr Edkins, knew nothing of the Byzantine collection, and could not profit by the subsequent labours of M. Berthelot, and yet it is exceedingly curious to note that the researches of the French savant do in no sense explode the hypothesis of the Chinese origin of alchemy, or rather, for once in a season to be in agreement with Madame Blavatsky, perhaps not the origin so much as a strong, directing, and possibly changing influence. The Greek alchemists appeal, it is true, to Egypt, but, as already seen, there is no answer from the ancient Nile, and China at precisely the right moment comes to fill up the vacant place.

The mere fact that alchemy was studied in China has not much force in itself, but Mr Martin exhibits a most extraordinary similarity between the theorems and the literature of the subject in the far East and in the West, and in the course of his citations there are many points which he himself has passed over, which will, however, appeal strongly to the Hermetic student. There is first of all, the fundamental doctrine that the genesis of metals is to be accounted for upon a seminal principle. Secondly, there is the not less important doctrine that there abides in every object an active principle whereby it may attain to 'a condition of higher development and greater efficiency'. Thirdly, there is the fact that alchemy in China as in the West was an occult science, that it was perpetuated 'mainly by means of oral tradition', and that in order to preserve its secrets a figurative phraseology was adopted. In the fourth place, it was closely bound up with astrology and magic. Fifthly, the transmutation of metals was indissolubly allied to an elixir of life. Sixthly, the secret of gold-making was inferior to the other arcanum. Seventhly, success in operation and research depended to a large extent on the self-culture and self-discipline of the alchemist. Eighthly, the metals were regarded as composite. Ninthly, the materials were indicated under precisely the same names: lead, mercury, cinnabar, sulphur, these were the chief substances, and here there is no need to direct the attention of the student to the rôle which the same things played in Western alchemy. Tenthly, there are strong and unmistakeable points of resemblance in the barbarous terminology common to both literatures, for example, 'the radical principle', 'the green dragon', the 'true lead', the 'true mercury', etc.

In such an enquiry as the present everything depends upon the antiquity of the literature. Mr Carrington Bolton includes in his bibliography certain Chinese works dealing with Alchemy, and referred to the third century. Mr Martin, on the other had, derives his citations from various dates, and from some authors to whom a date cannot be certainly assigned. Now, he tells us, without noticing the pregnant character of the remark, that 'one of the most renowned seats of Alchemic industry was Bagdad, while it was the seat of the Caliphate'—that an extensive commerce was 'carried on between Arabia and China'—that 'in the eighth century embassies were interchanged between the Caliphs and the Emperors'—and, finally, that 'colonies of Arabs were established in the seaports of the Empire.' As we know indisputably that Arabia received Alchemy from Greece, it is quite possible that she communicated her knowledge to China, and therefore, while freely granting that China possessed an independent and ancient school, we must look with suspicion upon its literature subsequent to the eighth century because an Arabian influence was possible. But, independently of questions of date, comparative antiquity, and primal source, the chief question for the present purpose is whether Chinese Alchemy was spiritual, physical, or both. Mr Martin tells us that there were two processes, the one inward and spiritual, the other outward and material. There were two elixirs, the greater and the less. The alchemist of China was, moreover, usually a religious ascetic. The operator of the spiritual process was apparently translated to the heaven of the greater genii. As to this spiritual process Mr Martin is not very clear, and leaves us uncertain whether it produced a spiritual result or the perpetuation of physical life.

2
ON THE ESOTERIC LITERATURE OF THE MIDDLE AGES

And on the Underlying Principles of Theurgic Art and Practice in Western Christendom

[Printed as the 'Introductory Essay' to *The Magical Writings of Thomas Vaughan*, 1888. It was not incorporated in Waite's edition of *The Works of Thomas Vaughan*, 1919, and has never been reprinted.]

This essay, the earliest in the present collection, represents Waite's thoughts on alchemy and mysticism as a young man and suffers from his repetition of inaccuracies in the sources available to him—as in his conviction that medieval black magic was in large part a Jewish creation. But the same sources were those used by the founders and early members of the Hermetic order of the Golden Dawn, and the essay provides a perfect illustration of the manner of thought common to Hermeticists of the late nineteenth century. It is also clear from the conclusion of the essay that Waite was already planning, in 1888, his series of major works on the Secret Tradition in Christian Times.

THE magical writings of Thomas Vaughan constitute an explanatory prolegomena not only to the general history of practical transcendentalism, and to the philosophy of transcendental art, from the standpoint of a Christian initiate, but they are specially directed to the interpretation of alchemical symbolism; they claim to provide the intelligent reader with a substantially fresh revelation of that mysterious First Matter of the *Magnum Opus* which endows those who know it, and can avail themselves of its manifold potencies, with a full and perfect power for the successful conduct of all classes of theurgic experiment. Adopting the terminology of Hermetic adepts, Thomas Vaughan enlarges the theoretical scope of alchemical processes, and delineates the spiritual evolution of humanity, completely and scornfully rejecting the merely mineral work, and claiming for the true hierophants of mystic science a personal interest and participation in the whole creative *opus*. In offering for the first time to the modern student of ancient mysteries a reprint of these curious and really important treatises, it seems needful to attempt a plain statement of the reasons which have led to their reproduction, and of the exact nature of the interest which now attaches to them. The vast literature of ancient occultism has till recently possessed little but an archæological interest, of a naturally relative kind, as the remains of discredited high thinking in past ages, and a certain bibliographical value, on account of the extreme rarity of all esoteric works. This interest and this value would be an insufficient warrant for their revival in an era of positive science or in the absence of any message of vital import to this veridic age, and, therefore, on philosophical, as well as practical and, I may add, commercial grounds, they would have remained archæological monuments and book-lovers' treasures alone. But the sudden revival of psychic research amongst us, and certain discoveries made in the psychic world, of which many are now well known, and others remain *in abscondito*, have placed the position of old mystics in an utterly different light, and have created a presumptive probability that prior claimants have also a right to be heard, and that the conductors of early psychic experiments in ages of single purpose may have advanced beyond ourselves, and may be qualified for our teachers and guides. Here are the broad *a priori* grounds for the revived interest in the entire circle of esoteric literature. But when the whole faculty of an impartial and sympathetic mind, cognisant already of those ascertained facts to which I have just alluded, is brought to the adequate study of 'the philosophers', as they were collectively termed, this general interest is speedily merged in a far more absorbing feeling, for we find ourselves in the presence of a titanic claim, advanced in a number of cases by intellectual giants and joined to a height of aspiration, a wealth of spiritual suggestiveness, a cosmic breadth of view, and a degree of apparent personal sanctity, which are sufficient to profoundly impress the most unemotional minds, while vistas of vast possibilities unveil to the prepared imagination at the magic word of the hierophants. Here are the more particular grounds for the new interest in ancient esoteric literature, and here once more the accepted facts of modern psychology are presumptive evidence for the truth of these claims, and evidence, moreover, which is, in my opinion, sufficiently strong not only to warrant their exhaustive and practical investigation on the lines of the mystics, but to make investigation imperative with those who, like myself, are unconditionally devoted to the progress of psychic science. To place within the reach of like-minded students the works of an acknowledged adept, which are otherwise almost *introuvable*, and thereby to set new sympathetic investigators on the track of the grand mysteries, is the *raison d'être* of this reprint. It is due to the work of the modern theosophists to state that they were substantially the first to draw attention to the connecting link between the psychic phenomena of today and the ancient thaumaturgy, and the second spring of magic and of magian thought in England is directly owing to their influence.

Having paid this just tribute, it becomes necessary to explain the nature of the psychic facts to which I have several times alluded, as much to prevent misconception as for the use of inquirers at the early stages of their progress.

The ascertained facts which I consider, in common with numerous qualified persons, to be presumptive evidence for the truth of the magical claim, taken broadly in its totality, are quite independent of any mystical theory, are not confined to any special circle of esoteric students, and are wholly unconnected with the results which may or may not have been attained by such colleges of oriental adepts as theosophists proclaim to exist among the politically unapproachable fastnesses of the Thibetan highlands. I speak with all deference of an opinion which is held by several intellectual persons, and with due appreciation of such evidence as exists on the subject; I am personally quite uncommitted to any opinion in the matter, except on the *a priori* ground of magical possibility. The psychic facts in question may be verified by any intelligent person who is possessed of sufficient perseverance, and is capable of appreciating the issues which are at stake in such a manner as to conduct his researches with a view to those issues. They are concerned with the higher classes of hypnotic phenomena, with ecstatic and trance clairvoyance, with thought-transference, the transcorporeal action of mind upon matter, and with such phenomena of modern spiritualism as unbiased inquirers agree to be well substantiated. These facts offer a rational basis for the belief in another form of subsistence than that of the physical life of man on earth, and naturally terminate the age of spiritual faith in the first auroral light of an age of spiritual knowledge, revealing for the first time, openly and to all mankind, that it is possible, even in earthly life, to enter into another form of perception and to establish communication with planes of intelligent existence which are normally beyond our range.

This communication at present is exceedingly hampered, and the progress, which has at best been slow, seems at the present moment to be almost completely arrested, partly owing to the insincerity of experiment, which is attempted on the lowest planes of physical subsistence with coarse, degraded, and sometimes diseased instruments, yet is concerned with the spiritual altitudes, while the ignorance of a proper method of procedure— the 'true process' of alchemical allegory—creates another and apparently insurmountable barrier. In this difficulty, the earnest student who turns for illumination to the sanctuaries of ancient mystic wisdom and for counsel to its grand hierophants, finds himself face to face with the departed but still eloquent representatives of a sacerdotal and royal science which claims to be exclusively acquainted with the One Way of Rectitude and the Unerring Path of Light. He discovers that the prodigies of the elder world are substantially identical with those modern phenomena with which he is already familiar, of whose actuality he is convinced, and which have prompted him in his further quest. The hypnotic trance, as we know it today, is clearly and frequently alluded to in ancient writings; modern clairvoyance is paralleled by the magical 'vision at a distance;' for thought-transference, we have mystical methods of communication with persons however remote and in the absence of any material means; while an exact fundamental correspondence may be easily established between many marvels of American Spiritualism and the ghostly mysteries of necromantic and magical evocation. But whereas our modern phenomena have all the characteristics of a merely initial experience, the thaumaturgic results obtained by the initiates of old are of another and loftier order, the fruit of matured methods and of a long sequence of experimental investigations.

There is no doubt or hesitation in the teachings or claims of the hierophants; they are ever positive, unflinching, and practically unanimous, and they write under the shadow of a vast and unlimited subject, embracing the depths and the heights, and fortified by the sublime consciousness of eternity.

As at present conducted, our modern experiments are devoid of practical results; the lines of investigation reach a certain point and there leave us, but the old pioneers of mysticism would appear to have discovered some hitherto inscrutable means of passing the barriers which confront us, and in so doing they tell us that they have come into the possession of a tremendous secret, which they declare to be of a divine character, and which they dare not publicly reveal, for incalculable penalties attach to the profanation of the Grand Mysteries. In their books they protected their knowledge from the vulgar by means of allegorical language and the use of symbols, leaving their veritable meaning to be divined by the sincere student with the help of an insight imparted from the spiritual world. They also perpetuated their secrets by the initiation of tested disciples of undoubted discretion, to whom they seem to have liberally laid open the precious treasures of their knowledge, and in this maner some of the secret colleges of magic, once apparently numerous, came to be formed in the West.

Thus, the study of the mystics presents us with obvious difficulties which at the beginning appear insurmountable, but, speaking from personal experience, I do not hesitate to say that there is no ground for discouragement in a pure, patient, and active intelligence, for the elementary phenomena are identical, and thus the modern psychologist is already in possession of the outer doors of the sanctuary; but he must carefully bear in mind that a large proportion of Hermetic literature is concerned with a physical process for the conversion of 'base metals' into gold, and that it is equally vicious and fruitless to force upon merely alchemical writings a psychic meaning which is completely at variance with the lives and undoubted aims of their authors. The literature of esoteric psychology in the past is large enough without the wholesale annexation which has been rashly, though not inexcusably, attempted by several critics.

The theurgic and mystical literature of Western Christendom, with which I am exclusively concerned in the present essay, is only a branch of universal occultism, but it admits of classification into several distinct divisions, all requiring consideration which will be much simplified by a brief preliminary reference to the history of Christian magic, or rather of magic as it was practised in the Christian countries of Europe.

The philosophical principles which underlie the theory and practice of theurgic art are mainly derived from the Platonic School of Alexandria—the school of Ammonius Saccas, Proclus, and Hypatia, the school of Synesius, the theosophical dream-interpreter, and of the angelical mysticism of pseudo-Dionysius. The neo-platonists were practically the inheritors of the Magian wisdom of Egypt, Greece, and Rome, and the mystical works of Hermes Trismegistus, which were the product of this period of Alexandrian illumination, were no mere inventions of a semi-Christianized sage, but probably embodied the traditional secrets and cosmic theories of a very considerable antiquity. The central doctrine of the high theurgic faith, professed by the grand masters of Alexandrian philosophy, was that by means of certain invocations, performed solemnly by chaste, sober, abstinent, and mentally illuminated men, it was possible to come into direct communication with those invisible powers which fill the measureless distance between man and God. A divine exaltation accompanied this communication with the superior intelligences of the universe, and man entered into a temporal participation of deific qualities, while the power and wisdom thus acquired submitted many hierarchies of spiritual beings to the will of the Magus.

The proscription of the old pagan cultus and the bitter and continual persecution of all professors of secret and magical arts, which took place in the reign of the infamous emperor Constantine, and was continued by Valentinian, Theodosius and other shining lights of imperial Christianity, did not eradicate polytheism or destroy the adepts. The old religion and the old theurgic art took refuge in remoter places; they were practised in stealth and in silence, and thus were presumably originated many of those mysterious secret societies which perpetuated the traditions of the Magi through the whole period of the Middle Ages, and in numerous magical rituals betray their connection with neo-platonism.

The proscription of magic and paganism was eventually followed by the proscription and persecution of the Jews, who, in like manner, were reduced to practise their religious rites in secret, and whose oriental vindictiveness was frequently roused to frenzy by their intolerable sufferings and humiliations. Professors of Kabbalistic arts, firm believers in the virtues of invocations and verbal formulæ, and addicted from time immemorial to every species of superstitious practice, they directed their mystic machinery to do injury to their enemies, and the infernal magic of the Middle Ages, with its profanation of Christian mysteries, its black masses and impious invocations is, in part at least, their creation.

Thus, medieval occultism was essentially of a composite character. It borrowed, on the one hand, from the rabbinical wisdom of Israel, and, on the other, from pagan sources. The crusades made it subject to Arabic influence, which was definitely increased by the spread of alchemical notions from east to west, while from the debris of every vanished cultus which in barbaric times had ever flourished among the Teutonic and Celtic nations was built up the mythology of nature-spirits, the elfin world, and the strange doctrines concerning elementary intelligences.

Over this many-coloured garment was invariably spread the sacerdotal cope of Christianity, which may have been adopted at first as a disguise, but which in the majority of cases came eventually to be beyond suspicion the official religious belief of most European adepts. The voice of esoteric literature is positively unanimous on this point. Whatever the secret-teachings which entered into the traditional science of the Magi, they were not of a nature to interfere with the sincere profession of Christianity among their later initiates, or they were modified into harmony with orthodox Christian teaching. Admitting the claims of magic, it is indeed probable that the secret knowledge which was perpetuated was concerned more with esoteric power than with esoteric doctrine—a view which is wholly consistent with the universal history of magic, for in all ages and nations we find the same claims to the same preternatural powers advanced in the interests of the most various systems of religion.

The magical literature of Europe abounds in potent formulæ for the evocation and control of all classes of spiritual beings, and these to a large extent are directly taken from the hierarchic liturgies of Christendom, the miraculous powers inherent in the names of Jehovah, Jesus, Mary, and similar sacred names, are explained in the rituals, and the numerical mysticism of Pythagoras is interpreted in the interests of Trinitarian doctrine.

There is therefore no ground for supposing that western initiates had discovered a 'religion behind all religions'; they were simply Christian mystics who never dreamed of looking further than Christianity for light, and what they pretend to have possessed was the key of miracles and not the key of religious symbolism. The professors of goetic magic and the infamous frequenters of the Sabbath may have denied and rejected Christ, but they did not deny his power, and if they served another master it was in search of an immediate recompense, and with a full consciousness of the penalties that they incurred.

The amount of misunderstanding which exists on this point among even sympathetic inquirers calls for a positive statement to check the general tendency to read into the writings of Christian adepts a significance that utterly eliminates all the positive elements of their faith, which generally was held in sincerity, and too often in the midst of persecution at the hands of their fellow-believers.

The sincere profession of Christianity by medieval and later adepts is, on a cursory view, unfavourable to the gigantic claim of magian art and science, for, at least in its exoteric presentment, I recognize, in common with the general concensus of modern mystical thinking, that the Christian scheme does not provide us with an intelligible theory of the universe, and we might reasonably expect that illuminated persons, who 'enjoy free perspicuity of thought in universal consciousness', would have entered into possession of a more adequate cosmogonical doctrine.

As one who is a partisan of no special opinion, and as one who deplores the extreme intellectual folly of making haste towards unstable and futile convictions on the most important problems by help of premature theories, I have no wish to minimise the importance of difficulties like this, but it is equally easy to overstate their value. Our modern discoveries in psychology have hitherto assisted us towards no definite theory of the universe, and it is impossible in their present condition that they should ever provide us with such. Their possibly indefinite development in the hands of the ancient mystics may have equally failed to enlighten them, for the power of working wonders within the domain of natural law and the exaltation of the intuitive faculties so as to enlarge the sphere of perception within the Cosmos may not place the observer in such a position as to make successful philosophic generalisations. On the other hand, if the Great Secret which is declared to be possessed by the Magi involves a veritably universal science, if it takes the observer without the domain of natural law, he is possibly wrapt beyond the domain of theory, and the temporary enjoyment of a transcendent and deific form of subsistence eliminates for the time from the mind all consciousness of the common forms of thought and normal intellectual limitation.

There are three broad divisions of medieval esoteric knowledge. The first is described as Natural Magic, the second as Spiritual or Transcendental Magic, and the third, under the comprehensive title of Alchemy, embraces a philosophy and a physical practice which are of the first and consummate importance to the modern student. The philosophy of the whole subject is embodied in two priceless collections, the so-called works of Hermes Trismegistus and the Jewish Kabbalah, which to all intents and purposes is contained in the Baron de Rosenroth's *Kabbala Denudata*, a part of which has been recently translated into English. The expositions of these philosophical text-books are numerous, and they vary considerably in value. There is much interesting and important matter to be found in Cornelius Agrippa's 'Three Books of Occult Philosophy', albeit this author, so exalted by Thomas Vaughan, is not included among adepts of the loftiest order.[1] The Hermetic and Kabbalistic writings are both in great part devoted to the mystical history of creation, to which the evolution of humanity is

---

[1] 'Cornelius Agrippa, who was a seeker all his life, and who attained neither knowledge nor peace, belongs to another category. His books abound in erudition and audacity; his personal character was fantastic and independent, which obtained him the reputation of an abominable sorcerer and the persecution of priests and princes; he subsequently wrote in condemnation of studies from which he had derived no happiness, and he perished in desolation and misery.'
Eliphas Lévi, *Histoire de la Magie*, pp. 346, 347.

considered rigorously parallel, in virtue of the magical doctrine of correspondence, and thus an esoteric significance is attributed to those portions which deal with the development of the material cosmos out of the chaotic storm of elementary forces.

The Kabbalistic books, in addition to this, treat largely of pneumatology, of the hierarchy and classification of spirits, the circular progression of the soul, its nature, origin, and destiny, the divine progress of the Royal Intellectual Essence from star to star and from sun to sun through the endless chain of existence, and of the highest problems of transcendental psychology. Their philosophical interest at the present stage of exoteric spiritual investigation is scarcely diminished by the uncertainty of their origin, and the occasionally fraudulent manner in which individual treatises have been given to the world, for they undoubtedly embody an antique tradition, and are wholly in harmony with the sombre sublimity of Jewish genius.

An important division of the Kabbalah is devoted to practical magic, and may be described as at once the source and synthesis of all the existing rituals from the days of the Enchyridion, not excepting those of the Black Art, which are simply infernal perversions of normal and lawful magic.

The nature, processes, and results of Natural Magic have been variously described by its professors, and its scope is frequently extended till it includes a large proportion of the spiritual or transcendental branch, as, for instance, the prediction of future events which are beyond the calculus of probabilities, and therefore can only be ascertained by the ecstatic transference of the intellectual faculties into another form of subsistence. It is properly the manifestation of the arcana of physical nature by means of art. In more common and definite terms, it is the production of apparently thaumaturgic effects by means of physical laws which are not generally known, and it has therefore no connection with psychology. Experimental chemistry produces at the present day innumerable phenomena which to the vulgar mind are distinctly thaumaturgic. 'That most secret and arcane department of physical science, by which the mystical properties of natural substances are developed, we denominate Natural Magic,' says Robert Fludd in his *Compendious Apology for the Fraternity of the Rosy Cross*; he cites the three Magi, who were led by the Star in the

East to the cradle of the Grand Christian Initiator, and the mythical King Solomon, among the most illustrious adepts of this elementary branch of esoteric wisdom, which culminates in the celestial science of astrology, for astrology is the calculation of future contingencies, based on the traditional and observed facts of stellar influence on the life of humanity at large. It is impressive in its antiquity, and important by the respect which it has commanded from great minds in the past, but neither this nor any species of Natural Magic are of service to the psychic student.

Spiritual or Transcendental Magic comprises in itself several distinct subdivisions of esoteric art and science. Considered in its totality, it is the synthesis of those methods and processes by which the ancient mystics claim to have developed their psychic potencies so as to establish communication with such forms of intelligent finite subsistence as are without the physical horizon, and therefore normally invisible, to form a correspondence with the underlying principles of nature, and thus develop the possibilities which are secreted like seeds in the heart of all material substances, and so perform on the physical plane what is beyond the scope of common physical science, and, lastly, as the crowning aim and *magnum opus* of experimental mysticism, to enable the 'highest fact in man' to hold 'immediate intercourse with the highest fact in the universe'.

The wonders of Spiritual Magic are said to be accomplished by means of a certain method of life and a certain sequence of ceremonies, all of symbolical significance, but unanimously considered by the highest adepts to be devoid of inherent virtue, and simply adopted to direct and develop the psychic faculties of will and imagination which are the grand agents in every magical process. Eliphas Lévi recommends the postulant in the pronaos of the Spiritual Temple to 'rise daily at the same hour, and at an early hour, bathe summer and winter before daybreak in spring water, never wear soiled clothes, to wash them himself if necessary, to exercise himself by voluntary privations that he may be better able to bear involuntary ones; finally, to impose silence on all desires save that of achieving the *magnum opus*.' But this is simply the preliminary discipline; the preparation of the mystic 'sulphur of the wise' is of another and higher kind; the student of Thomas Vaughan will find it described in various parts of his writings, and especially in the *Anima Magica Abscondita;* it is a process of psychic chemistry of a triadic and absolutely supernatural character, for the diatribes of modern mystics against the use of the term supernatural are founded on a fundamental misapprehension of occultism, and are due to the influence of materialistic philosophy. It is a doctrine of magical science that there is an inherent imperfection in Nature, and that there is an absolute perfection which transcends Nature; now, the testimony of the visible universe and the unceasing aspiration of man's higher consciousness are in harmony with this doctrine.

The triadic process of which I have spoken is the transmutation of the physical body by the soul within it, the exaltation and transfiguration of the soul by the overshadowing spirit, and the illumination and deification of the spirit by contact with the Universal Consciousness. This process accomplishes that regeneration of the whole man, which is the true object of transcendental philosophy and the only safe basis of practical magic. All operations attempted by the vulgar and the uninitiated, in other words, by unregenerate persons, are either dangerous or unsuccessful, or, as in the case of Black Magic, of a dark and abominable nature.

Contemplation and quietism are the keys of this mysterious process, which seems to have been carried to its highest point among Oriental nations. It is described by Roger Bacon as the modification of the body by alchemy, which puts much of Hermetic allegory in a new and more intelligible light.

When this modification, or New Birth, has been accomplished, the Magus is placed in communication with the creative forces of the universe, and the avenues of spiritual perception, which are narrow, difficult, and full of barriers to the psychologist of today, are freely thrown open for unlimited exploration—such, at least, is the claim of the magical text-books—and the initiated epopt may proceed to the invocation of the celestial intelligences, the souls of the great departed, and to the assertion of intellectual dominion over the hierarchies of elementary being. The depths and heights of his own immortal nature are also revealed to him, and from the pinnacles of his spiritual life he may soar into ecstatic yet conscious communion with God Himself. On the physical plane he may peform, by the adaptation of natural laws, many prodigies which seem to the uninitiated observer in defiance of all law; he may endue inert substance with the potency of his individual will, and this is the philosophical principle of talismanic magic; he can search all hearts and read all destinies; perceive events happening at a remote distance; and can impart to suitable subjects a portion of his own prerogatives, inducing trance, clairvoyance, prophetic foresight, &c.

Such is the great claim of Spiritual Magic, and it involves at least an aspiration of the highest conceivable kind. Its antithesis exists in the counter claim of the Black or Infernal Art, with all its grotesque horrors and barbarous, perverse processes, by which the initiates of forbidden knowledge employed their developed physical faculties in operations of darkness and destruction.

The third division of medieval esoteric science is, in some respects, the most important of all, for alchemy is not only the foundation of that experimental method which has transformed the face of the earth; it is not only the historical radix of modern physics, including chemistry, it is not only an arcane process for the manufacture of material gold, but it has originated a theory which is of the utmost importance to all present students of psychology.

I have traced the connection between ancient thaumaturgic mysticism and modern mystic action, I have shown that the hierophants of old were familiar with the spiritual phenomena of today, and they claim to have made such advances in the paths wherein we are slowly and painfully travelling, that they had entered into the permanent possession of a power and knowledge which it was dangerous or impossible for them to reveal, which they consequently spoke of in veiled language, but which they nevertheless endeavoured to extend to others, in order that it might be perpetuated, and to this end they invented their symbols and allegories in the hope that a divine light would illuminate deserving seekers and enable them to penetrate to their inner significance. Now, the grand initiates of ancient magic were the princes of alchemy in a large number of cases, and these two branches of esoteric wisdom are intimately and curiously connected both in principle and practice. The doctrines of mystical and magical regeneration were expounded by alchemical philosophers, and the psychic manufacture of gold was taught in return by the magicians. Astrology lent to both the assistance of her traditional observations and the resources of her archaic symbolism. Alchemists and magicians lay claim to the possession of the same tremendous secret, the same indicible power; they worked with the same weapons after rigorously identical methods but in various fields of achievement—the material world was the province of the followers of Geber; to the disciples of the Magi were delivered the realms of mind. The highest inspirations of both schools appear to have been derived from the Hermetic books, and though the practical alchemy of the Christian age originated with the Arabian Geber, its sources must thus be sought in the theosophy of the later Platonists.

Now, whether from hints contained in the Hermetic books or whether from some adaptation of Kabbalism, or from what source soever the seeds came which germinated in the minds of the alchemists, a theory of universal development, capable of application in almost any direction, was enunciated in this division of esoteric literature, and constitutes the general and explainable principle of the Secret Doctrine of Mysticism. I have described this theory at considerable length, and, I believe, with a certain precision, in an account of the true principles of the *magnum opus*, prefixed to the *Lives of Alchemistical Philosophers*, recently published in London. This biographical work endeavours, by a consideration of the careers of adept philosophers, to determine the true nature and object of practical alchemy, and, so far as this plan is fulfilled, it constitutes a suitable and necessary introduction to the study of historical Hermetics. I do not propose to make in the present essay any substantial repetition of what I have already stated there. The alchemical theory of universal development includes a philosophical forestatement of the modern evolutionary hypothesis which, considering the scientific ignorance and darkness of the Middle Ages, is simply bewildering, and justifies the indignant demand of one theosophical writer for the restitution of its rightful property to 'a spoliated past'. But the alchemical theory was originated by thinkers who believed in the paramount reality of spiritual things, and their doctrine of evolution was extended to the soul and spirit of man, though its practical application was scarcely attemped by alchemists outside the metallic kingdom. I would direct the particular attention of earnest psychological inquirers to this grand and important doctrine, the highest outcome of Hermetic speculation which has been openly transmitted from antiquity. It is founded on a general assumption that the philosophers claim to have demonstrated as experimentally true in at least one kingdom of Nature, namely, that all existing substances whatsoever—the substance of spirit and soul, of animal and vegetable life, of metals and of stones—contain elements or seeds of a higher perfection in any given direction than they can normally manifest, that there is no practical limit to their progress towards perfection, and that man is the agent and dispenser of Divine power for the development of his own and the latent energies of all earthly things. The union of individual consciousness in the universal consciousness of God was the culminating point of this theory in its extension to man, and the extraction of a tincture which would transform a million times its own weight into gold was its last assigned development in its relation to metals.

The unity and solidarity of Nature in the midst of infinite formal differentiation was the first logical outcome of this assumption, the universal potentiality of improvement constituting the bond of union. From this dual doctrine of fundamental solidarity and latent power a practical conclusion was drawn—that the processes for the development of inherent energies in the various kingdoms of Nature should be rigorously parallel, but with due regard to formal difference. *Quod superius sicut quod inferius, et quod inferius sicut quod superius ad perpetranda miracula rei unius.*

The alchemical doctrine of evolution is the philosophical basis of the sublime claim of transcendental or spiritual magic which I have already considered at such length, and the full consequent psychic importance of the literature of alchemy may be shown in a few words. Though it conceals the first matter of the *magnum opus*, it describes the processes which, given the first matter, will ultimately eliminate the imperfections of metals. These processes are parallel by the theory in every department of Nature, and thus the magical evolution, transfiguration, or reconstruction of man is to be accomplished in a manner which is rigorously similar to the reconstruction in the mineral world.

As man is the subject of spiritual chemistry, the first matter does not need seeking in this division of the art, and as man, in the same manner, is that mystic *vas philosophorum* which has always been a *crux* for seekers from the days of Geber downwards, it is a plain case that the development of his latent spiritual energies may be accomplished along the lines of the avowed Hermetic processes as they are described in alchemical works, provided the assumptions contained in the general Hermetic theory have a basis, as claimed, in fact. Now the processes in question are delineated with a tolerable amount of perspicuity, and I submit to those numerous students of psychology who are turning for light to the writings and to the alleged achievements of the old mystics, that here is an adequate warrant for their earnest and exhaustive study, and some ground for believing that we may strike upon an unwrought mine of spiritual possibilities in the hidden but not unattainable mysteries of alchemy.

The practical outcome of my own studies in this direction must be reserved for the present, as it would be unwise in the limited space of the present essay to forestall what I subsequently hope to treat in a comprehensive and complete manner. My present object is to draw the attention of other investigators to the only lines of research which are likely to produce a definite and desired result, and if possible to elicit their collaboration in the first serious attempt at the mystical reconstruction of humanity. From the practical magic of the Middle Ages we may learn the identity of new and old psychological phenomena, from theurgic philosophers we may ascertain the true nature of the psychic achievements which transcendental magic claims to have accomplished, for the actual processes by which it attained its grand results we must study the *turba philosophorum*—the long line of alchemists— and that in a consecutive and exhaustive manner. But we must carefully bear in mind that we are in search of the psycho-chemical process, which is connected, but not identical, with the metallic process of the *turba*, that the transmutation of material substances into material gold was the object of alchemy itself, and that it can only provide us with a parallel. But the exactitude of this parallel is guaranteed by the theory, 'From the greater to the lesser, from the lesser to the greater, the consequences are identically connected, and the proportions progressively rigorous.'

The student will also do well to avoid discouragement at the antiquated forms of reasoning and the exploded physical notions of all the Hermetic philosophers. Their conceptions are crude enough, and sometimes seem scarcely consonant with sanity, but their psychic knowledge is not to be measured by their progress in physics, and even a true process for metallic transmutation is not incompatible with a disconcerting ignorance of numerous natural laws.

All persons connected with the present revival of mysticism should endeavour by its logical and consistent study, on an unbiased historical method, to recover some positive knowledge from its secluded sanctuaries. That is an inconsequent interest which is manifested only in spasmodic investigation; rash and illiberal theories are its normal results. The secrets of esoteric literature will only surrender to the searching analysis of sympathetic minds which have been duly equipped for the task by an acquaintance with psychic progress in the present, and are endowed with a height of aspiration which is parallel to the aspiration of the hierophants.

3
HAUNTS OF THE ENGLISH MYSTICS

1. ROBERT FLUDD

['Robert Fludd' and 'John Dee' were printed in *The Unknown World*, Vol.1, Nos. 3 and 4, October and November, 1894.]
These two slight, but entertaining pieces say little about their subjects but much about Waite. The account of Fludd enabled Waite to eulogize the Kent countryside that he loved so well and at the same time to assail Hargrave Jennings over his inexhaustible fund of ignorance—he had already savagely reviewed Jennings's most famous book, *The Rosicrucians: their Rites and Mysteries*, in Walford's *Antiquarian Magazine* (Vol. 11, June 1887 pp. 423–5) when Arthur Machen was its editor. Like Machen, Waite had enjoyed wandering through the rural suburbs of London and his description of Dee at Mortlake is principally an excuse to rail against the urbanization he so detested.

THE late Mr Hargrave Jennings, an 'esoteric littérateur', once made a pious pilgrimage to the quiet village of Bersted in Kent, where beneath the nave of the church the dust of Robert Fludd has rested for a period approaching three centuries. Poor Mr Jennings, of whom one would like to speak tenderly, remembering the hackneyed adage, *de mortuis nil nisi bonum*, in several editions of his curious theosophical *mélange*, entitled *The Rosicrucians: their Rites and Mysteries*, posed as a serious exponent of the philosophy of Robert Fludd, but there is nothing to lead one to suppose that he had done more than dip into his writings in the dilettante manner of a *littérateur*, more especially when he is dubbed esoteric. He certainly never attempted a comprehensive exposition of his philosophy, and it is doubtful whether his inquiry extended much beyond the English version of Fludd's *Mosaicall Philosophy*. One thing at least is certain: the list which he gives of his writings in the last edition of his book is simply a transcript, quite unacknowledged by the way, from Fuller's *Worthies*, and, although he does not seem aware of the fact, is really unreasonably imperfect. So, also, when he undertook the pilgrimage to Bersted, as he states that he actually went there and remained in profound meditation before the monument of the reputed Rosicrucian, one must implicitly believe that he did, but it is not apparent from his narrative, which contains some notable inaccuracies, and any other man than poor Mr Hargrave Jennings might have been called to account in the matter. Now Bersted is not a remote place, being under three miles along a dull main road from Maidstone, and at least at the present day there is a railway station close by the village green. As a matter of enterprise it is no great achievement to have visited the place, which has been done for the purposes of this paper by the present writer.

Bersted village lies off the Maidstone road, and while the church occupies a site which is below the level of the road it is still above the level of the village itself. It is a peaceful pleasant spot ringed by hills in the distance, a sweet and scented place, green with a hundred gardens of hops, an illustration of perfect retirement, but otherwise marked by no special individuality, for the church itself is void of any distinctive character, though at the same time, it is well enough to look at it, above all on its ivied side. It is dedicated to the Holy Cross, and its architectural style is mainly perpendicular, for example, the picturesque tower and the eastern window. There is an aisle on the north side and something in the way of a minute transept which contains a minute organ has been added of recent years on the south side of the chancel. Within, the stained glass window of the chancel depicts somewhat vividly the Descent from the Cross, and there are panelled figures on the walls of apostles and female saints. On the floor and the walls of the aisle there are many memorials of the Cage family, numbers of whom are interred underneath. With these there is no concern here, but upon the eastern wall of this same narrow aisle there is an elaborate tablet, which he, who perhaps is *par excellence* the most illustrious 'philosopher by fire', erected to the memory of his mother.

Mors ei quæ bene vixit Luerum.

Elizabeth Andros being of the Ancient Familie of the Andros of Tavnton in Somerset Shire was ye first wif vnto Sr Thos Fludd of Millgate Knight: By whom he had divers sonns and davghters whose names are expressed on his Monument. What Her matchless Industrie in Houswifry was, and how amply she expressed herself in the entertainment of her friends, and in what lavdable manner her hospitality was extended towards ye poore we need not to expresse in writing, being that ye essentiall characters thereof are engraven even to this very day in the hearts of svch as are yet living who were conversant with her in her lif time; she changed this mortall lif for an immortall on ye (25)* of (Jan. 1591).*

Accept (O blessed soule) as sacrifice,
A filiall signall of obedience,
And let this marble memorie suffice,
Although but in a part of recompence
To maifest the loyall duty of your sonne
Before his toylesome pilgrimage of lif be done.

Robert Fludd, Esquire and Doctor of Medicine, erected this monument as a pious memorial of his most beloved Mother.

Besides the armorial bearings at the top and angle of this tablet, there is a curious winged skull, the wings of which are painted blue while the skull itself is brown.

Some interest naturally attaches to this memorial, more especially as the inscription is likely to have been the work of Fludd himself. Far more important, however, is a cross on the floor of the chancel hard by the altar steps, and bearing the following legend.

In Jesu qui mihi omnia in vita morte resurgam.

Under this stone resteth the Body of Robert Fludd Doctor of Phisicke who changed this transitory life for an imortall the VIII day of September A^o D^{ni} MDCXXXVII being LXIII years of age, whose Monument is erected in this chancel according to the forme by him prescribed.

Most people who, in times recent, have undertaken to write

---

*At these points the inscription is almost obliterated.

upon Fludd, have not failed to affirm that an exceedingly curious, not a little elaborate, and altogether occult monument was erected to his memory, as the above inscription indicates, within the chancel of Bersted Church. It has survived the spoliation of civil war and the fanaticism of puritan iconoclasts, and it is there, so they say, to this day. It is there also that Mr Hargrave Jennings performed his profound meditation. Will it be believed after all that the monument is not in the chancel, and that, on the authority of the Vicar of Bersted, the Very Reverend Canon Scarth, it must be something like forty years since it was removed to the vestry under the tower. There is no doubt about the matter, and, it is to be feared, there is no doubt after all that poor Mr Jennings, who describes his walk to Bersted, in the mellow pleasantness of a summer morning, did not go to Bersted at all, or at any rate did not enter the church, or again, if he did enter, had 'conditionated' into the seventeenth century. Mr Hargrave Jennings says further that the tomb is 'an oblong square of dark slate-coloured marble on the left as you stand before the altar looking up the body of the small church towards the door.' Nothing of the sort. The *tomb* is a plain flat stone with a small brass let into it, and is part of the chancel floor. Moreover, it is on the right and not on the left, as you look west, which is what Mr Jennings meant but has expressed so clumsily. His reference is really to the monument, concerning which he goes on to inform us that there is a 'seated half-length figure of Fludd', but again nothing of the sort. The figure is not seated and is really little more than a bust. Finally, our misguided instructor gives part only of the Latin inscription, and prints its metric portion as if it were not metric. The inscription is actually as follows:

Sacred to the Memory of the illustrious physician and man, Robert Fludd, alias de Fluctibus, Doctor of both Faculties, who after some years of travelling beyond seas, undertaken successfully for the improvement of his mind, was at length restored to his Fatherland, and was not undeservedly received into the Society of the London College of Physicians. He peacefully exchanged life for death on the 8th day of the month of September, A° D^{ni} MDCXXXVII, in the 63rd year of age.

The inscription is wholly in Latin, and is accompanied by the following verses:

> Magnificis hæc non sub odoribus urna vaporat
> Crypta tegit cineres nec speciosa tuos
> Quod mortale minus, tibi Te committimus unum
> Ingenii vivent hic monumenta tui,
> Nom tibi qui similis scribit, moriturque; sepulchrum
> Per tota æturnum posteritate facit.

Thomas Fludd, of Gore Court, Otham, in Kent, Esquire, erected this monument to the happy Memory of his most beloved Uncle, on the — day of the month of August, MDCXXXVIII.

The entire monument is enclosed by an arch. There are armorial bearings behind the head of the bust, and on each side there were originally four books arranged one above the other. Two only remain, respectively inscribed *Misterium Cabalisticum* and *Philosophia Sacra.*

A rugged and precipitous footpath brings the traveller going south-east of the church once more to the main road and opposite the lodge gate of Milgate House, in which Robert Fludd was born. Its external appearance which is quite in one of the best manners of the country seat of the seventeenth century. At the time of the writer's visit the lodge was empty and open-windowed, the bosky winding road which led from gate to manor was somewhat wild and weedy, the cluster of tiny cottages, amidst fern on the left, with an occasional suspicion of deer, were untenanted, and the house itself was empty. Here, beyond all doubt, was the reviewer's best opportunity, which he lost no time in successfully improving, and for the first time on record, whether for Kentish histories, like that of monumental Hasted, or for still more archaic 'Visitations', the house itself was visited, and that in all exhaustiveness, even from roof to cellar. With much of the same seriousness which imbued Mr Hargrave Jennings, the writer mused before the strange mythological paintings which adorn the fine staircase, trod the echoing floor of the library and admired its beautiful oaken panelling, speculated in the splendid chimney corner of the great kitchen, passed with due reverence upstairs to the quaint and not too roomy drawing room, retreat for the ladies of quality in the reign of James I, and traversed the innumerable bedrooms, in one of which Fludd was born. From almost every window there are charming views of a well-kept English lawn and English woodland vistas. The whole impression was fascinating enough, but here again there was nothing specially distinctive, and Milgate House, like Bersted Church, may be seen in one of its varieties in almost any English county, provided church or manor be 'four miles from any town'.

2. JOHN DEE

ABOUT the astrologer of Queen Elizabeth a century of marvels gather. Learned in the courses of the stars, he was also reputed an alchemist; possessed as people supposed him to be of the secret of transmuting metals, he had also the complement thereof, the elixir which prolonged life and even renewed youth; man of the exact sciences, accomplished and inventive mathematician, he yet practiced magic and interrogated the spirits of the crystal. Protected by the royal favour, honoured by the court, visited by foreigners of distinction, he was still in danger from the fury of the common people who regarded him as a wizard. Himself an upright man, so far as it is possible to judge, whose private manuscripts reveal him also as sincerely devout and religious, he yet was associated intimately with one who is accused of rank imposture, is supposed to have been pilloried for forgery, and afterwards to have lost his ears. These are some of the anomalies concerning Doctor John Dee. Add to this that the date and manner of his death are matters which have been held to be uncertain, and that some have not hesitated to affirm that he was in reality alive for nearly a quarter of a century longer than is generally supposed, so that he passed the centenarian period; add also that one among the latest hypotheses in account with the Rosicrucian Mystery refers the foundation of that order to the Elizabethan doctor; add further, in this connection, that a work said to have been written by Dee in the year 1564, though it was not published till 1581, albeit in no sense Rosicrucian itself, became of Rosicrucian importance. Dr John Dee, it is evident, take him altogether, is a man of no small glamour or mystery, as also that excellent romance testifies which was written by one, Ainsworth, concerning the plot and treason of Master Guido Fawkes.

The special local habitation which connects with the subject of this paper is the banks of the Thames at Mortlake. Kentish Bersted, noticed last month as the place of the birth and burial of Robert Fludd, is a nest of hillside fragrance hushed within the charmed circle of protecting downs, but Mortlake at the present day is a vulgarized suburb of London, indisputably associated with priggish and cocknefied Putney, with woeful and marshy Barnes, and never wholly unconnected with the suspensional horrors of Hammersmith Bridge. It has some historic associations not much worth a reference, but the League of the White Rose may still shudder at the traditional house rather gratuitously referred to the Lord Protector and another once consecrated, or otherwise, by the presence of his General, Ireton. From such memories as these it is pleasant to turn and contemplate the peaceful figure of Dr John Dee. He is under rather than above the middle height; he is stout rather than thin; he is most usually habited in black, with silver buckles on his shoes, with knee breeches, with a skull cap. So far as silken lace and fine velvet will permit of it, he attires richly when alchemy has flourished with him, but sometimes his vestments are worn, that is when his crucibles have broken and his varlet has misgoverned the fire. At such times royalty will send him so many crowns or florins with which to keep his Christmas, or so many angels because the right honourable, the Earl of Leicester, would dine with him 'two daies after'. You may picture him with his wonderful crystal, the great, genuine, clouded, and potent pebble, set in an ominous frame, over which he prayed and invoked, and wherein his 'skryer', the gifted, unscrupulous, much-abused Edward Kelly, beheld and spoke with spirits, with Uriel, Ariel, Orfiel, Metron, Anatron, and so on to infinity, as a certain 'faithful relation' testifies to this day. There are many portraits of Dee looking usually serene and collected, and hinting little of the mysteries by which he was encompassed. That which appears[1] at the head of this brief memoir has not been selected as the best or most authentic, but rather as the nearest to hand, for those which are most to be preferred are unfortunately least accessible. That of his companion Kelly, reproduced at this point, is, so far as our knowledge goes, the only one which pretends to represent him, though on what authority is unknown. It is derived from Sibley's well-known but

---

[1] [Neither the portrait nor the view of the church are here reproduced. RAG]

not altogether respected *Illustration of the Occult Sciences.* Mr Ebenezer Sibley, albeit he forecast horoscopes, is not an altogether credible gentleman, and his vast volume contains some notable absurdities.

The memory of John Dee has perished from the drowsy, riverside town which he once adorned and mystified. Probably few people, even if they have been modified by mysticism, are aware that he lies in the churchyard of Mortlake. Yes, he is there, in spite of the Great Elixir, medicine of men and metals, and in spite of Rosicrucian hypotheses, unless indeed it be that the tradition of Mortlake lies, and that John Dee himself departed eastward to join the undying alchemist Flamel, and to be followed in due course by the whole Turba of migrating Rosy-cross adepts. For the Rosicrucians have orientated long ago, as one Neuhusius testifies. However this may be, there is nothing at the present day which identifies Mortlake with one of the most distinguished of its inhabitants. Poets, as the author of *Philip Van Artevelde*; premiers, as the first Lord Sidmouth; Lord Mayors of London, as Sir William Barnard; actors even, as Phillips, the friend of Shakespeare, are among the celebrities who abode here in life or rest here in death. House or site of house, monument or tablet—some relic—witnesses concerning most of them, but of Dee there is nothing. He may have been buried beneath the stones of the church floor, or he may lie beneath the grass of the crowded and now closed churchyard. No one knows. The site of his cottage is forgotten. Of the church which existed at his day only the tower remains; the body of the building belongs to the Georgian period; the chancel, with its fine Eastern window, is of yesterday. Yet some interest still attaches to the edifice, for it was over against the church wall that Dr Dee exhibited on one occasion his crystal to Queen Elizabeth, who had come to visit him accompanied by the whole Court and Privy Council, and the royal gentlewoman is said to have found great contentment and delight over that which she beheld therein. Here then is the picture of this church, since it is well to know by what walls an English Sovereign and an English Mystic, who held a special license in Alchemy, once 'skryed' in a crystal. One reason for giving it is to save well-intentioned persons from the misery of visiting Mortlake, more especially on a day in November when the river is abject and melancholy, the banks are damp and dripping, and on the waste of the Middlesex side the horrible spectres of iron cranes loom through the mist. It is ghostly enough at Mortlake in November even at the close of a pleasant Sabbath Day, but the ghostly quality is devoid of any fascination. Dead leaves are on the tow-path; desolate empty houses, with faded worm-eaten shutters, and countless broken windows, stare sadly at the forlorn prospect. Repulsive debris float slowly with an unnoticeable tide up-stream. It is precisely one of those waterlogged, weedy places where mere wretchedness would drive a materialist into mysticism, and where deadly dulness would tempt a mystic into transcendental trickery. It would probably be a good place for evocations; at least there could be no difficulty in transferring the mists of the river into the cloud which precedes vision in a magic crystal. There are quaint, old-fashioned, creeper-clad houses in rows here and there, which would be picturesque anywhere except in immediate contiguity to that particularly sordid railway bridge which spans the river. There is vacant land unlimited declared eligible by its agents, but to be shunned by all ghost-fearing persons. O hopeless and incurable dulness merged mostly in the mist of the river at its most dull and hopeless bend! Wapping may sometimes look winsome, and attractive the reaches of Ratcliffe, but Mortlake will never spell anything but misery to the mind capable of sentiment.

In these 'Haunts of the English Mystics' which illustrate the local habitations affected by some great names of transcendentalism, it is not designed to touch otherwise than with extreme lightness upon the histories of the personages that are concerned. The life of Doctor Dee and his associate Edward Kelly is a veritable romance of alchemy, none the less fascinating reading because, so far as Kelly was concerned, it has a reasonable leaven of trickery. It has also its tragical element, as becomes Hermetic biography. Of all these matters a full and authentic account will be found in an extended introduction to the *Alchemical Writings of Edward Kelley*, issued recently by the publishers of this magazine.[2]

Here it is sufficient merely to mention in passing that one of them is said to have discovered the red and white powders

---

[2] [i.e. James Elliott and Co. Waite wrote the 'Biographical Preface'. RAG]

of projection at Glastonbury, that afterwards they travelled in alchemy, visiting many continental countries, and performing fabulous exploits in transmutations, besides incessant divinations in the magic crystal. But the Emperor Rudolph II imprisoned Kelley hoping to extract his supposed Hermetic secrets, and he died in attempting to escape. Doctor Dee survived him many years, and became warden of Manchester College, but his life closed in poverty; the services which he rendered to mathematical science were obscured by his necromantic reputation, and to be forgotten even while alive was the fate which befel the Queen's own alchemist and the author of *Monas Hieroglyphica*.

4
THOMAS VAUGHAN AND HIS *LUMEN DE LUMINE*

[Printed as the *Introduction* to *Lumen de Lumine, or A New Magical Light*, by Thomas Vaughan, 1910. Waite did not reprint it in *The Works of Thomas Vaughan*, 1919, and as only 300 copies of his edition of his *Lumen de Lumine* were printed, the essay is virtually unknown.]

Waite looked upon *Lumen de Lumine* as Vaughan's most important work, for he saw it as representing Spiritual Alchemy as an expression of mystical experience in clearer terms than in any other English alchemical text. His essay comprises a detailed, comparative analysis.

THE intellectual and literary life of Thomas Vaughan belongs to a period which was not, perhaps, especially considerable in Wales, his native country, for preoccupations that were similar to his own. But in England it was sufficiently remarkable for interests of the occult kind, as distinguished from mystic interests, and so also in those parts of Western Europe which were most in communication, mentally and otherwise in Britain. I do not propose to dwell upon the incidents of Vaughan's external life, about which I have written sufficiently in other memorials; the few words in my preface will stand for the little that seems necessary in this respect; moreover, the known facts are few, and they offer practically no landmarks in respect of his inward life, or that part of it especially which is exhibited in his writings and with which we shall be here concerned. The compass of his literary work is small; he produced little books only in place of those vast treatises of which Robert Fludd had set the fashion in England a generation or so previously, and he issued everything within a period of six years. There is no means of gauging what impression his work produced in its own day, for the animadversions of Henry More cannot be counted as the formulation of more than an individual opinion. Vaughan, after his manner, was an alchemist—as we shall see with some detail presently—and it is certain that a century and more after his death he was disesteemed in this particular rôle, as alchemical bibliographies make evident. This is to be accounted for readily, as the makers of such lists reflected the feeling among seekers after what is called the physical work, and Thomas Vaughan—in spite of certain vagaries—was too much on the metaphysical side to be appreciated, or perhaps understood, in such circles. At the renewal of Hermetic learning in England, about the year 1850, a change came which is part of a general transition in critical or interpretative opinon on the whole subject of alchemy. It had then come to be regarded as the expression of a purely spiritual mystery under the veils of physics, and Thomas Vaughan was accepted as a typical example of the true concern, almost ready-made and close at hand. He was exalted at once to a high throne of adeptship, and, as criticism of the opposite kind can be scarcely said to exist, he has so remained to this day— at once prized among the few and neglected by all others. Now, it is not my present object to consider his titles to an advance place among adept-mystics in any sense that might be called catholic; an investigation of this kind, supposing that it requires to be made seriously, would introduce more suitably the text of his collected works, which still remains in my mind as something for which an opportunity is desirable, and hence may be sought hereafter. I propose only to enlarge upon the purport, horizon and inference which belong to the individual text presented here for the first time to modern readers. It is just possible that the conclusions arising therefrom will stand virtually for the whole. *Lumen de Lumine* is in several respects the most considerable tract which has appeared under the name of Eugenius Philalethes; it is much more important than *Euphrates, or the Waters of the East*, although this was his last work, and it is much more mature as a fruit of thought than the little things that preceded it, though those which I have already edited contain traces of attainment as well as abundant promise.

While I have intimated that he is not entitled to any considerable place as a prose writer, Vaughan's style has the charm of its period, which is not to be accounted for entirely by the archaic manner; but the reader who passes from these introductory pages to the work itself must be prepared for the particular difficulties which attach to the terminology of occult literature in English of the seventeenth century. To write on the subject in the vernacular was then almost a new experiment, and that which had been expressed obscurely enough, so far, in the universal medium of the Latin tongue, fared worse in the unaccustomed vesture. The difficulty is of two kinds: in part initial, on the surface and therefore superable; but in part it is also essential—that is to say, inherent to the matter—and in this aspect it prevails indifferently in all the tongues and dialects which have contributed their resources to the expression of the mysteries in terms of the logical understanding. The unassuming task of an attempt to clear some, at least, of the issues is all that is designed in the present introductory discourse; and if it should prove helpful to those who are concerned, I shall consider that my part is done.

Now, it is said that some books are written within and without, and we know of one, at least, which is so described under the most mystical of all conditions, concerned as it is with that epoch when the last things of time will suffer dissolution into eternity. In a much lower sense, there are many other books which correspond to this diagnosis, and among them there are some also which seem to be written in an inverted manner, so that to get at their real message it is better to begin at the end and to work backwards. Their real and ultimate meaning is in any case reached more easily after this method. Thomas Vaughan's *Lumen de Lumine* is one case in point, though it does not follow this cryptic plan consciously, for the confusion of the issues or otherwise. If I have personally broken up its veils to my better satisfaction by such a process, it may, of course, mean only that I have followed what has proved for myself the line of least resistance. The angels came up and went down indifferently on Jacob's ladder, and it does not signify materially how the task of disentanglement is initiated, if at the end I shall have found some part of that which lay within the author's mind when he wrote it— of that which appears very badly on the consecutive side of the surface, firstly, through his plan of concealment, and, secondly, through his imperfect power of intelligible expression.

The tract is offered by its title as a new magical light communicated to the world: let us see therefore what he has to say about Magic. Well, those who understood it of old divided it into three parts—elemental or physical, celestial or astrological, and spiritual. The first and second are not to be understood in any conventional sense, for Vaughan despised common processes of alchemy—to cite a single example—and he did not consult almanacs or ephemerides either. At the same time, there were some aspects of practical alchemy which he acknowledged and proficiency in which he sought: this branch of Hermeticism was included implicitly in his first division of natural magic. And he recognised also the subtlety, the power and the universal permeation of the stellar influences, wherein, under God, both soul and body—except in complete regeneration—would be said by him to live and move and have their being; but hereof was his natural magic on the astrological side. Respecting the third division, it is plain throughout the discourse that an alternative description for spiritual or divine Magic is the root and mode of experience which lies behind the mystical doctrines of theology. Having reached this point, it will, I conceive, be unnecessary to say that Vaughan's Magic was a secret wisdom, distributed after definite manners and was not evocation or necromancy, dealings with angels or demons, trafficking with elementary spirits, the confection of talismans or sigils, or anything approaching, from whatever distance, the dregs and lees which have been gathered into Keys of Solomon, Almadels, Arbatels and Grimoires. The intellectual fools of these subjects and devices he left to their foolishness, and the cultus-mongers of diabolism to the disease of their black arts.

According to Vaughan, the three divisions which I have cited are intermarried, and it is indispensable that they should so be for the accomplishment of any great work. This, however, is when they are comprehended at their height, for normally they are now dismembered. Once they were united in a single natural subject; but man separated them, with the result that they became dead and ineffectual. As our mystic does not speak further, or at least from the same point of view, concerning this Natural Subject, and as we know otherwise that there is one and one only to which these branches of research and implied attainment are attributable, I conclude that man is the synonym thereof, his body the ground of the occult physics, his soul—or psychic part—the one sphere in which the stars can be read with a true judgment, and, finally, that of things divine the criterion or key of discernment is in the spirit of a man. If therefore it pleases anyone—who seeks to make use of a veil—to term the knowledge of this subject Magic, I conceive that it will be scarcely worth while to dissuade him—always on the understanding that he can show such reasons for concealment as may excuse the recourse to veils under any circumstances. At the very end of our inquiry we shall have to decide whether all this phenomenal mystery wherewith we are surrounded in the hidden sciences—so called officially—may cover an experience about which it is unsafe to talk openly in the public day, and, if so, whether we can make a guess as to its nature. We shall then have received that magical light which Thomas Vaughan set out to communicate in his treatise; we shall be in a position to judge whether his veils failed him as a warrantable and catholic medium, and how far he was hampered by the inchoate physics of his period as well as by his personal inhibitions.

We can say at once that *Lumen de Lumine*, in a stricter understanding of the respective terms, is an alchemical rather than a magical discourse, and out of this arises the question whether his alchemy is after all or not that of the mines, or whether it is of the holy spirit of man. For this purpose I shall begin almost at the end of his little book. In his day, he tells us there was one section of a perverse generation which commonly called themselves chemists, and these abused the Great Mystery of Nature by applying thereto the name and nonsense of *Lapis chemicus*, whereas the gold and silver of the philosophers are a soul and spirit, while the common metals of alchemy, as it was known to Geber, are in no wise adaptable to the purposes of the adept. We can discern, I think, here that Vaughan is again talking—but still in the language of subterfuge—concerning that subject which we have agreed to regard as man. His medicine is a spiritual substance, his gold is wisdom, his stone is the touchstone which transmutes everything. And, again, the medicine can only be contained in a glass vessel, by which I understand the purified body of the adept. Connected with this, there is the theory of a metempsychosis, which is the last transmutation, and thereby the mercurial nature of man is endowed with the constancy of symbolical gold. They key of all is the Kabalistic septenary of man, it being understood that these distinctions of faculty are without division of essential personality. The septenary is composed of two triads and unity in the middle thereof; or, seeing that such distributions are essentially fluidic, there is an alternative key which is formulated as one ruling over three, three over seven, and seven over twelve, the name of one being *Deus Rex fidelis*, the Divine part of man, in its union with the Divine in the universe, governing and co-ordinating the triad of its chief phases, the heptad of its gifts or faculties, and the duodenary of its fruits in manifestation. 'This and no other,' says Vaughan, 'is the truth of that science which I have prosecuted a long time with frequent and serious endeavours'. We seem already to stand in the upper room of a great palace, with great windows looking out over a far country; but to translate the cryptogram in this sense, though it is, of course, something, is not sufficient to justify Vaughan or our own concern in his reveries. If a given cipher decodes in the official language of a theosophy which is already familiar, we have had our pains to no purpose, but we shall see at the end whether, in his concealed fashion, the author intimates anything concerning that *Rex fidelis* by which his kingdom may be declared with power in the consciousness of the heart.

Proceeding a little further in our reverse process, we shall come to understand more openly the sacred and religious nature of the metempsychosis— or soul transfer—which is here under notice, because its alternative word is defined very simply as transmutation, and salvation itself is nothing but the synonym of both. When it is understood that these three are one, their product is yet another familiar term which stands for them all—that is to say, conversion, being a deep, mystical, substantial change, by which the hard and stubborn flints of this world become chrysolite and jasper in the eternal foundation. It is the same process as that which is referred to in the old Rosicrucian counsel: *Transmutemini, transmutemini de lapidibus mortuis in lapides vivos philisophicos*—'Do ye suffer transmutation, and be changed from stones that are dead into living and philosophical stones.' It is in this sense that the *ars chemica transmutoria*, in its vulgar understanding, was, according to the claim of the Rosicrucian brotherhood, least and most negligible of their secrets. By the virtue and effect of such conversion, it is said by Vaughan that we may ascend from our present distressed church, which is in captivity with her children, to the Jerusalem which is above and is the mother of us all. Man attains thereby the state of the septenary, which is the true Sabbath, the rest of God into which the creation shall itself enter at the close of the great, symbolical week.

But Thomas Vaughan is like some schools of the mystics which are working at this day, and which draw their oracles of interpretation from many branches of symbolism artificially combined and indeed confused together. He discourses now of physics, now of astrology, now of alchemy—often meaning all the time that highest conception of religion which he has been able to attain—and he pauses here and there to serve a righteous vengeance upon those who have sophisticated and degraded these sciences, which in their proper understanding are aspects of the one science of sanctity. So also, as an extrinsic office of divergence, he introduces that convention attributed to Zoroaster under the name of Prester, which, unfortunately for us, has come to have rather ridiculous associations at this day. He is showing, in his halting and ineffectual way, that the earth itself is not only the Lord's, as well as the fulness thereof, but that it is bright with the glory of God and glowing with His intelligence. To that which thus animates and illustrates he ascribes the name of Prester, otherwise the fire-spirit of life, or, according to pseudo-Zoroaster, 'the priest that governeth the works of fire'. This, says Vaughan, is an influence of Almighty God—that is to say, it is life of life, and it comes from the land of the living, which is the Supernatural East and the Second Person of the Divine Trinity. The elucidation offered is that the supernatural light was first manifested in the Second Person, or—literally speaking—in Christ, even as the sun is first manifested in the East, morning by morning. I believe, and it is indeed certain, that all this is an allusion to the work of Christ in the soul; but again we shall have got no further than we had reached very long and long before we had opened the closed gates of *Lumen de Lumine*, unless, as the term of all, he has something so far undemonstrated to tell us of this operation and that which lies behind its experience at first hand. It is in the true sense of this oracle that Vaughan also explains the Kabalistic maxim which tells us how every good soul is a new soul coming from the East, that is to say, from the *Sephira* called Wisdom, which, according to the Christian Kabalists—whose school may be said to have been founded by Picus de Mirandula and carried some steps further by William Postel, while at the very period of Vaughan it was putting forth a great light of arbitrary reasoning in Germany—which, according to these interpreters, was Messias, the Son of God. Hereof is therefore the mystery of being born of God. This birth and rebirth is not, however, exactly an operation of time, or of God in the soul while it dwells in an earthly body, for it is also the theosophical doctrine of emanation—or, in other words, the descent of the soul is from God by the way of the Second Person, and in this sense it is antecedent to the night of the body. Vaughan, however, was not especially versed in Kabalism, for his opportunities were few in England; he wrote prior to the publication of Rosenroth's *Kabbala Denudata*, and, as I have intimated, he does not, with the best intention, express himself too clearly. Against his apparent contradictions at this point, the reader should understand that Kabalistically the descent of souls took place by the way of the two Sephirotic pillars, that at the head one of these there is the supernal *Sephira Chokmah*, and at the other that of *Binah*—respectively, Wisdom and Understanding, *ex hypothesi* answering to Christ and the Holy Spirit, but in reality to *Abba* and *Aima*, the Supernal Father and Mother, who are in no sense these Persons of the Christian Trinity. To put it shortly, there was emanation or creation from both sides of what is called the Tree of Life. Among the later Kabalists, no two excogitated along quite the same line of doctrine, and criticism is disposed to regard most of the scholia and commentaries as works of reverie. But the complete independence of each consideration in respect of antecedent consideration is really in the spirit of the *Zohar*, the materials of which are equally vast and confused, while their common exclusiveness was reduced to artificial harmony by a presiding genius of compulsion, which was always out of expectation and always worked wonders. When, finally, the Christian Kabalists intervened with other unheard-of curiosities, they were arbitrary after their own manner and exhibited strange lights of enforced conformity.

The truth is that the doctrine of our descent from the Divine according to the Sephirotic system of Jewish theosophy scarcely adjusts itself to Christian interpretation, or rather the doctrine presented under that light is much more involved than Vaughan and some other interpreters recognise. It is not therefore surprising that, as he proceeds in his short commentary, he gets further and further away from recognised mystical philosophy, more especially in his statement that it was the Most Holy Spirit which breathed into Adam the breath of life. He records also another failure when he seeks to justify this statement by identifying the Third Person with the Kabalistic river flowing forth from Paradise, and with the Kabbalistic *mater filiorum*. The Sephirotic *Binah*, or Understanding, has nothing to do with the river symbolism of the Sephirotic scheme, as this springs from the *sub-Sephira* which is called *Daath*, or Knowledge, while the principle of womanhood in the Divinity does not reside in the Third Person but in the First, as I have sought to explain elsewhere.

For our present purpose it signifies little in the last resource whether Vaughan misconceived, or even if he embroidered, Kabalism; what is much more important is that at this point we approach what may be termed his actual presentation of secret doctrine, and this I shall state substantially in his own words, leaving the necessary developments till all is collected at the end.

The first intimation begins fantastically enough by the comparison of souls to flowers in the land of the living, and it is for this reason that the Prester is called in the *Oracles* a flower of thin fire. The reference, of course, is to flowers in a world of light, and this world is seemingly the supernatural centre upon which Nature was founded at the beginning, or the Throne of the Quintessential Light. Now, it is said that the operation of what Thomas Vaughan has elected to call Magic is to attain this centre, while its supreme mystery or practice, the *modus* of the operation in question, is to multiply—which means to manifest—the centre. The reference that is here intended is not to the centre which gives up no form—the abyss of Saint-Martin—but rather to the circumference thereof, which is the fountain of all forms, and of him who enters therein it is affirmed by the mystic that he will know why the fire descends and, having found a body, why it again goes up to heaven—this being an allegory—perhaps among other things—of the soul's outward progression and ultimate return within. The alternative, correlative expression of this mystery declared in doctrine is that the Prester is the 'secret light of God', while its knowledge is that also of the Hidden Intelligence and the vision of the Inexpressible Face. Herein is the categorical statement, and hereof it is the evidence that we seek, or, if it must be expressed so clearly, the theory is insufficient to arrest when completely set apart from the practice.

In some other respects the spiritual philosophy of Thomas Vaughan was like that of the period which he represents; it recalls Robert Fludd, Reuchlin the Kabalist, from each of whom something was drawn, and many others who, possessing certain lights for the explanation of the mystery of the soul, were conscious also of an uninspired but feverish anxiety to probe the mysteries of Nature and carry to its last consequences the Hermetic doctrine that the things which are above correspond to the things that are below, that the macrocosm is summarised in the microcosm, and that the first is only the second on a greatly extended scale. There is a heart of truth in this fantasy, because the means of Divine Grace are abroad in Nature, though the correspondences between Nature and Grace are not understood in their confusion but in their parallel distinction.

Very often Thomas Vaughan, who confesses everywhere to a policy of concealment, is liable to be credited with more subtlety than he possessed, for his method of expression—as I have more than once sought to point out—is as much unintentionally involved as it is wilfully cryptic. His discourse concerning the æther is a case in point. It is said to be that of the lesser world, of the microcosm, and he likens it to the Heaven which Anaxagoras called his country, believing that he would return thither after death, so that, within the limits of theoretical philosophy, though not really, we seem at once and obviously outside the microcosmic region. The æther heats, but does not burn; its region is above the stars, in the circumference of the Divine Light. It is that empyrean which receives warmth direct from God and conveys it to the visible heavens and the inferior creatures; it is the reflection of the First Unity. On the surface all this is crude enough, as it is also preposterous enough, even on the understanding that Vaughan is speaking in his heart of

Divine offices in the soul, using primitive language of physics. That his concern is this, and not, except far away and in virtue of dubious analogy, the mode of communication between the spiritual and material worlds, is made evident when he says that the microcosmic office of the æther is to bring news of another world and to show that we live in a corrupt place. What can this be other than the descent of the Divine Light into human consciousness? When therefore the alchemist Sendivogius—or alternatively Alexander Seton, standing behind his disciple as the true author of the *New Light of Alchemy*—affirms that with this æther he watered the lunar and solar plants, I can only infer that he spoke, or was held by Vaughan to be speaking, of the powers and graces of the soul and spirit—as it may indeed be—of the seven gifts of the Spirit, and the twelve fruits previously mentioned. And when the Kabalist, also quoted, says that this æther is Divine, that when joined with Divinity it makes Divine substances, I conceive again that hereof is the work of God in man's soul. The æther is therefore the Divine virtue in the macrocosm and in the microcosm—the rest is wilful verbiage or unintended confusion. And I suppose further that its identification with the mineral tree of the alchemical philosophers is the one or the other as whosoever may please to regard it. Or in reality it is both, and out of those two there comes a third as their natural issue, for, as I have intimated already, according to theosophical cosmogonies of this kind and of this period, the creative work in the mines is like the formative work in the soul, and God raises plants and vegetables to life as He restores the inward man from the bonds of mystical death. Thus also, as *Luna* is held to correspond with the psychic part of man in virtue of a nature-born symbolism which seems almost as old as history, so Vaughan says that there is a *Luna* of the mines; and as there is a *Sol* which is the spirit within us, in the same immemorial correspondence of symbolism with *Sol* in the greater world, so also our mystic supposes an *astrum solis*, a mineral sun, to which in his obscure fashion he attributes power that he calls spiritual. There is no need to say that the institution of such analogies could not help physicists or the seekers after metallic transmutation, and Eugenius Philalethes fell therefore reasonably into disrepute among them.

Now, I think that enough has been gathered by way of

quintessence from the mixed elements of *Lumen de Lumine* to show that its author, though he elected to write of eternal and divine things under the regrettable term of Magic, was concerned with these things primarily, and was therefore before all else a mystical philosopher. We have thus established a proper canon of criticism and have secured a *terminus ad quem* for the whole discourse. We can now proceed to a short consideration of his tract in its opening sections, leaving to the last that Rosicrucian document which is not his work, but by which it is justified and wherefrom it arises as an elaborate commentary. Now, as I have intimated, Vaughan was also an occult philosopher, and, as such, he carried the warrants of his school at the period for an explanation of the cosmogonical universe. To this end he had his one catholic and Hermetic axiom for the root-principle of philosophy, and this—to reproduce it literally— was 'that the things which are above are equal to things that are below, and things which are below are equal to things that are above.' It has been already the subject of reference; it is called otherwise the doctrine of correspondences and forms part of the document known as the *Emerald Table*, attributed to Hermes Trismegistus on the authority of a Latin version which is exceedingly late, and the claims of which no scholar would, I believe, accept at this day. The question does not signify, for its real authority is not resident in its imputed source and still less in a simple difficulty of date; it is of universal acceptance in all branches of Hermetic wisdom, and it is at the root of mystical religion, which explains Nature by Grace, man by God, that which is without by that which is within, and the things that are seen by means of the things which are invisible. It is *par excellence* the universal sacramental doctrine; but it is to be distinguished, on the one hand, from the false teachings of pantheistic identity and, on the other, from the aberrations which characterised the occult philosophy of physics in the seventeenth century, though it was thought that they drew from Nature.

Having excogitated in the light of his masters certain spiritual principles which illustrated mystically the dealings between God and man, and additionally, if we care to say so, having passed through various grades of spiritual experience, which he expounds hermetically, and comprehending thus—or in part—

how the soul grows under the light of Divine Grace, he proceeds to theorise physically along the same lines, with results which are readily intelligible, seeing that in such matters he was in the rear rather than the van of scientific knowledge at his period, while neither van nor rear can be held as anywise advanced from our present standpoint. He speaks therefore on the authority of similitudes representing things that are within concerning that which is without, and he is dark and dubious enough. In a word, he declares in the macrocosm who should declare in the microcosm only. This is how at the beginning of their wisdom the wise exceed the measures. He had many of the modes and dilections for the great subjects, and he knew well enough that there is a mystical marriage to be made between things without and things within. But it was not given him to proclaim the banns, and so I think that he went astray, as so many have done both before and after this illuminated disciple. It is almost impossible to extract anything consecutive from the continual superincession which he effects between the spiritual and physical works. As a theoretical alchemist—though not utterly apart from practice—he went also astray wonderfully over the generation of metals, though it would have been none of our concern if he had been right therein. He began his intellectual life as a follower in particular of Henry Cornelius Agrippa, and perhaps it was in this manner that he came to call his philosophy of things, as he believed that they were, by the name of Magic. Of such was his first predisposition. He had another, and this—as we have seen—was alchemy, which became his ruling passion in physics. It was a preoccupation which he never overcame, and this is why it is not merely so difficult to separate what is highest in his memorials from what is external and phenomenal but why the process secures so little by comparison in the residue. If, therefore, for the satisfaction of my readers, in dealing with an obscure subject, I proceed to speak in more detail concerning the earlier and negligible sections of *Lumen de Lumine*, they must appreciate my standpoint that there is no need to trouble about anything which Vaughan says in physics; because, although it is exceedingly occult science, it does not, for such reason, contain any hidden treasures: in some respects it is certain that he was taught of the spirit, but the spirit told him nothing that is or was of moment about the material world. I believe that he had what he regarded as a true theory on the spiritual side, and he spoke of it as darkly as other adepts about the great practical work. His only extant manuscript seems proof to my mind that personally he had not advanced very far in the physical experiments, and, indeed, there is little reason to conclude that he was on the right track or met with decisive success even in respect of the *minima*. For the rest, let it be assumed at the moment that he had, by rumour, or otherwise, some notion of an important spiritual practice: now, the point is—as we have seen—that he attempted sometimes to apply it in the physical order; and, accepting his own tentatives with high seriousness, as occult philosophers will, he describes how he obtained recognition and credentials from Thalia, the Spirit of Nature, as a reward of his zeal and his service. In the course of a visit paid in her company to the mineral kingdom, she communicated to him some of her mysteries under the seal. it does not transpire what they are in any clear maner; but he returned with two gifts, of which the first is an hypothesis concerning the generation of minerals and metals in the bowels of the earth after a mode which is analogous to that of animals and vegetables; but the second was that cryptic similitude, in virtue of which he borrowed the language of alchemy to speak of the soul's transmutation. As regards both, it is certain that the one was taken over by Thalia from Paracelsus and the chemists of his extensive school, while the other looks like a draught on open account from Jacob Böhme, though otherwise there is little evidence that he was especially known to Vaughan.

There is only one thing more to say of this wonderful interview, which went into things so deep and yet suffers anti-climax from a *mise-en-scène* and light sentiment couched in indifferent verse and rather suggesting comic opera than the centre of things physical in the course of their solemn exploration. It is certain, again, that Vaughan is adapting his mystical doctrine by the help of Hermetic correspondences to the physical world; he is really endeavouring to get at the first matter and the principle of metallic life; he is not therefore discoursing of spiritual mysteries under a veil. At the same time, and because he is applying a spiritual principle to things external, there is here also superincession in his language; in other words, he is talking of one subject in the technical terms of another. It would be easy to reconstruct the visit *ad interiora terræ* so that it would read like a very carefully formulated mystery of introspection, a visit *ad interiora animæ*, characterised by the chief signs which are presented symbolically at their reception to initiates of the instituted mysteries. We should find the great but not hostile darkness with which such experiences and ceremonies always open; the hush of expectant anxiety; the breathing of the spirit; a certain light which goes before manifestation in the spirit; the approach to the sanctuary; the intimations concerning a way of ascent and descent; and so forth. The sanctuary and altar at the centre of the material universe would become those in the deep place of a man's inward nature, from which the fire goes up towards a higher mode of life; and as no man knew better than Vaughan that the way is indeed within, his higher dedications may have been scarcely less present—although unintended—to his mind when he talked of the growth, transmutation and tincture of physical things than when his subject in all frankness was the descent of the soul into generation. Here and there he seems to offer profound suggestions that we have not touched the fringe of that great and mysterious providence which was at work in the fall of man; he mentions here and there an ascent and fermentation which, whether he thought or not that it had a root in the material side, is unintelligible except as the *ascensus mentis in Deum* and as the ferment of the new life; in fine, he seems to hint at the repose of the body in trance, and recalls the Sabbatic rest of the soul, as it is so described by the great Kabalists, in the hour of translation.

Speaking generally, it is because of his recurring preoccupations of the better kind that when he is least to our purpose in his actual matter, we find allusions and side-lights in Vaughan's writings which are true and rare and precious. I think that he realised, for example, the Divine Presence and the Divine Immanence at the centre and root of material things, and he may even have recounted his symbolical journey to the mineral region as if he were passing into the realisation thereof. For him that Immanence was declared externally in Nature; for him it was at work everywhere—in generation, even in corruption; it was shown forth also in man by that light of conscience wherein we abide under the shadow of the Divine Light. Thus the first matter of the spiritual work is always within us; we are thus wonderfully made; an inner heaven and an earth are ours, even by Nature. If naturally also we are comparable spiritually to a realm without form, there is a cosmos to be declared within us, a desirable term in harmony to be manifested. If Vaughan recognised the hand of God in any physical work, it was because in the spiritual order no other power obtains or counts for anything. If he affirms that the secret fire to which he refers so often has the place of its abode in the Divine Nature, it is because it is the root and essence, the life of all our life: as such, his theoretical intention was perhaps an inquest beyond the regions of knife and scalpel into the very heart and marrow of our being. He dealt, and only too often, with other matters; but he knew that the true subject of philosophy is the man within. And he was by no means alone in his school over this dedication, for even the physical alchemists, who sought for the gross elixir, held this notion before them, and their minds were so polarised—if I may use such a strange term—that they could scarcely help combining man's physical and spiritual welfare. The divine experience could occur to man in flesh; his higher part is indeed a holy ground; it is the vessel and recipient of heaven, the mystical Horeb on which the Law is promulgated, whereon falls the Divine seed. Vaughan's reference—which I have mentioned already—to the Hidden Intelligence looks very much like getting to the Palace of the King; he is indeed as a prophet who, having seen God manifested in a burning bush, comes down from the Mount of Horeb that he may apply the particulars of his vision to the explanation of every cosmos. How far he could have expressed the position to himself in this direct language I do not know, and perhaps have little encouragement to think; but he is speaking continually, to the extent that any power has been given him, of the mystery of a grace above all grace made known in the heart.

 I believe, therefore, that I am within the reason and the evidence if I repeat that Thomas Vaughan was *per essentias* a mystical philosopher, and that his school, as such, was that of the Hermetic tradition, with important derivations from other and especially Kabalistic sources. But *per accidentia* he was a Hermetic philosopher of the school of metallic transmutation, and he worked upon a fantastic adaptation of the Divine promise contained in the Divine counsel: 'Seek first the Kingdom of God and His justice, and all other things shall be added unto you.' That notebook of his, to which I have before alluded, exhibits his devotion to certain lines of experimental research which he never left and of which he died ultimately, at a comparatively early age. According to the common report, perpetuated by Anthony à Wood, he was killed by an explosion in the midst of operations upon mercury. It seems evident from the manuscript that he proceeded largely by guesswork, which he may have regarded as a kind of inspiration; and the fact that he was once successful in performing a specific experiment was no guarantee that he could repeat it. On one occasion, which he regarded as signal, he failed through forgetting his materials; another inspiration came, and then he remembered and achieved. It is not after this manner that the Great Work was performed—if performed indeed—in physical alchemy. Vaughan was, otherwise, a man of transparent sincerity, and so it should be added and noted that he never claimed final attainment in respect of the mystery which absorbed him on the outward plane; so also he arrogated nothing to himself in the grades of mystical achievement, but he had reached after some manner the degree of certitude.

And now there are only a few points which remain over, but they are really the main points of my thesis—its term and conclusion. Intellectual certitude or conviction on the basis of experience, if this had come into his soul, what is the message which he bequeaths to us who study and are concerned with him only as a mystic? He has illustrated the hopeless nature of the material quest when he says that, although nothing can be effected in its absence, the *secretum artis* has never been published and is a secret of God. But there is another secret, which is *Donum Dei*, and is therefore, I presume, more disposed for dispensation to those who are prepared and seek it—though neither is, of course, incommunicable. The few who receive it must, before all things, beware of sin; for, albeit repentance is possible, the super efficacious grace, which is the tincture of this gift, is lost thereby, or alternatively has been turned to poison, and there is no record of its second reception. It is obvious that this reference can be only to some state of the soul which is above the two states recognised by official theology, namely, sufficing and efficacious grace. There is, I believe, an exotic theology which admits of a sudden *élan*, a sudden illustration, a call and response so instantaneous and so absolute that the soul overleaps everything, even repentance, and does not merely partake of sanctity but becomes it. This is the condition of the tingeing stone, which can diffuse only what it has, and hence sanctifies by its presence. If such a state is ever reached—God knoweth—I should suppose that sin is impossible, for the soul is no longer under the law of God's Immanence but of God's Transcendence. Accepting this, the condition descried or experienced by Thomas Vaughan lies somewhere between a region which we can look at only through a glass darkly and the world of efficacious grace. I suggest that it responds to the first-hand realisation in consciousness of the most approximate *locus* of the Divine Immanence— which *locus* is within us. The bond between that Immanence and the Great Transcendence is the link and chain by which we are 'bound about the feet of God'. Herein is the recognition—and after some high manner, the manifestation—of the *Deus Rex fidelis*, the sight of 'the secret light of God', and the 'vision of the Inexpressible Face'. Assuredly, those who have received these gifts need never sin; such gifts are health of the body, health of the soul, pearls without price.

Now, the Key of which we are in search to unlock these mysteries further is not given by Vaughan, but is found in the *Rosicrucian Epistle* which he published, and of which his visit to the mineral region is a variant and reflection on a kind of eternal plane. The *Epistle* describes, under the allegory of a mountain, a certain profound state of introspection, the experience of which, in one or other of its aspects, is shown forth—like his own allegory—by the pageants of the instituted mysteries. Once more, the darkness is always there, the Guide is there also, and so are the Dwellers on the Threshold, who are conquered by complete purgation, even as the presence of the Guide is ensured by a preparation which is more literally perfect prayer than is prayer its veil and symbol. The revelation comes in a stillness which is as if after tempest; it is then that the darkness dissolves, the sun rises and the treasure is found. That treasure is, according to Thomas Vaughan, a mystery of Christ, and, according to the Rosicrucians, it is the deep secret of a meeting in the Spirit—that is to say, where the House of the Holy Ghost lies hidden from the world. It is the 'secret incubation of the Spirit of God' upon the chaos of the natural man. It follows from the context of the *Epistle* that the practice is a work which is done by a man on his own part, proceeding from his own basis. To attain therein, I conceive that it is essential and imprescriptible that at any and every hour we should abide—at least by conformity of the will—in communion with the Divine, and that, whether we eat or drink, whether we are dejected or exalted, we should never permit any lesser interest to interfere with that communion, because there is nothing to be gained in the whole world which is of any value in comparison with the Gift of God, wherein He offers Himself and is received. But this is the high commonplace of eternal truth.

There are three other things only—the concealment practised by Thomas Vaughan, the unity of the mystery which is the subject of cryptic writing in Christian times, and after what manner it is rooted in Christian doctrine. These three are intermarried by an underlying bond, and, as they can be taken in any order and the exhaustion of the one will almost determine the other, I will begin by speaking of the peculiar artifice of language which is adopted in *Lumen de Lumine*, so that it shall at once intimate and cover the parts that are most vital in the subject of discourse. I have scarcely occasion to say that the art was common to the whole school of occult philosophy, and, to all intents, it was a creation of Christian times. There is no proper sense in which it can be said to have existed in old Greece or Rome. Plato was deep and suited little enough to men and women of the crowd; Plotinus was deeper still; we know also that there were the oracles of Zoroaster, and there was so much as may have passed into the writing of the original Pythagorean wisdom. The instituted mysteries were never made known in the open day, or at least till the time came when the divine spirit had departed and there was perhaps little but their corruption to hide. But there were no concealed literatures; there were no subjects which, by claim or attribution, were exceedingly high, as a *gloria in excelsis*, about which for some inscrutable reason it was necessary to write books that dealt with the subject largely from a standpoint of intimate familiarity and yet never made it known. It was, of course, *Hekăs, hekăs, este bébēloi* for those who were foreign to the sanctuary, and the schools of philosophy were protected from intrusion by a graduated scheme of instruction; but there is no analogy between these facts and the successive production, for centuries, of books—let us say—on alchemy. Except in the sense that all great books are cryptic—that is to say, are mysteries of art, and yield up the inward essence of their meaning to the fellow-artist only—there is no concealed writing at the present day. If I, for example, had such a predisposition and so pursued it that I learned how to transmute metals, I should either make known my process or reserve the fact of its discovery. I should not write mystery-theses to announce that I possessed the secret and place it under impassable veils, while affirming that I was revealing the whole art. I am not in the seat of judgment on this matter *per se*, and, though I know that all this was done in the past, I am not prepared to say—except upon a single assumption, to be specified later—how or why it appealed to those who adopted it in the old days. But as alchemy is not the only concealed literature, and as it has two aspects, while in respect of its more exalted part it does not differ in the term from all spiritual traditions, the question arises whether there is a mystic secret, the existence of which can and should be intimated, but is at the same time too vital to speak of openly—either from the danger which may attach to it—apart from certain conditions—or from its possible abuse, either because it is only transmitted by initiation or because its expression is not possible in the terms of the logical understanding. I feel that the first set of alternatives offers no adequate explanation, though both forms were used indifferently by alchemists. In the second set, I do not care to entertain too definitely any question of things which are held to exceed expression because of the wilful obscurantism which may seem to be implied thereby to the normal mind. It is obvious that the thoughts conceived in the brain can pass into the symbolism of language and are not otherwise formulated. *Ex hypothesi*, however, we are dealing with an experience which, according to the intimations concerning it, lies behind the common field of consciousness and is attained only in a non-external state. Yet, this granted, then the greater the truth of the view the more idle it must appear to write books about that which neither has entered nor will enter at any time into the formulæ of language.

The cryptic literatures on this supposition would be held therefore stultified; but it should be observed that they do not confess to inability of such kind, though they allude and testify plainly to a restriction imposed by duty. When Eirenæus Philalethes claims that he has spoken more openly than any adept who preceded him, he also admits that he was ever in fear of his vow—lest he should betray that part of the mastery which he had covenanted not to record. We find everywhere the intimations of a hindrance belonging to this order; and though, again, I do not like to regard a matter of experience as communicable solely in a sanctuary of initiation, and although there is otherwise little trace of such initiation in the books of Thomas Vaughan, the process of exhaustion seems to leave no other explanation open, and this therefore is the assumption to which I have once referred. If we accept it, the whole position is simplified; we have no longer to consider whether the law of concealment was itself justified, or perhaps even essential, for we are dealing simply with a code of honour, or at most with some pledge which lay between the hands of a secret tribunal that was able to enforce its covenants. As the mystery was received, so it was also passed on, and the texts came into being, demonstrably or otherwise to keep alive the tradition. It will be asked, after what manner? How could they act as recruiting sergeants? Supposing that one of them fell into hands prepared, how did the simple fact and how did the untutored study bring such a person to the door of any sanctuary? It may be suggested that the student was put thereby upon the quest and that, if he followed it with untiring patience, he came at length to the right quarter and among the right people. It may be said, on the other hand, that, if he were indeed prepared, what Eckartshausen calls the inner sensorium was in part opened by aspiration, stimulated by reflection and the study of the texts; that at a certain point it might happen that he was joined on to the chain of tradition; that he entered and took his place in the secret church, company or assembly. In a word, he grew up into the sanctuary. This is the only justifying and catholic construction: we know how our meetings come about naturally and everywhere in the normal consciousness and how our consanguinities are declared; but if—as we can and should know—there is an experience possible in a higher form of consciousness, then it is reasonable to suppose that therein are other meetings—of those who have grown up into the same degree, and that there other bonds are declared. Those who have followed the path of astral workings, and who are acquainted with the kind of encounters which take place in that region, will understand well enough that very different doors may be opened in the world of sanctity. Those also, and such still more, who in the repose of the heart receive the intimations of the Union will not need that I should add more thereof or of the communion of saints in a common medium of experience. They understand that we need not go either to the east or west to reach our peers or masters. The experience is spoken of diversely in all the schools; but I have not found that the draperies conceal other than the same form, and I end as I began, therefore, by affirming that it is one mystery concerning one experience and the deeps and the heights thereof. It does not differ in Thomas Vaughan, who set out to use language that he might hide his thoughts, or in Jacob Böhme, who had no pledges to maintain and is yet darker still because in the heights and the deeps he saw indeed plainly but found no adequate tongue. And I place these two cases in apposition to show that initiation—though it is usually the shorter road—is one thing; but the work of the Spirit is not confined within those limits, and the high experience is everywhere. That is why the great mystics of the Latin Church reached terms in their consciousness which it was given to them to expound more fully than the exponents of most other schools. But these confess also how language failed them respecting that which eye hath not seen nor has the sensible ear heard. So there is something—and those who have undertaken the great journey will be aware otherwise—to be allowed for the impediments which are of this nature, as well as for the holy jealousy that is special to the secret sanctuaries.

In this manner we begin to understand why the mystic and adept philosophers had recourse to their veils; there was the difficulty of initiation with covenants, and there was the difficulty of translating an experience in the deeps into the terms of the surface. Our own mystic has perhaps spoken as best he could, subject to the personal confusions which made his veil a patchwork; and I hold that, to us who are seekers on our own part of the mysteries which are within, he does bring reports of a fuller understanding concerning the work of God in the soul than we are used to hear except from his peers and brothers. And this is the summary which arises out of the present inquiry— that the holy centre is manifested in consciousness, or, as Thomas Vaughan says in his crude terminology, the Prester is multiplied—that is to say 'the influence of Almighty God' and the life of life. To conclude therefore: he testifies on many occasions in all his books that his mystery was in Christ and that Christ was the Key thereto. The Incarnation is the Key in particular of his mystic chaos. I should add that the schools to which some of my subsidiary references[1] are made were also Christian schools; but, because the first-hand experience at what the spiritual alchemists called the fount of Nature is of all tongues and nations and ages and climes, I think that the Divine Saviour has been known by other names in many places of God. He is the ground of union which union has been attained everywhere. It is in this wide sense that all his sheep are not of the same fold, and Christ delivers up the Kingdom to His Father in all regions of the universe.

[1] [i.e. Waite's footnotes to the text of *Lumen de Lumine*. RAG]

5
A HERMETIC APOCALYPSE

[Printed in the *Occult Review*, Vol. 17, No. 1, January 1913, pp. 20–6.]

Between 1908 and 1913 Waite produced a series of papers for the *Occult Review* on the most significant pictorial works of the Spiritual Alchemists of the sixteenth and seventeenth centuries. Khunrath he perceived as being among the most important of these alchemists, because of his blending of alchemical and apocalyptic images in his engravings. Waite looked upon these engravings as providing a source of inspiration for later Rosicrucian symbolism—itself utilized by the adepts of the Golden Dawn.

THE name of Heinrich Khunrath is rather a vague portent to most of us here in England, for his record in Hermetic archives was either in the Latin or German language, while he was somewhat disposed to the disastrous literary fashion set a few years previously by Paracelsus; that is to say, he interspersed his Latin with German, so that in his chief work he is a crux to the reader of either language only. When, therefore, the time came for his most important memorial to be put into a French vesture—now some years ago—I do not on my own part envy the competent translator to whom the task was committed. That rendering is unknown here, except by a very few indeed, and the rumour regarding Khunrath depends either from intimations given by myself or from references by Eliphas Lévi, most of which I have been responsible for putting into English. The reader may be aware possibly that he was an alchemist, but of a strange, exotic kind, and it has been suggested, with a certain temerity, that he belonged to the Fraternitas R∴ C∴.. Eliphas

Lévi says that he is worthy in all respects to be saluted as a Sovereign Prince of the Rosy Cross, but this has to be understood in the symbolical and not the historical sense, as if it were a point of fact. The brilliant French occultist indeed specifies that he applies it scientifically or mystically, much as it might be conferred on himself. The title was, in any case, unknown to Rosicrucianism of the seventeenth century and is borrowed from a Masonic High Grade, belonging to a period which was very generous in the distribution of exalted dignities.

Khunrath was an illuminated Christian Kabalist, and in so far as the secret doctrine of the brotherhood may have set forth then, as later, the mystic theosophy of Israel under the light of the New and Eternal Covenant, so far the author of the *Amphitheatre of Eternal Wisdom* is on common ground with Rosicrucians, with whom he has been for such reason identified. Being also, as I have said, an alchemist, though bizarre in his manner of expression, so far as the fraternity included Hermetic Mysteries among its implied possessions—which it did indeed and certainly—so far it was in near relationship the the German Philosopher. But Khunrath was born in or about the year 1560; he died in 1601, before Rosicrucianism had appeared on the horizon of history; and there is no evidence (*a*) that he was concerned in any secret movement which led up to its foundation, or alternatively (*b*) that he caused its antecedent existence to transpire, supposing that it is much older than the available records show. One student of the subject with whom I was once in correspondence—Dr George Cantor, of Halle—even went so far in the opposite direction as to suggest that there is a veiled attack upon Khunrath in the *Confession Fraternitatis R. C.*, under the disguise of a stage-player 'with sufficient ingenuity for imposition.' This tract belongs to the year 1615, when the death of the supposed subject of reference should have tended to shield his memory, while the period of time that had elapsed would have removed all point from the allusion, which is obviously to some man of the moment. Moreover, the mystical aspect of alchemy, which was the particular concern of Khunrath, should have drawn rather than repelled a society which protested against 'ungodly and accursed gold making'.

There is some evidence in his books that the alchemist was irascible enough, and abusive like Thomas Vaughan, in dealing with those from whom he differed, but there is nothing tangible to show that he made a figure at his period. How obscure he was is indeed evident from the few facts which have transpired concerning him. He was a native of Saxony who led the wandering life of so many struggling physicians before his day and after. Having taken his degrees at Basle, he made a certain stay at Hamburg and ultimately settled at Dresden, where he is said to have died in poverty at about 42 years of age. He published three small tracts in 1599; one was entitled *Symbolum Physico-Chemicum*; another was on the Catholic Magnesia of the Philosophers; and the third was on the alchemical Azoth, by which he understood the First Matter of creation, otherwise, the Mercury of the Wise. One of them at least was reprinted in the eighteenth century, but there is nothing to suggest that they were important at their own epoch, in the opinion of that epoch. His really great work did not apear till 1609. He is to be distinguished from Conrad Khunrath, another writer on alchemy, who began to publish about 1605 and may have been his kinsman, but I have no particulars concerning him.

It is the *Amphitheatre of Eternal Wisdom* which occasioned some glowing panegyrics by Eliphas Lévi, who also chose for the motto on the title-page of his enchanting *History of Magic* the definition which Khunrath gives of his own book, *opus hierarchicum et catholicum*—a catholic and hierarchic work. He points out, however, that in the matter of official religion, the German theosopher was a resolute Protestant, adding that herein he was 'a German of his period rather than a mystic citizen of the eternal kingdom'. Perhaps this is more an aphorism than an apology; but Lévi recognized assuredly that on another side of his nature Khunrath abode in the freedom of the spiritual Zion and not under the ægis of reform, in Germany or otherwise. I have long felt that his apocalyptic presentation of the Kabalistic and Hermetic Mystery should be known among Students of the Doctrine in England, but the brief notice which is possible in the present place can only summarize the design.

I offer to the consideration of my readers three reduced plates out of the total series of nine most curious engravings on copper which form an integral part of the work with which I am concerned. They represent (1) the Oratory of an Alchemist, the device belonging to which is *laborare est orare*; (2) the Gate of

Eternal Wisdom, being that of the Knowledge of God; and (3) the sum and substance of the whole work, termed by Eliphas Lévi the Rose of Light; but this is the explanation of one symbol in the terms of another. It is the central point of all wisdom, human and Divine, which point is Christ. The suggestion of the designs as a whole is that the work of the alchemist belongs to the path of devotion, notwithstanding (*a*) the material vessels with which the kneeling figure is surrounded in the first and on which his back is turned somewhat significantly; (*b*) the message of the Latin dictum—that work is prayer. I conclude that here inward work is adumbrated. The suggestion of the second plate is that the Gate of Wisdom is one which is opened by prayer, but

The Oratory of the Alchemist

The Gate of Eternal Wisdom

the latter is not to be understood in any formal and conventional sense. It opens in the darkness and seems like a journey to the centre, meaning the inward way and the great path of contemplation. The third design indicates that Christ is not only the Way but the Truth, understood centrally, and the very Life itself. This is the Christ of Glory, no longer the Man of Sorrows and acquainted with infirmity. Yet is He still in the human likeness, not the Mystic Rose in the centre of the Macrocosmic Cross. The reason is that as what is called theologically and officially the scheme of redemption is an operation within humanity, for the manifestation of a glory to be revealed, so in its utmost attainment humanity is not set aside. The Christ

The Vision at the Centre

manifest is not apart from the Lord of glory, and the Christ within is ever the Son of man in us. So also our great Exemplar in Palestine could not do otherwise than come to us in human form, or He would have been never our pattern and prototype. He could not do otherwise than speak in the clouded symbols of our earthly language, or He would have brought us no message. There seems no question that in the opinion of Khunrath the knowledge of Christ gave that of the Philosophical Stone, in the ordinary alchemical understanding of this term, for a medicine of metals and of human nature, but he deals on his own part only with the mystic side of attainment, though in such language that it shall preserve the likeness of alchemy. Many of the old seekers may have sought to understand him literally and went astray accordingly.

The thesis is veiled under the guise of a new translation, with commentary, of certain passages extracted from the Book of Proverbs and the Apocryphal Book of Wisdom, the versicles being arranged so that there shall be one for each day of the year, and each with its annotation might well afford food for thought even at this time and amidst all the hurry of our ways. The new rendering—as such—is, I think, negligible, but it is printed side by side with the Vulgate. The commentary explains that in alchemy, as in religion, Man is the Matter which must be purified, the physical part being brought into subjection by that which is within and above. God is the soul which vivifies; the Holy Spirit is the bond of union that leads to the Everlasting Kingdom and gives admission therein through the work of regeneration. The part of co-operation which lies with the alchemist must be performed in the deeps and solitude of his own spirit, separated from sensible things, as by a withdrawal into God. The way of contemplation and Divine colloquy will open the Book sealed with Seven Seals—which is the Divine Book of the Scriptures, Nature and the Self. The end is a marriage of Divine Wisdom with the soul, and therein is the Blessed Vision wherein all things are beheld.

In addition to the allegorical plates, the text already mentioned and the commentary, there are some curious tables, and the significance of one is likely to escape the penetration of all but the most careful reader. It is a summary of the whole subject; and it suggests that those who are called to the work should realize under Divine leading, that the knowledge (*a*) of God, (*b*) of Christ Whom He has sent, (*c*) of the greater world, (*d*) of the Self within each of us, and (*e*) of the Stone sought by the Wise under so many names, is one knowledge which is attained by one gift within ourselves, as in a clear mirror or fountain.

Such was mystic alchemy at the beginning of the seventeenth century and on the threshold of the Rosicrucian Mystery.

6
KABALISTIC ALCHEMY

[First printed in *The Journal of the Alchemical Society*, Vol. 2, Part 9, January 1914, pp. 43–58. Reprinted in *The Alchemical Papers of Arthur Edward Waite*, but omitting the *Abstract of Discussion*.]

The association of alchemical and kabalistic symbolism in one text fascinated Waite, and he dealt with the anonymous *Aesch Mezareph* (Purifying Fire) in *The Doctrine and Literature of the Kabalah* (1902), analysed it in depth in the present paper, and returned to it again in *The Secret Tradition in Alchemy* (1926). The eighteenth-century English translation of *Aesch Mezareph* was familiar to members of the Alchemical Society through Westcott's reprint of 1894 (as Vol. 4 of his *Collectanea Hermetica* series), but Westcott's brief introduction had been inadequate for a proper understanding of the text, and Waite's commentary—in the form of his paper, *Kabalistic Alchemy*—was both welcome and necessary. Waite gave four papers to the Alchemical Society during its two years of active existence (from 1913 to 1915) and of them *Kabalistic Alchemy* seems to have been the most successful.

IT IS my intention on the present occasion to enter a very curious and unfrequented byway of Hermetic research, but it is one which repays visitation, at least in a certain sense, and though I feel that within the limits of a single paper, I can only touch very lightly on the main part of my subject, we may be brought to another Gate of Alchemy, beyond which the field of spiritual aspects unfolds a wide horizon. It is not an easy byway to travel and, therefore, although I shall assume no familiarity on the part of my hearers, I must ask for their particular attention. If afterwards, in their own studies, they will seek to pass through the Gate, they may find that the opening of the eyes in Alchemy is like the opening of the eyes which befell the disciples at

Emmaus, so that they knew Him Who was their Master. At the same time, all that is understood as Alchemy—its concepts, phraseology and remains in literature—will be left behind as they proceed.

Among the writings of Zosimus, the Panopolite, which formed part of the great collection of works by the Byzantine alchemists, there is a tract entitled *The True Book of Sophe the Egyptian*, which appears to regard Lead as the First Matter of the physical work and Copper as the Tingeing Agent. In a word, the practical part has nothing to suggest that it conceals spiritual operations under terms borrowed from material things, even if the metals mentioned have to be philosophically understood; but the little text has a preamble of one paragraph concerning the Divine Lord of the Hebrews and the Powers of Sabaoth. This creates a noteworthy distinction between the science and wisdom of the Egyptians and that of the Jews. Both have come down from the far past; neither investigates material or corruptible bodies; the operation of each is sustained by prayer and Divine Grace; but that of the Hebrews is rooted more solidly in Divine Justice. There follows a passage which I have quoted already elsewhere [*The Doctrine and Literature of the Kabalah*, 1902, pp. 451, 452] and which accounts for the recurring comparison between the work of Alchemy and that of God in creation. 'The symbol of chemistry is drawn from creation (in the eyes of its adepts), who save and purify the divine soul enchained in the elements and, more than all, who separate the divine spirit entangled with the flesh.' This is sufficiently remarkable as a definition of the work of adeptship, but there is also presumably a key to the sense of certain terminology used subsequently in the text. 'As there is a sun, the flower of fire, a celestial sun, the right eye of the world, so Copper, if it becomes flower (that is, if it assume the colour of gold) by purification, becomes a terrestrial sun, which is king on *anciens Alchemistes Grecs*, 1887, 1888. Greek text, pp. 213, 214, French translation, pp. 206–208).

My object in giving these citations is not to show that it is easy—as it is certainly—to find mystical aspects of Alchemy in the Greek remains, but to introduce my particular subject by proof positive that thus early in the records, we find the people of Israel accredited with science and wisdom like that of Solomon, namely, greater than the Egyptians, but—*ex hypothesi*—like theirs a science and wisdom of Alchemy. We may leave it, at least for the moment, as an open question whether the wisdom and science were purely mystical and transcendent or whether there was also what is called a practical side in the sense of physics. That 'flower of fire', the spiritual sun of the adepts, is obviously a concept drawn from the material luminary; and the flower of earth, denominated by later Alchemy 'the Son of the Sun', the divine manifestation below of that which is Divine in the universe, was probably unfolded by processes regarded, in the Hermetic dream, as reproducible analogically in the laboratory of the adept, when he was at work, in the metallic kingdom.

Here, then, and in any case, is our first intimation concernjng the possible existence of a Kabalistic Alchemy at an early period of the Christian centuries. In the opinion of M. Berthelot, the tract—but more correctly there are two tracts—which Zosimus refers to Sophe, or Cheops, contains elements of considerable antiquity, belonging to the period of the oldest texts passing under the name of Hermes. It is not a very clear intimation, being confined to the statement of an alleged fact, from which nothing appears to follow. There is, however, a much longer treatise—by way of commentary on Zosimus and some other philosophers—referred by tradition to Olympiodorus, an Alexandrian philosoper, and possibly the preceptor of Proclus. In this it is affirmed that Democritus and the rest of the adepts, belonging to anterior times, concealed their science by the use of common and inappropriate terms, so that it might be reserved to the Egyptian kings and that they, on their own part, might be enabled to maintain their rank among the prophets. The Jews notwithstanding attained knowledge of the practice and expounded it in clandestine books. [*Ibid.* Greek text, p. 90; translation, p. 98.] It is said further by Zosimus himself that the Jews, having been initiated, transmitted that with which they had been entrusted, namely, suitable processes in the mystery of natural tinctures. [*Ibid.* Greek text, pp. 242, 243; translation, pp. 233, 234.] So also he went in quest of a certain 'instrument' but could find nothing concerning it till he had recourse to Jewish books. [*Ibid.* Greek text, p. 138. Translation, p. 140.] Finally, under the pretext of describing furnaces and other apparatus, the same Zosimus gives an account of the vocation, habits and aims of philosophers which incorporates a very curious mysticism concerning man in his original perfection, the fall of man, his redemption and restoration to Paradise. All this he claims to have drawn out of Jewry, and it is not a little in the likeness of what we now understand as Kabalism, but permeated by Gnostic and Christian elements. [*Ibid*, Greek text, pp. 229–233. Translation, pp. 222–226.]

Now it is difficult to suppose that these testimonies do not establish the fact that not only was the Secret Doctrine in Israel beginning to exceed the measures of Talmudic literature, but that there were at least a few alchemical treatises, presumably written in Hebrew, outside those of Maria the Jewess, to whom the Byzantine alchemists refer so frequently. Zosimus, it should be remembered, belongs to the third century of the Christian era and pseudo-Democritus is referred by Berthelot to the very beginning of Christianity. The Hebrew literature is, however, lost—unless, after that manner which is dear to the heart of occultists, we prefer to say that it is in concealment.

Kabalistic Alchemy is represented at this day by a single tract, or rather by so much of it as can be found in a piecemeal translation into Latin of the later seventeenth century. The original has disappeared, and it is indeterminable whether it was written in Hebrew or Aramaic, though one of the modern editors has decided in favour of the latter, but without assigning his reasons. The text in question is called ASH MEZAREPH, the 'refiner's fire' of Malachi ii, 3, according to the Authorised Version, but translated *ignis conflans* in the Vulgate, and hence the alchemical work is called in the English rendering of 1714, *Purifying Fire*. It was put into Latin, as I have said, by the pains of Baron Knorr von Rosenroth and is incorporated into that great Lexicon or Apparatus which forms the first volume of his *Kabbala Denudata*. The incorporation has no pretence to completeness, which was not to be expected, having regard to the purpose in view; and the extracts are described by Rosenroth on his first title-page as forming a *Compendium Libri, Cabbalistico-Chymici, Ash-Mezareph dicti, de Lapide Philosophico*, etc. When the unknown student who called himself 'A Lover of Philalethes', made the English translation at the period I have mentioned, he collected all the excerpts scattered through the

Kabalistic dictionary and reduced them into logical order, taking considerable pains. His work has been reprinted, with certain revisions and some useful notes, under the editorship of Dr Wynn Westcott [*Collectanea Hermetica*, Vol. IV, 1894]. What proportion the collated text, as we know it, bears to the original seems likely to remain as it now is, a matter of speculation, though a preface to the latest edition mentions that it is 'still extant as a separate treatise'. About this there must be some misapprehension, unless it is in that statement of hiddenness to which I have alluded. In any case it does not seem to have been available for the purpose of the edition in question.

In the absence of the original we are as much in the dark as to its date as we are about the comparatively unimportant question of its authorship. It is transparently that which it claims to be, a genuine remnant of Kabalistic Alchemy. At the same time, it belongs to late Kabalism, as it postulates the existence of ten *Sephiroth* or Numerations in each of the Kabalistic Worlds, and this is not countenanced by the *Zohar*. There is one reference to Geber, the Arabian philosopher, but, at least to my own mind, it suggests an acquaintance with the Latin author who assumed that name. The *Zohars* are rather numerous in Hebrew and there is one mention of one of them which treats of medicine, but this I have failed to identify and believe that it may be a confused reference to the anonymous *Zohar Al Harrephua*, or *Splendor super Medicinam*, which was printed at Venice in 1497. Could we rest certain that the 'Lover of Philalethes' had made all his extracts from Rosenroth correctly, the *terminus ad quem* in respect of antiquity might be settled out of hand, for *The Book of Purifying Fire*, in its English form, quotes *The Garden of Pomegranates*, which is the work of Moses of Cordova, and this Rabbinical Master is either of the fourteenth or sixteenth century—probably of the later date. On referring, however, to the Latin text of Rosenroth, it seems certain that a mistake has been made and that a short passage referable to the German compiler has been credited to the alchemical text. In this case, four lines at the head of Chapter III call to be deleted. I should imagine, in conclusion as to the point of date, that we shall be safe in assigning the *Ash Mezareph* to the sixteenth century, or subsequently to the appearance of the *Sepher Ha Zohar*, in its first printed forms at Cremona and Mantua, between 1558 and

1560. There is no doubt in my own mind that it was the publication of these editions which gave an impetus to the study of Kabalism, both in Christendom and Jewry; for, although what I have called late Kabalism, largely an extension of Zoharic doctrine and its interpretation, had already begun, the works by which it is best known are of posterior date.

<pre>
                    1.
                  KETHER
               (WHITE HEAD)
                 The Crown

      3.   2.
     BINAH   CHOKMAH
  (THE MOTHER)   (THE SON)   (THE FATHER)
  Understanding   Wisdom   Wisdom

      5.   4.
   GEBURAH   CHESED
   Severity   Mercy
                      6.
                  TIPHERETH
                    Beauty
      8.   7.
     HOD   NETZACH
    Glory   Victory
                      9.
                    YESOD
                  Foundation

                     10.
                   MALKUTH
                (THE DAUGHTER)

                  The Kingdom
</pre>

Fig. 1. The Sephiroth and their Significations.

Kabalistic Alchemy

Having now finished with the preliminary and bibliographical part of my subject, I will take up the question as to the way in which the little Kabalistic treatise on Alchemy should be approached if we are to find anything to our purpose in its pages. In so far as it embodies Kabalistic elements regarded under a Hermetic light, we must have recourse to the *Zohar* in its study. Following *Sepher Yetzirah*, or *The Book of Formation*, this great monument of Hebrew theosophy postulates ten *Sephiroth* or Numerations extended through Four Worlds, beginning with pure Deity and ending with the manifest creation. There is

1.
KETHER
Metallic Root

3.
BINAH
Tin

2.
CHOKMAH
Lead

5.
GEBURAH
Gold

4.
CHESED
Silver

6.
TIPHERETH
Iron

8.
HOD
Brass

7.
NETZACH
Brass

9.
YESOD
Mercury

10.
MALKUTH
Medicine of Metals

Fig. 2. The Sephiroth and metals. First scheme of allocations.

neither place nor occasion to speak of them in detail here. In a broad sense the gulf between the Divine and the world of earthly elements was bridged by means of the *Sephiroth*, and hence they have been called emanations, but the Zoharic system is not, strictly speaking, emanationist, or at least it includes counter aspects which modify or perhaps cancel some apparent leanings in that direction. The *Sephiroth* are tabulated as shown on the previous page. KETHER = The Crown; CHOKMAH = Wisdom; BINAH = Understanding; CHESED = Mercy; GEBURAH = Severity; TIPHERETH = Beauty; NETZACH = Victory; HOD = Glory; YESOD = The Foundation; MALKUTH = The Kingdom.

These titles are conventional, for the most part, and will be familiar to many, but have been enumerated, this notwithstanding, for the purpose of the subject in hand. In ancient Kabalism the first three form the *habitaculum* of Deity, the essence of which is triadic. This is the world of ATZILUTH, *fons Deitatis*, the true region of emanation, but it is that of Divine Persons, proceeding one from another, though having very slight correspondence with the Christian Trinity. The next three *Sephiroth* constitute the world of BRIAH, or of creation. From one point of view, this world is archetypal, the pattern or idea in Divine Mind which became manifest afterwards; from another it is the realm of highest created intelligence; understood broadly as archangelic. The world of YETZIRAH or Formation comprises three further *Sephiroth*. From one point of view, the universe was formed therein, but it was not externalised; from another it is the angelic world. ASSIAH, the factual, manifest, material world is constituted by the tenth *Sephira*, MALKUTH. This is one Sephirotic system, but there is another of high importance which postulates BRIAH and YETZIRAH as the body of the Divine Son and ASSIAH or MALKUTH as the Daughter of God. Between them they contain all created intelligence, from Seraphim to human souls, and the Daughter is more especially the Community of Israel, the synthesis of elect souls. So far concerning the *Zohar*, but the masters of rabbinical theosophy who discourse therein knew nothing of Alchemy.

Later Kabalism had, however, yet another classification, as I have intimated already, and this repeated the decade of *Sephiroth* through each of the Four Worlds. Now, it was possible

1.
KETHER
Philosophical Mercury

3.
BINAH
Philosophical Sulphur

2.
CHOKMAH
Philosophical Salt

5.
GEBURAH
Gold

4.
CHESED
Silver

6.
TIPHERETH
Iron

8.
HOD
Copper

7.
NETZACH
Tin

9.
YESOD
Lead

10.
MALKUTH
Metallic Woman
or Moon-Lady

Fig. 3. The Sephiroth and metals: Second system of allocations.

obviously to say things about KETHER in ASSIAH which were not possible about KETHER in ATZILUTH, and so of the rest. But the author of *Ash Mezareph* goes further, even than this and affirms that the *Sephiroth* are found, from first to last, in the Mineral Kingdom; and on this basis he produces two further classifications, as they now follow. (1) KETHER = The Metallic Root, from which all metals originate, as the remaining *Sephiroth* from KETHER in the worlds above. (2) CHOKMAH = Lead, which is the first-born of the Metallic Root and is called Father in relation to the rest of the metals. (3) BINAH = Tin, being of old evolution in the series, as shown by its age. (4) CHESED = Silver, and the reason of this allocation is said to be the metal's colour and use. (5) GEBURAH = Gold, because in the late Kabalistic Diagram called the Tree of Life, GEBURAH is on the left or northern side, and according to *Job, xxxvii*, 22, gold 'cometh from the North'. With this rendering the Latin Vulgate agrees, but our Authorised version substitutes 'fair weather' for the precious metal. (6) TIPHERETH = Iron, because it is said to be like a man of war, presumably having the kind of beauty which belongs to the array of battle. (7 and 8) NETZACH and HOD = Brass, because this is the hermaphrodite of metals and because the two pillars of Solomon's Temple were made thereof. (9) YESOD = Mercury, because it is the foundation of life and quicksilver is a living water, which is the basis not only of metallic art, but of Nature herself. (10) MALKUTH = the Medicine of Metals, because they are metamorphosed thereby into gold and silver, under the auspices of Judgment = GEBURAH = Gold, and of Mercy = CHESED = Silver, on the right and left sides of the Tree.

The alternative classification is equally acceptable for the reason that 'all systems tend to the one truth'. According to this, the first three or Supernal *Sephiroth* represent the three alchemical Principles, thus KETHER = Philosophical Mercury; CHOKMAH = Philosophical Salt; BINAH = Philosophical Sulphur; CHESED = Silver; GEBURAH = Gold; TIPHERETH = Iron; NETZACH = Tin; HOD = Copper; YESOD = Lead; and MALKUTH = The Metallic Woman, the *Luna* of the Wise; the Water of Gold and that mysterious field 'into which the seeds of secret minerals ought to be cast.' I should add that, his liberality notwithstanding, the author of *Ash Mezareph* prefers the first

Kabalistic Alchemy

classification, as it is that which he uses chiefly in the text.

The next question before us is that which we can learn from our text about metals and their allocations, the Three Principles, the Medicine and the Water of the Wise. As a Kabalist, the author was quite naturally concerned with the tabulation of all important references to the seven metals found in the Old Testament. On these he allegorised, computed the sum of the numbers produced by the consonants of the names, and sought further light by comparison with other names and words from which the same numbers could be derived. Herein he followed certain familiar methods—I mean, familiar among Kabalists—but if I were to enter into this part of the subject and deal adequately therewith I should fill a volume. If anyone should be disposed to pursue it, I can promise him much that is curious, a few analogies which are striking, but he will not find that *latens Deitas* lying, by the hypothesis, behind the processes and experience of mystical Alchemy, not yet the secret of metallic transmutation. In a word, it is not a research that I can recommend specifically to the *sodales* of The Alchemical Society.

It is possible, no doubt, to work so long at the decade of *Sephiroth* and dwell upon it so steadfastly that you will see the one thing everywhere. Had it not been for the saving virtues of the sovereign reason, I might have been in such case myself, considering my years of immersion in Kabalism, its schools and its literature. The 'adept anonymous and lover of learning' who discoursed of Purifying Fire must have taken a high degree in this kind of persuasion, for he discovers the decade in Gold, which has ten orders or degrees, all devised from the Scriptures and beginning with the KETHER of the precious metal, being that 'head of fine Gold' celebrated in *The Song of Solomon*, v, II, and ending with the 'Gold of Ophir' mentioned in *Job*, xxxii, 25. Silver has also its decade, and if anyone is in search of its KETHER, he will find it in *Exodus*, xxxviii, 17, where the chapiters of the pillars in the Court of the Tabernacle are said to be overlaid with this metal. But the MALKUTH of Silver is that Silver 'seven times purified' which is compared to the Word of the Lord in *Psalm*, xii, 6. The *Sephiroth* of Lead are in a state of occultation, which means literally that the number of references to this metal in Holy Writ falls short of the decade, so that it has to be completed by splitting the reference in *Zechariah* v, 7, 8 into two parts. Lead in alchemical doctrine is the Primordial Salt of the Wise. Now, as it is impossible to discover more than five references to Tin in all the Law and the Prophets, the author is in a position to elicit a purely Hebraistic reason for the inconsequence of this metal so far as the Work of Wisdom is concerned, and he says therefore that it remains separate from the Universal Medicine'. Moreover, vileness and tenuity are its conspicuous vices and hence—in addition to the obvious Scriptural reason already intimated—it is not suggested that Tin contains a Sephirotic decade. On the other hand, this is found easily in Brass, which term there is reason to believe signifies Copper; but silence reigns concerning the decade in respect of Mercury or Quicksilver. The reason seems to be that this metal was unknown in ancient Jewry, though our Hermetic scholiast pretends that its mystery lies hidden in the name of Mehetabel, who was the wife of a king of Edom. [*Genesis*, xxxvi, 29]. I do not know why the decade of Iron is omitted from *Ash Mezareph*, unless it be that this kind of invention maketh even the heart of the artist grow sick within him; but we learn for our consolation instead that Iron is the Male and Bridegroom, 'without whom the Virgin is not impregnated', which Virgin would seem to be the philosophical *Luna*, or Medecine of Metals, already mentioned. Turning for one moment to the second tabulation and in particular to the three alchemical Principles, no canon of distinction seems to be offered between *Mercurius Philosophorum* and mineral Quicksilver; on Philosophical Sulphur I find nothing that lends itself to quotation; while the discourse on the Salt of the Wise seems to be one of the lost sections.

So far it will appear that the intimations of *Ash Mezareph* are remote from the practical side of things in Physical Alchemy; they are an exaggeration in part of Zoharic principles of commentary, interpretation and so forth, while for the rest they draw upon the artificial and arbitrary devices of what is called the practical Kabalah. There is of course no reason to question that its domain is that of metals, literally understood, or at least that it begins therein. What it presents, however, in rough and broad lines is an hypothesis of evolution or generation from a Metallic Root, operating in several directions with various results, according to the places of the *Sephiroth* on the Tree of

Life. As such, I consider that the first tabulation is almost manifestly incorrect, but if the second should be preferred to the first, it is not therefore unimpeachable. I have met with other attributions in more secret Kabalistic systems and these are still better, though not perhaps perfect; but they do not concern us now. To the hypothesis there is a process added for the production of the White and Red Tinctures. This rests on the authority of Rabbi Mordecai, but I do not find an alchemist of this name in the great bibliography of Bartolocci. [*Bibliotheca Magna Rabbinica* 4 vols., folio, Rome, 1675–93].

Hereof is Kabalistic Alchemy, as it stands in the text, and I should think that scientific criticism would be disposed to turn and rend me, did I suggest that it should be taken seriously, or even as a contribution of any discernible moment to the most cryptic side of the literature. There is, however, another point of view, and to approach this we must set aside the wonderful but arbitrary verbal gymnastics of *Gematria, Temura* and *Notaricon*, in virtue of which Kabalism of a certain sort deduced anything that it wanted from the words of Scripture by the transposition of Hebrew consonants, the substitution of one for another and the computation of their numerical values. There are a few people in Israel who believe in these kinds of methods even at this day, but they are the antithesis of philosophical Kabalism. When the *Zohar* draws from the fountains of the higher mind, it knows nothing of such devices; it knows and cares very little concerning them in moments of pure fantasy. It is arbitrary enough, very often and too often, after its own manner, but it has other tricks than these. The ill-equipped occultism of the late nineteenth century, when it betook itself to Kabalism in ignorance of the real authorities, though that there were great mysteries in all these follies of artifice.

We must set aside the putative process of *The Book of Purifying Fire*, and then there will remain the attribution of metals and their suppositious planets to certain *Sephiroth* in the Tree of Life, together with that of alchemical Principles and so forth to the *Sephiroth* which remain over. Now, I have followed the quest of the meaning which lies behind these ascriptions through no common paths of research, and I have found some things that belong to our subject as members of an Alchemical Society which is concerned with the mystical side of Hermetic literature as much as with the physical. If metallic transmutation is possible, then in the hope that it may become actual, we know enough to be certain that the experiment has to be approached from the direction of modern scientific chemistry and not from that of the old alchemical texts. There are seven planets of the ancients as there were seven metals; the names given to the planets in the Western world have become in the course of time almost interchangeable with those of the metals. At least this is certainly the case so far as Alchemy is concerned. The history of the interlinking is obscure and it is beyond my present horizon. I may say that it is not explicable by analogies of colour, though there are certain thin analogies, as, for example, between the Sun and Gold. It is not entirely explicable by an hypothesis of astrological influence, as there is nothing on the surface of this to connect Saturn with Lead. It is a western doctrine of correspondences, and as such, has been extended to the Signs themselves; but this does not now concern us. The Hebrew names of the planets are not only entirely distinct from those of the metals, so far as the metals were known to ancient Jewry, but they were never interchanged with these. The seven planets were: *Sabbathaï, Tzedeq, Maadim, Hamâ, Nogâ, Cokhab, Lebanâ*; that is to say, Saturn, Jupiter, Mars, Sun, Venus, Mercury, Moon. This is on the authority of the *Zohar*, Part III, fol.. 287a. The seven metals are: Lead = *Ophereth*; Tin = *Bedel*; Iron = *Barzel*; Gold = *Zahad*; Copper = *Nehuseth*; which except in *Ezra*, viii, 27, is always translated 'Brass' in the Authorised Version; Mercury = *Aspirika*; Silver = *Cheseph*. The connection with which I am dealing between the metals and *Sephiroth* cannot be said to exist in the *Zohar*, though we are told in one place that Silver = CHESED = Mercy, and Gold = GEBURAH = Severity, or alternatively, Gold = BINAH = Understanding, while Brass is the union between Severity and Mercy, which might be held to answer by way of reflection to NETZACH = Victory and HOD = Glory [*Zohar*, Part II, fol. 138b.] So also Iron is once referred to MALKUTH and once to TIPHERETH. I must add the great text knows little and next to nothing of a connection between the planets and *Sephiroth*, because the planets belong to ASSIAH. The distinctive name of the planetary world is '*Galgooleem*', which is here taken as a synonym of ASSIAH, and, as we have seen, this world corresponds to MALKUTH, the repetition of the Sephirotic decade in each world being a later invention. Our particular author dwells, however, on a mystical interconnection between all the worlds and between the kingdom of metals and the kingdom of heaven. 'The mysteries of this wisdom differ not from the superior mysteries of the Kabalah. For the same consideration obtains respecting the predicaments in holiness as respecting those of the impure region. The *Sephiroth* which are in ATZILUTH are the same as those in ASSIAH.' It is added that 'their excellency is always greater on the spiritual plane.' It follows from this that the author of *Purifying Fire* recognises that there is a correspondence, not, however, developed, between the metals hidden in the earth and the planets which move in heaven: herein he is at one with alchemical literature, taken as a whole, and, I presume, with certain aspects of astrology. He recognises further that there is a higher, more momentous, correspondence between the metals and *Sephiroth*, extending through all the worlds recognised by Kabalism: herein he is particular to himself, and it is at this point that his thesis begins to emerge, if anywhere, into a mystical light.

The *Sephiroth* in the Zohar are a ladder of sanctity by which man can be united to the Holy One, and the allocation of certain *Sephiroth* to certain metals, though comprehensible in a text belonging to Hermetic literature, which is committed to the Doctrine of Correspondences, is a stretching of that doctrine to breaking point, unless the metals themselves are spiritualised. As much must be said, in my opinion, concerning the planets themselves; and I do not suppose that, on either side, the alternatives can be regarded as lying within the field of legitimate or tolerable discussion. Now, in orthodox Kabalism it cannot be said that there is any trace of symbolism concerning the Metallic Kingdom, save and except in so far as the Sephirotic correspondences which I have mentioned may imply—as I hold that they do—not only a marriage in symbolism, but an uplifting into a spiritual order. The question of planetary allocations is in much the same case. The sun, according to the *Zohar*, is in correspondence with TIPHERETH and the moon with MALKUTH, and these luminaries are spiritualised after the same manner as will be found in Holy Scripture. For example, the light which rules the day is the Sun of Justice and of Righteousness that 'shall arise with healing in its wings', according to *Malachi* iv, 2. I must not make myself responsible for the content of a colossal text like the *Zohar* on the face-value of memory, but I do not believe that there are any other express allocations of planets to *Sephiroth* found therein. Yet it would be difficult to affirm that much which passed into expression and extension at a later period is not by implication in the *Zohar*, and at the dawn of the sixteenth century, or some fifty years before thre text in question was printed, the following notable attributions are registered by Cornelius Agrippa in his *Three Books of Occult Philosophy*, which was in the hands of Abbot Trithemius in 1510, as appears by his letter prefixed to this work. The planet Saturn is referable to BINAH, the third *Sephira*; Jupiter to CHESED; Mars to GEBURAH; the Sun to TIPHERETH; Venus to NETZACH; Mercury to HOD; and the Moon to YESOD [*Op. cit.*, Book III, Ch. 10]. These ascriptions differ from both tabulations of *Ash Mezareph*, but the author of this work testifies that 'if anyone hath placed those things in another order, I shall not contend with him, inasmuch as all systems tend to the one truth.' Cornelius Agrippa invented nothing on his own part, being only a diligent compiler, and it follows that on this subject he drew from early Kabalists, but I have no means of identifying them. I regard his scheme as preferable to those of later date, and it assuredly implies that the *Sephiroth* connected with the planets had also an influence on the metals which correspond to these, a correspondence which he develops fully elsewhere in his work. [*Ibid.* Book I. Chapters 23 to 29.]

Let us take, however, the second classification of *Ash Mezareph* and see what it implies in the light of Zoharic theosophy.

We have seen that the three alchemical Principles are in the place of the supernal *Sephiroth*, which is the world of Deity. Philosophical Mercury is in analogy with the Metallic Root of the alternative list and belongs to KETHER, wherein is the Great White Head of the Zoharic Holy Assemblies, being That which resulted from the first movement of the Unknowable God towards the state of being declared and manifest. Out of KETHER, by a simultaneous development, there proceeded the co-equal *Sephiroth* which are called CHOKMAH and BINAH, being the

Divine Father and Mother of Kabalistic theosophy, both implied in KETHER and not in separation therefrom. In *The Book of Purifying Fire* these correspond to Philosophical Salt and Sulphur, which are not in separation from Mercury, for the Principles are a trinity in unity, like the three *Sephiroth* of ATZILUTH. But the triad of these Supernals produces a second triad, being CHESED, GEBURAH and TIPHERETH, or the world of highest created intelligence. In Alchemy they generate Silver, Gold and Iron, or the perfect metals and what, I suppose, might be called alchemically the first degeneration from these. But Philosophical Iron, according to *Ash Mezareph*, is the Sun of the Wise, the Male or Bridegroom, as we have seen, in correspondence with the Divine Son, begotten by the Divine Father and Mother. A third triad follows, which is another world of created intelligence, namely NETZACH, HOD and YESOD, or metallically Tin, Copper and Lead. There is no philosophical Tin, but Copper has an influence from Gold, as HOD draws from GEBURAH and philosophical Lead, according to our text, has the whole system of the universe concealed therein, because YESOD represents generation and the Kabalistic organs of sanctity by which this is operated. Hence Lead is called also the Father.

Finally, there is the fourth world of ASSIAH or MALKUTH, the region of manifest things, in correspondence with the Metallic Woman, Moon-Lady, and Medicine for the White, 'so-called because she hath received a whitening splendour from the sun.' There is only one way to explain this allocation, and it is by recourse to theosophical Kabalism on its highest mystical side. The sun is that Divine Luminary which is termed Jehovah in the *Zohar*, but also by other Sacred Names, and the Moon-Lady is Shekinah, connected in her manifestation with MALKUTH.

We are now in a position to understand something of the entire scheme. The outward development of transcendental *Sephiroth* produced, *ex hypothesi*, a perfect manifest order, which, according to tradition, subsequently fell; but the Divine Presence of Shekinah is still on this earth of ours and the return journey by which all things are consummated in God is by and in union with her. She is the leader of the human into the beatific state of ATZILUTH, and the nature of the travelling is adumbrated by the qualities ascribed in the Zohar to the *Sephiroth* above MALKUTH, up to and including *Chesed*. There is no opportunity here to specify these qualities, but they can be ascertained by a collation of Kabalistic texts and more readily by integration in those orders which are inheritors at this day of the old secret traditions.

On the alchemical side it is testified by the entire literature that the intention of Nature was always to make Gold or by inference at least Silver, as an alternative perfect metal; but owing to effective hindrances the so-called inferior metals have been produced instead. In the *Malkuth* of the metallic Kingdom, there is, however, that which *Ash Mezareph* denominates a certain 'field', a place of 'whitening splendour', a realm of medicine and of healing, wherein is the Moon-Lady, who is also the field. Herein lies the restoration of metals, so that they shall enter into the perfect state, which is to be understood as the free operation within them of the Three Principles in the Supernals of the World of Metals. This analogy constitutes what I termed at the beginning that other Gate of Alchemy which, if opened by the student, may lead into strange places, even to the Heart of the Master.

In conclusion, I think that the little tract on *Purifying Fire* deals, as I have said, with literal and material metals, but is written in the light of its statement that the greater excellence is always on the spiritual plane. So far as it puts forward physical processes seriously, it is the dream of a fantasiast, who held that a described order on the spiritual place is repeatable of necessity on the material. I would dissuade any one from supposing that the tract contains cryptic chemical science of an advanced kind; but if another should pretend that its alchemical terminology is a pretext to direct seekers towards the true object of research, I would scarcely contend with him, for I do not know certainly.

ABSTRACT OF DISCUSSION

Miss Clarissa Miles said that she would be glad if Mr Waite would supply some information concerning the Kabalah and the texts containing it for her benefit and for the benefit of other members who had not studied Kabalism. She wanted, in particular, to know in what language and at what date the books of the Kabalah were written, and whether there was any evidence that the alchemists were acquainted therewith. She would also be glad if Mr Waite would explain further the expression 'Moon-Lady' which he had used in his paper.

Dr ELIZABETH SEVERN asked to what extent, in Mr Waite's opinion, did the alchemical processes of Kabalism offer points of correspondence with the mass of recorded experiment commonly known as Alchemy.

Mr SIJIL ABDUL-ALI asked whether Mr Waite regarded the *Sephiroth* only as mental concepts to bridge the gulf between Deity and the created world. He asked, further, whether in speaking of KETHER as corresponding to the Metallic Root, Mr Waite was referring to the alchemical 'first matter'. He added that he had seen this attributed to YESOD as the Foundation of the world.

The CHAIRMAN[1] said that he considered Mr Waite's paper as a particularly interesting one and likely to give rise to many questions. He supposed that Mr Waite would agree with him that it was most probable that the *Ash Mezareph* did not appear until after Cornelius Agrippa, because had it been accessible to him, it is most likely that he would have followed it in his allocation of planets to *Sephiroth*, the names of the planets and metals being practically interchangeable in the minds of the alchemists, as Mr Waite had pointed out. He did not think it necessary to assume that Cornelius Agrippa had derived his allocations from an earlier Kabalistic book. No doubt he derived the general theory of correspondence from the *Zohar* as from the writings of the Neo-Platonists, but the details might, in many cases, have been the product of his own fancy. In the particular case under discussion, he seems merely to have arranged the planets in the order of their positions in the geocentric scheme, commencing with the outermost. Of course, this raised, the speaker said, the whole question of the connection between Alchemy and Kabalism. It seemed quite probable to him that the alchemists may have gone on developing Alchemy and the Kabalists developing the Kabalah, the two never having been married until the appearance of the *Ash Mezareph*. No doubt some of the alchemists might have learnt of the doctrine of correspondence through the Kabalah, but here was an earlier source, namely the Neo-Platonists, whose views were diffused at an early date through the works of

[1][i.e. H. Stanley Redgrove.RAG]

Pseudo-Dionysius—an author whose influence on the mystical philosophy of the Middle Ages seems not always to have been adequately estimated. It was very probable that the Kabalists also owed much to the Neo-Platonists.

Mr A. E. WAITE said, in reply, that the point raised by Dr Severn was one of considerable interest, but there was unfortunately only a single process in *Ash Mezareph* which it was possible to compare with other cryptic formulæ in alchemical literature at large. It stood out conspicuously from the rest of the text, because the Kabalistic terminology which prevailed otherwise was dropped suddenly and completely, so that the putative process emerged in the prevailing language of western Alchemy. It might be thought that it did not really belong to the work, but the explanation was that it was quoted from R. Mordecai, mentioned in the lecture. The Chairman was correct—at least from the speaker's point of view—in suggesting that *Ash Mezareph* was later than Cornelius Agrippa, though perhaps on other considerations than that which had been mentioned more especially, as there was no reason to suppose that the occult philosopher of Nettesheim had taken all Kabalistic literature for his province. As an instance in point, his acquaintance with the *Zohar*, though theoretically possible, was not at all clear from the material available in his *Three Books*. As regards Jewish theosophy and Alchemy, the *Ash Mezareph* was the one and only sign of any marriage between them, and it seemed to have produced no issue in the literature on either side. In reply to Mr Abdul-Ali, it was not possible for the modern mind to regard the *Sephiroth* as other than mental concepts devised to bridge the gulf between Deity and the created world; but it must be remembered that for Kabalists they were spheres of created or alternatively of begotten intelligence, as indicated in the lecture. The 'Metallic Root' probably signified what western Alchemy understood as the First Matter, but the second classification referred philosopical Mercury to KETHER and Lead to YESOD, which does not seem to be the place of the First Matter, according to either list. Yet it would be a possible allocation if the principle of the text were accepted—that 'all systems lead to the one truth'. It was not possible to answer adequately the questions asked by Miss Miles. The primordial text of Kabalism was *Sepher Yetzirah*, which the speaker ascribed tentatively to the fourth century of the Christian era. The most probable view concerning the *Zohar* was that it embodies old materials with much that is of modern authorship comparatively—that is to say, of the thirteenth century. The term 'Moon-Lady' represented the lecturer's rendering of 'Luna of the Wise', 'Metallic Woman', etc., used in the Kabalistic text.

7
THE HERMETIC AND ROSICRUCIAN MYSTERY

[Printed in the *Occult Review*, Vol. 8, No 4, October 1908, pp. 207–21.]

During the decade between his reconstruction of the old Golden Dawn in 1903 and his final closing down of the Isis-Urania Temple in 1914, Waite brought to maturity his thesis of the Secret Tradition and especially its central concepts of a Hidden or Interior Church. The first major statement of his thesis occurs in *The Hidden Church of the Holy Graal* (1909), but it is implicit in many of his early contributions to the *Occult Review*. It is most clearly stated in *The Hermetic and Rosicrucian Mystery*, in which Waite combines the common elements of the varying traditions of the Kabalah, of alchemy and of Rosicrucianism.

WE ARE only beginning, and that by very slow stages, to enter into our inheritance from the past; and still perhaps in respect of its larger part we are seeking far and wide for the treasures of the mystic Basra. But these treasures are of more than one species and more than a single order; for that measure to which we are approximating and for that part which we hold, we shall be well advised to realize that there are some things which belong to the essences while some are of the accidents only. I do not think that among all the wise of the ages, in whatsoever regions of the world, there has been ever any difference of opinion about the true object of research; the modes and form of the quest have varied, and that widely, but to one point have all the roads converged. Therein is no change or shadow of vicissitude. We may hear of shorter roads, and one would say at first sight that such a suggestion may be true indubitably, but in one sense it is rather a convention of language and in another it is a commonplace which tends to confuse the issues. It is a convention of language because the great quests are not pursued in time or place, and it would be just as true to say that in a journey from the circumference to the centre all roads are the same length, supposing that they are straight roads. It is a commonplace because if any one should enter the byways or return on his path and restart, it is obvious that he must look to be delayed. Furthermore, it may be true that all paths lead ultimately to the centre, and that if we descend into hell there may be still a way back to the light, as if one ascended to heaven; but in any house of right reason the issues are too clear to consider such intrinsic possibilities. Before I utilize these random and, I think, too obvious considerations to present the root-thesis of this paper, I must recur for one moment to the question of the essence and the accident, because on the assumption from which the considerations originate—namely, that there is a secret tradition in Christian times, the place of which is in the West—or rather that there are several traditions—it seems desirable to realize what part matters vitally among them. I will take my illustration from alchemy, and it should be known that on the surface it claims to put forward the mystery of a material operation, behind which we discern— though not, it should be understood, invariably—another subject and another intention. Now, supposing that we were incorrect in our discernment, the secret tradition would remain, this notwithstanding, and it would remain also if the material operation were a dream not realized. But I think that a tradition of the physical kind would have no part in us, who are concerned with another conversion than that of metals, and who know that there is a mystic stone which is unseen by mortal eyes? The evidences of the secret tradition are very strong in alchemy, but it must be accepted that, either therein or otherwise, I am not offering the proofs that the tradition exists. There are several schools of occult literature from which it follows that something was perpetuated belonging to their own order, as, for example, the schools of magic; concerning these latter I must say what to some persons may seem a rule of excessive severity—that they embody nothing which is essential to our purpose. It is time that we should set apart in our minds the domain of phenomenal occultism as something which, almost automatically, has been transferred to the proper care of science. In so doing it is our simple hope that it may continue to extend a particular class of researches into the nature of man and his environment which the unaccredited investigations of the past have demonstrated already as productive to those who can be called open to conviction. The grounds of this conviction were manifested generations or centuries ago, and along both lines the research exhibits to us from time to time that we—or some of us—who know after another manner, have been justified very surely when, as if from a more remote region, we have returned to testify that the great mysteries are within.

I have no need to affirm that the secret tradition, either in the East or the West, has been always an open secret in respect of the root-principles concerning the Way, the Truth and the Life. It is easy, therefore, to show what it is not, and to make the distinction which I have attempted between the classes of the concealed knowledge. It is not so easy to define the most precious treasures of the King—in respect of that knowledge—according to the estimate concerning them which I have assumed tacitly to be common between persons confessing to mystic predispositions at this day. The issues are confused throughout, all our high predilections nothwithstanding, by the traditional or historical notion concerning the adept, which is that of a man whose power is raised to the transcendent degree by the communication or attainment, after some manner, of a particular and even terrible knowledge of the hidden forces of nature. I have heard technical and imputed adepts of occult associations state that those who possess, in the actual and plenary sense, the gifts which are ascribed to themselves by the simplicity of an artificial title, are able so to disintegrate the constituted man that they can separate not only the body from its psychic part but the spirit also from the soul, when they have a sufficient cause in their illumination against a particular victim. If things of this kind were possible, they would belong to the science of the abyss—when the abyss has been exalted above all that is termed God; but there is no need to attribute an over-great seriousness to chatter and traffic of this kind which has been all too prevalent in a few current schools of inexactitude. The tendency contributes, as I have said, to confuse the issues and, though it may seem a perilous suggestion, one is tempted to say that, in all its higher aspects, the name itself of adept might be abandoned definitely in favour of that of the mystic—though on account of the great loose thinking it is only too likely—and there are signs sufficient already—that it would share a similar fate of misconstruction. There was a time perhaps when we could have listened, and did even, to descriptions of this kind, because we had only just begun to hear of adepts and sages, so that things were magnified in the half-light. The scales have fallen now, and though the light into which we have entered is very far from the high light of all, it is serviceable sufficiently to dispel many shadows and to dissipate many distractions. The difficulty which is here specified is increased by the fact that there are certainly powers of the height, and that the spirit of man does not in its upward path take all the heavens of aspiration without, after some manner, being set over the kingdoms which are below it. For ourselves, at least, we can lay down one irrevocable law—that he who has resolved, setting all things else aside, to enter the path of adeptship must look for his progress in proportion as he pursues holiness for its own sake and not for the miracles of sanctity. It will be seen that I am disposed to call things by their old names, which have many consecrations, and I hope to command sympathy—but something more even—when I say further that he who dreams of adeptship and does not say sanctity in his heart till his lips are cleansed and then does not say it with his lips, is not so much far from the goal as without having conceived regarding it. One of the lesser masters, who has now scarcely a pupil amongst us, said once, quoting from somewhere *Vel sanctum invenit, vel sanctum facit;* but I know that it must be long resident in our desires before it can be declared in our lives.

I have searched the whole West and only in two directions have I found anything which will compare with pure monastic mysticism; one of these is the mystic side of alchemy, while the other is that body of tradition which answers most fully to the name of Rosicrucianism. There are other places in which we find the same thing, or the substance of the same thing, and I believe that I have given faithful testimony already on this point; even in the lesser schools I am sure that it was always at the roots, but except in so far as a personal sympathy may direct us, or the accidents of an historical study, I do not know that there is a direct gain—or that there is not rather a hindrance—by going any distance afield for what is so close to our hands, and into side issues for what is in the straight road—whether this be broad or narrow. There is no doubt that from one point of view Christian mysticism has been on the external side bewrayed rather seriously by its environment, because of the inhibitions of the official churches; in saying this, I hope that the time has come to all of us when the cheap conventions of hostility towards these churches, and especially towards the Latin Rite, have ceased to obtain in our minds and that we can appreciate, in however detached a manner, the high annals of their sanctity. If so, we shall be able to appreciate also, at the proper value, an external and historical side on which the Latin Church approached too often that picture in the story of the Holy Graal of a certain King of Castle Mortal, who sold God for money. The difficulty which the Rite has created and the inhibitions into which it has passed arise more especially not alone on the external side but from the fact that it has taken the great things of symbolism too generally for material facts. In this way, with all the sincerity which can be attached to its formal documents, produced for the most part by the process of growth, the Church Catholic of Latin Christianity has told the wrong story, though the elements which were placed in its hands are the right and true elements. I believe that the growth of sanctity within the Latin Church has been—under its deepest consideration—substantially hindered by the over-encrustation of the spirit with the literal aspect, though this at the same time is indispensable to expression. I believe that in the minds of the mystics this hindrance has operated; of all men on earth they have recognized assuredly the working of the spirit; but they sought to attain it through the veils of doctrine and they did not utterly and wholly part the curtains thereof. The result was that these trailed after them and were an impediment as they entered the sanctuary. The process itself was, in one sense, the wrong process, though on account of their environment it was almost impossible that they should adopt another. We have agreed long ago that to work up from Nature to Grace is not really the method of the wise, because that which is below is the branches and that which is above is the roots, and the tree of life is really in this sense, and because of our distance from the centre, as it were, upside down. So also the true way of experience in the mystic life is to work outward from within. It is natural, of course, and this is of necessity also, that we should receive our first intimations through the letter, but when it has exhibited to us some reflections of the light which is behind we must not suffer our course to be hindered by the office of the letter, but should set it aside rather, to abide in the root-meaning which is behind the symbols. There is a later stage in which we shall revert to the external and to the meaning that is without, bringing back with us the inward light to interpenetrate and transform it. Perhaps an illustration will explain better the order of procedure than a formal statement merely, though I do not think that there is even a surface difficulty concerning it. We have been taught in the infancy of the mind the great story which is the root and heart of external Christianity. That is not the letter which kills but the cortex of a vessel behind which are the eternal fountains of life. I need not say that many of us do not get beyond this cortex and, unfortunately, it is not a dead husk, but a living body through which Grace flows to us after the measure of our capacity. But it may come to pass that the inward sensorium is opened—by the mediation, as it may well be, of the great books of the Church, or in what manner soever—and we then see that the great story, the old story, the story which is of all things true, is that of our own soul. I mean this not in the sense of the soul's geniture, but in the sense of its progress, as it is here and now environed. We are then looking towards the real road of our redemption, and it is at this stage that the letter should be set aside for a period because everything has to be enacted anew. The virgin must conceive and bear her son; in the grand rough outline of Saint Martin the son must be born in the Bethlehem of our human life; he must be presented in the temple which stands in the Jerusalem within; he must confound the doctors of the intellect; he must lead the hidden life of Nazareth; he must be manifested and must teach us within, in which way we shall return to the world of doctrine and shall find that all things are made new. It is not that there are new doctrines, but there is another quality of life; thereby the old symbolism has been so interpenetrated that the things which are without have become the things which are within, till each seems either in the power of the grace and in the torrent of the life. It is then that we cease to go out through the door by which we went in, because other doors are open, and the call of many voices, bidding us no longer depart hence, says rather: Let us enter the sanctuary, even the inmost shrine.

I desire, therefore, to make it plain that the Secret Church Mystic which exists and has always existed within the Church Militant of Christendom does not differ in anything from the essential teaching of doctrine—I mean *Quod semper, quod ubique, quod ab omnibus;* that it can say with its heart what it says also with its lips; that again there is no chance or shadow of vicissitude; but in some very high sense the ground of the essentials has been removed. The *symbolum* remains; it has not taken on another meaning; but it has unfolded itself like the flower from within. Christian Theosophy in the West can recite its *Credo in unum Deum* by clause and by clause, including in *unam sanctam catholicam et apostolicam ecclesiam*, and if there is an *arrière pensée* it is not of heresy or Jesuitry. Above all, and I say this the more expressly because there are still among us—that is to say, in those circles generally—certain grave misconceptions, and it is necessary to affirm that the path of the mystic does not pass through the heresies.

And now with respect to the secret schools which have handed down to us at this day some part or aspects of the secret tradition belonging to Christian times, I must leave out of consideration, because there are limits to papers of this kind, the great witness of Kabalism which although it is a product of the Christian period is scarcely of it, and although therein the quest and its term do not assuredly differ from that of the truth which is in Christ, there are perhaps other reasons than those of brevity for setting it apart here. Alchemy may not have originated much further East than Alexandria, or, alternatively, it may have travelled from China when the port of Byzantium was opened to the commerce of the world. In either case, its first development, in the forms with which we are acquainted, is connected with the name of Byzantium, and the earliest alchemists of whom we have any remains in literature constitute a class by themselves under the name of Byzantine alchemists. The records of their processes went into Syria and Arabia, where they assumed a new mode, which bore, however, all necessary evidence of its origin. In this form it does not appear to have had a specific influence upon the *corpus doctrinale*. The records were also taken West, like many other mysteries of varying importance, and when they began to assume a place in western history this was chiefly in France, Germany and England. In other words, there arose the cycle of Latin alchemy, passing at a later date, by the way of translation, into the vernaculars of the respective countries, until finally, but much later, we have original documents in English, French and German. It follows, but has not so far been noticed, that the entire literature is a product of Christian times and has Christianity as its motive, whether subconsciously or otherwise. This statement applies to the Latin Geber and the tracts which are ascribed to Morien and Rhasis. The exception which proves the rule is the Kabalistic *Aesh Mezareph*, which we know only by fragments included in the great collection of Rosenroth. I suppose that there is no labyrinth which is quite so difficult to thread as that the the *Theatrum Chemicum*. It is beset on every side with pitfalls, and its clues, though not destroyed actually, have been buried beneath the ground. Expositors of the subject have gone astray over the general purpose of the art, because some have believed it to be: (*a*) the transmutation of metals, and that only, while others have interpreted it as (*b*) a veiled method of delineating the secrets of the soul on its way through the world within, and besides this nothing. Many text-books of physical alchemy would seem to have been re-edited in this exotic interest. The true philosophers of each school are believed to have taught the same thing, with due allowance for the generic difference of their term, and seeing that they use the same language it would seem that, given a criterion of distinction in respect of the term, this should make the body of cryptogram comparatively easy to disentangle. But as one of the chief difficulties is said also to reside in the fact that many of them do not begin at the same point of the process, the advantage of uniformity is cancelled largely.

There are affirmed to be experimental schools still existing in Europe which have carried the physical work much further than it is ever likely to be taken by any isolated student; but this must be accepted under several reserves, or I can say, at least, that, having better occasions than most people of knowing the schools and their development, I have so far found no evidence. But there are testified otherwise to be—and I speak here with the certainty of first-hand knowledge—other schools, also experimental, also existing in Europe, which claim to possess the master-key of the mystical work. How far they have been successful at present in using that key I am not in a position to say, nor can I indicate its nature for reasons that, I think, must be obvious. It so happens, however, that the mystery of the processes is one thing and that which lies on the surface, or more immediately beneath the externals of the concealed language, is, fortunately, another thing. And, as often happens also, the enlightening correspondences are offering their marks and seals—if not at our very doors—at least in the official churches. Among all those places that are holy there is no holy place in which they do not abide *a mane usque ad vespertinum*, and the name of the correspondence-in-chief is the Holy Eucharist.

I propose now to tabulate certain palmary points of terminology which are common to all the adepts, including both schools indifferently, though we are dealing here—and this is understood—with the process of one school only. By the significance of these points or terms we shall see to what extent the symbolism of the higher alchemy is in conformity with mystic symbolism and with the repose of the life of the Church in God. It should be realized, however, that there is nothing so hard and so thankless as to elucidate one symbolism by the terms of another—and this notwithstanding an occasional identity which may manifest in the terms of each.

It must be understood further and accepted that all alchemists, outside the distinctions of their schools, were actuated by an express determination to veil their mystery and that they had recourse for this purpose to every kind of subterfuge. At the same time they tell us that the whole art is contained, manifested and set forth by means of a single vessel, which, amidst all manner of minor variations, is described with essential uniformity throughout the great multitude of texts. This statement constitutes a certain lesser key to the art; but as on the one hand the alchemists veil their hallow-in-chief by reference, in spite of their assurance, as above noted, to many pretended vessels, so has the key itself a certain aspect of subterfuge, since the alleged unity is in respect only of the term final of the process in the unity of the recipient. This unity is the last reduction of a triad, because, according to these aspects of Hermetic philosophy, man in the course of his attainment is at first three—that is, when he sets out upon the great quest; he is two at a certain stage; but he is, in fine, one, which is the end of his evolution. The black state of the matter on which the process of the art is engaged is the body of this death, from which the adepts have asked to be detached. It is more especially our natural life. The white state of the stone, the confection of which is desired, is the vesture of immortality with which the epopts are clothed upon. The salt of the philosophers is that savour of life without which the material earth can neither be salted nor cleansed. The sulphur of the philosophers is the inward substance by which some souls are saved, yet so as by fire. The mercury of the sages is that which must be fixed and volatilized—naturally it is fluidic and wandering—but except under this name, or by some analogous substitute, it must not be described literally outside the particular circles of secret knowledge. It is nearer than hands and feet.

Now the perfect correspondence of these things in the symbolism of official Christianity, and the great mystery of perfect sanctification, is set forth in the great churches under the sacramentalism of the Holy Eucharist. This is my point, and I desire to make it clear: the same exalted mystery which lies behind the symbols of bread and wine, behind the undeclared priesthood which is according to the order of Melchisedeck, was expressed by the alchemists under the guise of transmutation; but I refer here to the secret school of adeptship which had taken over in another and transcendent interest the terminology and processes of occult metallurgy.

The vessel is therefore one, but the matter thereto adapted is not designated especially, or at least after an uniform manner; it is said to be clay by those who speak at times more openly in order that they may be understood the less, as if they also were singing in their strange chorus:

> Let us open as the day,
> That we may deeper hide ourselves

It is most commonly described as metallic, because on the

surface of the literature there is the declared mystery of all metals, and the concealed purpose is to show that in the roots and essence of these things there is a certain similarity or analogy. The reason is that the epopt, who has been translated, again finds his body after many days, but under a great transmutation, as if in another sense the *panis quotidianis* had been changed into the *panis vivus et vitalis*, but without mutation of the accidents. The reason is also that in normal states the body is here and now not without the soul, nor can we separate readily, by any intellectual process, the soul from the spirit which broods thereover, to fertilize it in a due season. It is, however, one vessel, and this makes for simplicity; but it is not by such simplicity that the art is testified to be a *lusus puerorum*. The contradistinction hereto is that it is hard to be a Christian, which is the comment of the man born blind upon the light that he cannot see. There is also the triumphant affirmation of the mystical counter-position, that to sin is hard indeed for the man who knows truly. The formula of this is that man is born for the heights rather than the deeps, and its verbal paradox is *facilis ascensus superno*. The process of the art is without haste or violence by the mediation of a graduated fire, and the seat of this fire is in the soul. It is a mystery of the soul's love, and for this reason she is called 'undaunted daughter of desire'. The sense of the gradation is that love is set free from the impetuosity and violence of passion and has become a constant and incorruptible flame. The formula of this is that the place of unity is a centre wherein there is no exaggeration. That which the fire consumes is certain materials or elements, which are called *recrementa*, the grosser parts, the superfluities; and it should be observed that there are two purgations, of which the first is the gross and the second the subtle. The first is the common process of conversion, by which there is such a separation of seemingly external components that what remains is as a new creature, and may be said to be reborn. The second is the exalted conversion, by which that which has been purified is so raised that it enters into a new region, or a certain heaven comes down and abides therein. It is not my design in the present place to exhaust all the sources of interpretation, because such a scheme would be impossible in a single paper, and I can allude, therefore, but scantily to the many forms of the parables which are concerned with the process up to this point. The ostensible object, which was materialized in the alternative school, is the confection of a certain stone or powder, which is that of projection, and the symbolical theorem is that this powder, when added to a base metal, performs the wonder of transmutation into pure silver or gold, better than those of the mines. Otherwise, it prolongs life and renews youth in the adept-philosopher and lover of learning. In the second case, it is spoken of usually as an elixir, but the transmuting powder and the renewing draught are really one thing with the spiritual alchemists. It must be also affirmed that in virtue of a very high mysticism there is an unity in the trinity of the powder, the metal and the vase. The vase is also the alchemist on his outer side, for none of the instruments, the materials, the fires, the producer, and the thing produced are external to the one subject. At the same time the inward man is distinguished from the outward man; we may say that the one is the alchemist and the other the vessel. It is in this sense that the art is both physical and spiritual. But the symbolism is many times enfolded, and the gross metal which is placed within the vessel is the untransmuted life of reason, motive, concupiscence, self-interest and all that which constitutes the intelligent creature on the normal plane of manifestation. Hereof is the natural man enclosed in an animal body, as the metal is placed in the vessel, and from this point of view the alchemist is he who is sometimes termed arrogantly the super-man. But because there is only one vessel it must be understood that herein the stone is confected and the base metal is converted. The alchemist is himself finally the stone, and because many zealous aspirants to the art have not understood this they have failed in the great work on the spiritual side. The schedule which now follows may elucidate this hard subject somewhat more fully and plainly.

There are (*a*) the natural, external man, whose equivalent is the one vessel; (*b*) the body of desire, which answers to the gross matter; (*c*) the aspiration, the consciousness, the will of the supernatural life; (*d*) the process of the will working on the body of desire within the outward vessel; (*e*) the psychic and transcendental conversion thus effected; (*f*) the reaction of the purified body of desire on the essential will, so that the one supports the other while the latter is borne upward, and from such raising there follows this further change, that the spirit of a man puts on itself a new quality of life, becoming an instrument which is at once feeding and is itself fed; (*g*) herein is the symbol of the stone and the great elixir; (*h*) the spirit is nourished from above by the analogies of Eucharistic ministry; (*i*) the spirit nourishes the soul, as by bread and wine; (*j*) the soul effects the higher conversion in the body of desire; (*k*) it thus comes about that the essence which dissolves everything and changes everything is still contained in a vessel, or—alternatively—that God abides in man.

This process, thus exhaustively delineated in the parables of alchemy, is put with almost naked simplicity by Eucharistic doctrine, which says that material lips receive the supersubstantial bread and wine, that the soul is nourished and that Christ enters the soul. It seems, therefore, within all reason and all truth to testify that the *panis vivus et vitalis* is even as the transmuting stone and that the chalice of the new and eternal testament is as the renewing elixir; but I say this under certain reasonable reserves because, in accordance with my formal indication, the closer the analogies between distinct systems of symbolism the more urgent is that prudence which counsels us not to confuse them by an interchangeable use.

All Christian mysticism came forth out of the Mass Book, and it returns therein. But the Mass Book in the first instance came out of the heart mystic which had unfolded in Christendom. The nucleus of truth in the missal is *Dominus prope est*. The Mass shows that the great work is in the first sense a work of the hands of man, because it is he officiating as a priest in his own temple who offers the sacrifice which he has purified. But the elements of that sacrifice are taken over by an intervention from another order, and that which follows is transfusion.

Re-expressing all this now in a closer summary, the apparatus of mystical alchemy is indeed, comparatively speaking, simple. The first matter is myrionimous and is yet one, corresponding to the unity of the natural will and the unlimited complexity of its motives, dispositions, desires, passions and distractions, on all of which the work of wisdom must operate. The vessel is also one, for this is the normal man complete in his own degree. The process has the seal of Nature's directness; it is the graduation and increasing maintenance of a particular fire. The initial work is a change in the substance of will, aspiration and desire, which is the first conversion or transmutation in the elementary sense. But it is identical even to the end with the term proposed by the Eucharist, which is the modification of the noumenal man by the communication of Divine Substance. Here is the *lapis qui non lapis, lapis tingens, lapis angularis, lapis qui multiplicetur, lapis per quem justus aedificabit donum Domini, et jam valde aedificatur et terram possidebit, per omnia, etc.* When it is said that the stone is multiplied, even to a thousandfold, we know that this is true of all seed which is sown upon good soil.

So, therefore, the stone transmutes and the Eucharist transmutes also; the philosophical elements on the physical side go to the making of the stone which is also physical; and the sacramental elements to the generation of a new life in the soul. He who says *Lapis Philosophorum*, says also: My beloved to me and I to him: Christ is therefore the stone, and the stone in adept humanity is the union realized, while the great secret is that Christ must be manifested within.

Now it seems to me that it has not served less than an useful purpose to establish after a new manner the intimate resemblance between the higher understanding of one part of the secret tradition and the better interpretation of one sacrament of the church. It must be observed that we are not dealing in either case with the question of attainment. The analogy would remain if spiritual alchemy and Christian sacramentalism abode in the intellectual order as theorems only, or as part of the psychic dream which had never been carried into experience. It would be more easy (if there were here any opportunity) to offer the results of the experience as recorded in the lives of the saints than to discuss the traditional attainments which are held to have passed into actuality among the secret schools; but the veiled literatures must be left to speak for themselves, which—for those who can read—they do, like the annals of sanctity; as to these—those who will take the pains may seek verification for themselves. My task in respect of spiritual alchemy ends by exhibiting that this also was a mystery of sanctity concerned *ex hypothesi* with the communication of Divine Substance, and that this is the term of the Eucharist. It is this which the doctrine of sanctity offered, to those who entered the pathway of sanctity, as the foretaste in this life of the union which is consummated in eternity, or of that end beyond which there is nothing whatever which is conceivable. We know from the old books that it has not entered into the heart of man, but the heart which has put away the things of sense conceives it by representations and types. This is the great tradition of that which the early alchemists term truth in the art; the end is representation after its own kind rather than felicity, but the representation is of that order which begins in ecstacy and ends in absorption. Let no man say, therefore, that he loses himself in experience of this order, for, perchance, it is then only that he finds himself, even in that way which suggests that after many paths of activity he is at length coming into his own.

It might seem that I have reached here a desirable point for my conclusion, but I am pledged, alike by my title and one antecedent reference, to say something concerning Rosicrucianism, which is another witness in the world on the part of the secret tradition. There is one respect in which it is simpler in its apparatus than the literature of the purely Hermetic tradition, for it lies within a smaller compass and has assumed a different mode. It is complicated by the fact that very few of the texts which are available among the things of the outside world have a title to rank in its tradition. This, I suppose, is equivalent to an intimation that the witness is still in the world after another and more active manner, which is true in more than a single way. I am not the ambassador, and much less the plenipotentiary, of the secret societies in the West, and independently of this statement I feel sure that I shall not be accused of endeavouring to assume the rôle or to create the impression. I know only that the societies exist, and that they are at the present time one means of perpetuating that tradition. I do not suggest that there are no other means, because I have indicated even from the beginning that the door looking towards heaven and the sanctuary which is its ante-chamber was opened long centuries ago by the official churches. But the tradition itself has been rather behind the churches and some part of the things for which we are all seeking is to be found therein—all which is without detriment to the light of the East, because this is also the light of the West under another veil. Even in the esoteric assemblies which are now and here among us, the tradition is, in a sense, veiled, and, of course, in speaking publicly one has always to cloud the sanctuaries rather than to say: Lift up your eyes, for it is in this or that corner of London, Paris or Prague. If there is one thing more regrettable than the confusion in forms of symbolism, it is the identification of separate entities under a general term which has only a particular meaning so far as history is concerned. The name Rosicrucian, has suffered from abuse of this kind, being used almost interchangeably with that of Alchemist by popular writers. I must ask to be disassociated from this error when I say that the external history of the Rosy Cross, in so far as it can be said to exist, has only one point of correspondence with Rosicrucian traditions perpetuated by secret societies in a few centres of Europe. The point of correspondence is the legend-in-chief of the Order, detached from the pseudo-historical aspect which it bore in the early documents, and associated with a highly advanced form of symbolism. It is in this form only that it enters into the sequence of the mysteries, and exhibits how the priest-king does issue from Salem, carrying bread and wine. We have, therefore, the Eucharistic side in the higher Rosicrucian tradition, but if I may describe that which is greater in the terms of that which is lesser—because of the essential difficulty with which I am confronted—it has undergone a great change, not by a diminution of the sacraments but because they are found everywhere. The alchemical maxim which might be inscribed over the gate of any Rosicrucian temple is—

Est in Mercurio quicquid quærunt sapientes.

The Eucharistic maxim which might be written over the laboratory of the alchemist, in addition to *Laborare est orare*, would be—

Et antiquum documentum
Novo cedat ritui:
Præstet fides supplementum
Sensuum defectui.

The maxim which might be written over the temples of the official churches is *Corporis Mysterium*, that the mystery of the body might lead them more fully into the higher mystery of the soul. And, in fine, that maxim which might, and will be, inscribed over the one temple of the truly catholic religion when the faiths of this western world have come into their own—that which is simplest of all, and of all most pregnant, would be *mysterium fidei*, the mystery which endures for ever and for ever passes into experience.

In conclusion as to this part, Rosicrucianism is the mystery of that which dies in manifestation that the life of the manifest may be ensured. I have found nothing in symbolism which accounts like Rose-Cross symbolism for that formula which on one side is the summary expression of mysticism: 'And I look for the resurrection of the dead and the life of the world to come.'

And now in conclusion generally:

I have spoken of three things only, and of one of them with great brevity, because the published literatures have to be set aside, and of that which remains it does not appear in the open face of day. The initiations are many and so are the schools of thought, but those which are true schools and those which are high orders issue from one root. *Est una sola res*, and those whose heart of contemplation is fixed upon this one thing may differ widely but can never be far apart. Personally, I do not believe—and this has the ring of a commonplace—that if they came to understand one another they would be found to differ widely. I know not what systems of the eons may intervene between that which is imperishable within us and the union wherein the universe will, in fine, repose at the centre. But I know that the great systems ay, even the great processes—of the times that are gone, as of those which now encompass us—do not pass away, because that which was from the beginning, is now and ever shall be—is one motive, one aspiration, one term of thought remaining, as if in the stillness of an everlasting present. We really understand one another, and our collective aspirations are united, world without end.

8
REPORT TO THE CONVOCATION OF THE INDEPENDENT AND RECTIFIED RITE, R.R. et A.C.

[Unpublished typescript, contained in Waite's bound collection of Convocation Reports. It is undated but was delivered on either 15 or 16 June 1906.]

The Hermetic Order of the Golden Dawn was founded, by Westcott, Woodman and Mathers, in 1888; it expanded rapidly, reached its zenith in the years following the creation of the wholly magical Second Order, the *Roseae Rubeae et Aureae Crucis*, in 1892, and then declined through a series of alarms and diversions until its final dissolution in 1903. After this collapse Waite, in company with the more mystically inclined members, salvaged the Isis-Urania Temple, reconstructed the rituals, and created the Independent and Rectified Rite. Little has been published about Waite's branch of the Golden Dawn, for the discovery of his private papers came too late for Ellic Howe to make other than cursory use of them in his admirable history of the Order, *The Magicians of the Golden Dawn* (1972; reprinted, Aquarian Press, 1985).

Among Waite's papers was a bound volume of his Reports prepared for members of the Independent and Rectified Rite between 1904 and 1909. Each of the reports combines an account of the progress of the Order with the results of historical researches relating to its origin and structure. The report that follows is typical of the series; the negotiations to which it refers resulted in 1907, in the Concordat between the Independent and Rectified Rite and the Stella Matutina of Dr Felkin.

IN THE great and holy names with which we are here familiar, in the concealed names which are behind these mysteries and in the grace of these sacraments, I open this convocation of the Independent and Rectified Rite by the power in me vested.

Peace profound my Brethren. Health and benediction in the Lord.

Most of you will be acquainted by report at second-hand and by such exaggerated rumours with the fact of certain negotiations into which the Independent and Rectified Rite has entered with members of the Second Order believed to have remained unattached and unincorporated for a considerable period following the constitution of the G.D. and R.R. et A.C. as we have for some years now held both in the natural inheritance thereof. According to the information which we have received, these former brethren were subsequently collected into a group under the auspices of a temporary chief in the past, and it would seem that they have initiated several new members into the Outer Order. It was understood that the negotiations mentioned should remain private until a definite stage was attained but this notwithstanding the tentative subject would appear to have been freely imparted and canvassed among several persons belonging to the Society in question. We feel it advisable therefore to inform you firstly as to the stage which has been reached up to the present moment and secondly as to the motives which have actuated your Chiefs in being to any extent concerned therein. As regards the first point there has been no personal communication of any kind but merely an exchange of letters with a view to ascertain whether there was any ground by which an understanding could be reached and a recognition on both sides established. No conditions have been so far definitely agreed and it is possible that the matter will lapse entirely on certain questions of essentials. As regards the second point we have felt that if old members belonging to the Second Order, but not under the obedience of the Independent & Rectified Rite and therefore from our point of view unattached since the time of its creation, chose to incorporate it would be reasonable, if otherwise possible, that we should work under a concordat together respecting in all matters the independence and autonomy of each. It is obvious however that many necessary stipulations must precede such an understanding and that outside those which are necessary there are those which will be desirable if that which is begun through an anxiety for peace and goodwill is to work for the future in harmony. Until the actual and binding agreement is reached we do not recognise the existence of any separate section in the two Orders and we are without definite particulars concerning any other body than our own. In one of the reports delivered by your Chiefs it was affirmed that our rite constituted the two Orders of the G.D. and R.R. et A.C., and to this we adhere. We have however to remember that there has been for a considerable time a Society working under the obedience of a long expelled Chief and although this could not under any circumstances obtain our recognition, we have no wish to withhold it from other unincorporated members who may desire to work together, if an equitable basis can in any manner be reached. It happens however in cases of this kind that a minority with doubtful credentials will sometimes put forward claims which are not less than preposterous and will so render any agreement ineffective. It is believed that in the present position of the question this is all that it will be necessary to bring on our part to your notice, but in terminating to this extent the incident we would ask you to assist us over one matter, which is to read those persons who have been concerned with ourselves in the discussion at least one lesson of prudence by forbearing from premature speaking. If therefore you should meet with any unattached brother or with those claiming affiliation with other bodies we shall rely upon that caution and will for this purpose assume that you will say nothing, not even that the question has been the subject of any intimation, however vague, in this Temple or on the part of the Chiefs of your Rite.

There was one point left over from the report to the last Convocation and to this it was promised that I should recur as to something which could not fail to interest the Fratres and Sorores generally. Probably I have said to you already that in respect of historical connections we are comparable in a sense to Melchisidec the king mystic of Salem, since we are really without father or mother. At the same time I have tried to indicate that, so far as research has been possible, we are not disowned by the past. Here I am making, as you will infer, no reference to our symbols, the antecedents and identities of which belong to a very different category. I am concerned only with our possible affiliation with and descent from earlier fraternities known under other names. Such connections are not indeed vital, for they do not transmit mystically, but in spite of any disassociation on the higher intellectual ground, they remain exceedingly interesting, and though we may be disposed, as time goes on, to fall away from their quest in proportion as we become more and more dedicated to the greater interests, we shall yet recur to them with regret, wishing that more had been done and that we personally could do still more. Such enquiries have also their proper aspect of importance, and our descent after the incorporated manner from the Adepts of the far past would assuredly place us among the last links in a chain of transmission the external signs of which are not isolated from an inward ministry or unconnected with those higher laws which work also from within.

Well, as it was indicated in brief words on the last occasion, certain documents have been transmitted to the masonic headship as a derivation in part from the mystic side of masonry, and they have a distinct bearing on the antecedents of this Order, forming, as we conceive, links in a chain of evidence which if it still remains to be forged is at least in course of collection for that purpose. It will be readily understood that it is possible to speak of this only in a general way but so much as due reticence will permit may I think be sufficient to convey, under the pledges of our own fraternity, an intelligible conception of their purport.

I must remind you in the first place that the earliest published knowledge concerning the fraternity R.C. is not historically assignable to an older date than 1610, at which period, and so forward until the year 1615, it was rather a matter of rumour. When at that time certain documents, bearing what may be termed the sign manual of the Order, were printed and circulated in Germany there was still nothing which could be called historical evidence concerning the corporate existence and claims of such an association.

The documents put forth an intimation which many hundreds of persons came forward to accept gladly and there is practically no tittle of evidence to shew that any of them were accepted, unless indeed we make a tentative reservation in the case of Michael Maier. Concerning him, one, Benedict Hilarion, of whom otherwise we know nothing, gives out in a tract appended to some posthumous writings of Maier, a hint that his various defences of the Order had not been written in vain, or, in other words, that he was in fine received into the ranks of the brotherhood. Now all this is common knowledge among students, and there would be no call to recite it here except that it enables me to affirm that no researches subsequent to those which I undertook personally, now so many years ago, have contributed a single line of more satisfactory evidence than was then made available. It is commonly reported that associations in imitation of this Order which had transpired by its own act (or so at least *ex hypothesi*) but was not really in evidence, sprang up from time to time and the suggestion is that they were impositions on the credulity of the age and on the zeal of a certain part of it. As the true historical spirit is concerned with no side and is therefore impartial to all the issues, it is just here to say that the value of this view is not greater historically than that to which it is alternative, for to those who have advanced it the original and therefore genuine order, supposing that the published manuscripts issued from such a source, would have been assuredly in the same category. The next point in our summary is to note that a century later a great volume of alchemical processes, together with the laws of a similar Brotherhood, was published, also in Germany, and its contents constitute together strong presumptive evidence that a sodality was then working and had probably been working far earlier under the name of the Brotherhood of the Golden and Rosy Cross. It was followed in 1785 by the secret symbols of the Rosicrucians of the sixteenth and seventeenth centuries. Between these two dates, or precisely in the year 1777, those documents which have now passed into our possession in rough transcript were rendered into an ordered record. They contain the rites and ceremonies of the Most Ancient and Honourable Order of the Golden and Rosy Cross, as established by the Supreme Conclave of the Fraternity, and issued for the benefit of members in the year above mentioned, being that in which the headship had for reasons which have not so far transpired, but are to be inferred from the text of the documents, decreed its reformation and re-establishment upon another basis. Prior to this, and as we may perhaps assume in about equal proportions, it had been devoted to astral workings (which may well have corresponded to those that are still extant among us) and for the rest to what is termed in certain tabulated Regulations, the Great Mystery, by which the transmuting stone of alchemy was unquestionably designated. The Reformation set aside the astral working, though apparently for a period only, in favour of the alchemical work and it further required the Masonic qualification from everyone of its candidates. This is equivalent to saying that at that time women were not admitted into the Order, nor is there any trace of such reception at a period prior to the year 1809. I particularise this point because in attempting to trace certain analogies between this Institution and our own Order, it is well to put on record one factor of some importance in which there is a very clear distinction established. Outside the Masonic qualification, the conditions required from postulants contain several which are substantially similar to our own and among these, firstly, that in accordance with the old and new fundamental laws members shall seek above all the Kingdom of God instead of Mammon; secondly, that they shall strive to attain wisdom, art and virtue, following on the will of God and living in the service of their neighbour. It was further laid down that no candidate should be promised anything at his reception beyond that which he could attain by the mercy of God, the intervention of his Superiors and his own industry.

The documents, however, contain the grades of the Order as follows:

a. That of the Juniores or Neophytes.
b. That of Theorici.
c. That of Practici
d. That of Philosophi.
e. That of the Adeptus Minor.
f. That of Adeptus Major.
g. That of Adeptus Philosophicus, corresponding to Exempt Adept.

The existence of two still higher Grades is indicated by the manuscripts, but nothing transpires concerning them and they were probably reserved to the headship or Supreme Direction of the Sodality as a whole. It is difficult to say anything at length concerning the essential points of the several rites, which it will be noticed include everything familiar to ourselves, the Grade of Zelator excepted. The correspondence of this is, however, really with the Neophyte Grade of the Golden and Rosy Cross and the correspondence of our own $0 = 0$ Grade is, from this point of view, with the Masonic initiation as an indispensable condition of candidature. I may perhaps be permitted to mention one question which is asked in the First Grade concerning the candidate, as follows: What do you ask at our hands in this man's favour? The answer was, I ask you to kill the body and purify the spirit.

The second and third Grades are summarized very shortly and in the fourth degree, or that of Philosophus, the Candidate is offered pure rose-coloured water for the washing of his hands, during which he is asked to remember that the doors of the higher wisdom are closed to impure beings but set open to the virtuous and spiritually minded. The symbolic cleansing is followed by the obligation, and thereafter comes the anointing of the candidate. In the 5th Grade, or that of Adeptus Minor, the postulant, after being inducted to the vestibule of the Rite, proclaims his titles and dignities in the lower degrees as the claim in chief to his advancement, an analogy which will be assuredly familiar to all who are here and now among us; it is one therefore on which it is unnecessary to dwell. In the 3rd point of the ceremony the celebrants appear with veils upon their faces and the liturgical part is throughout of a striking character. In the 6th and 7th Grades I could not of course indicate the possible analogies in this place but the definite information in the manuscripts is rather non-existent than scanty. I would add that in all preliminary or advanced degrees the candidate is handed certain written instructions, as in our own order, and in the Neophyte Grade, for example, he receives special information concerning the four elements, with the characteristic signs thereto attributed. The signification of the planetary signs and the degrees of corrosion in metals are given at a later stage.

I trust that I shall not be misconstrued as to the limits of this sketch concerning the analogies between the two sequences of ritual. I have not sought to show that our grades as we have them are the same even with differences as those of the Rosicrucian Order in the year 1777. I believe that they have been developed independently from one Rite; that there are sufficient correspondences to indicate that the Rite is one; and that if this be actually so, we have made a distinct advance in our knowledge as to the genesis of our own sodality. I recognise out of hand and at once all that might be said by an intentionally hostile criticism, and if I do not deal with it here, it is because in too many fields of research I have found full opportunities of appraising such criticism at its true value. I am moreover looking for further lights along the same paths—in which, if attained, all such criticism will dissolve.

Fratres and Sorores, as I tried to make plain at the beginning, these things are not in the last resource of our great concern but they are a part on the external side of our laudable quest. Speaking for myself, they remind me of that matter with which I opened the present convocation. If our former unattached Brethren have really after any fashion contrived to incorporate themselves, it is well that we should extend to them our recognition. But if in view of any position which they should assume, or through any reason whatsoever, this should in fine prove impracticable then in fine this is also well. If further our researches should more fully disinter our past, I do not doubt that such an event will be for our increased consolation, but if not we shall still be consoled, since other lights are with us and in proportion as we follow them faithfully we know that they will increase; in the certain anticipation of which I now close this Convocation. Fratres and Sorores, for that light which is with us we are grateful and we look for the extension of the light!

9

AN ADDRESS TO NEOPHYTES

In addition to the six-monthly Reports, Waite delivered lectures and addresses to the members of the Independent and Rectified Rite, drew up a Constitution for the Order and constructed appropriate ceremonies and grade rituals. None of these was intended for publication, but Waite collected most of them and bound eighteen of them for his own use in a single volume of typescripts entitled *Studies and Rituals of the Rosy Cross*. From internal evidence they can be dated between 1906 and 1911.

The six essays and addresses (9–14) that follow illustrate the doctrines that lay behind the rituals of the Order and the manner in which Waite reconstructed the traditional teaching of the Golden Dawn to harmonize with his own beliefs. Because they were designed for use within his Order they are relatively free of the ambiguity that marks many of Waite's published works on the Tarot and on Rosicrucian symbolism—subjects that he felt were central to the working of the Order and that should be presented to the world at large under a veil.

After the demise of the Independent and Rectified Rite, in 1914, Waite felt less constrained to keep his essays secret, but he never found an appropriate occasion to publish them. Of the remaining twelve essays, five are on mysticism, three are rituals and four concern the structure and working of the Order; they are all of lesser interest than the six published here.

Fratres et Sorores, a discourse in the Neophyte Grade has at first sight some difficulties attached to it, because even in this earliest and partial mode of the communicated light, a Novice of the Golden Dawn is made acquainted, like the Entered Apprentice of Masonry, with the fact that there are grades beyond; and as we assist to dispense a peculiar knowledge within the limits of symbolism, it may be thought—and not unjustly—that at this gate of our outer Temple, it must be possible to speak only in a very superficial manner; that it may even be held necessary to evade and to cloud the issues, so that secrets—official or otherwise— may be protected in accordance with pledges. It is, however, out of such difficulty that a real opportunity arises. That could be assuredly no practical proposition which should suggest that the subject-matter of sermon, lecture, or discourse ought to exceed the capacity of hearers; it is rather desirable— and is, I think, of the essence of illumination—that the matter which is most ready to our hands should be held in such case to be the true matter. The King's craftsmen can work with any tools. To think otherwise is to limit the means of grace, and covenant thereto is really an affirmation that the precious things are always about us. This, after having tried many paths, is the conclusion at which I have arrived as a ground of experience, and it is from such a point that I propose to start here.

I will analyse at first for a moment the dedications and predispositions which bring men and women within the ranks of this Fraternity, I have had some opportunity to form a judgement concerning them, being one of the older members, and of course it would be mere commonplace to say that their name is legion—for, in truth, they are very many, and I must reduce them therefore under a few very broad heads. I am supposing a definite interest because mere curiosity goes the way of all vain things and, profiting on neither side, does not enter into account. Among the other departments, there are those who in one or other manner—obscure, as it may be, or patient—have failed to find satisfaction in official religions and are looking for some firmer support. There are those whom religion on the external side has never touched, perhaps because it has scarcely entered within their environment of life. There are again others—shall we say?—who have a certain ground in faith, but are deeply anxious to enlarge it for the experimental knowledge, who are drawn therefore in those directions where it seems possible that knowledge may be obtained. There are those, in fine—since it serves no purpose here to multiply the instances—who do indeed believe that there is a religion in Christ, who are haunted, by a sense of the depth, the wonders and height of all its unfathomed mystery; but these also are seeking for a demonstrative side of faith—not so much or not so exclusively for its ministry to their own needs as for a public witness in the world at large. Now, these dispositions are all true and good; they are titles for entrance into the Order of the Golden Dawn; but the question arises after what manner, and within what measure, it may prove possible that they shall be fulfilled in the term. It is out of this question that there arises the whole problem of initiation—what it is and how its purpose must be understood. Is there within this Order, or is there conceivably within any other association, differing from or greater than this, a Divine Secret which can be communicated in words, and when imparted shall unveil the Mystery of Being on the absolute side, so that those who receive it can say: I know, even as I am known. Let there be no deception on the part of the Novices among us, lest disillusion should follow at a later stage of their progress. The promise of all initiation is to communicate powers and graces, but those which are concerned with the first apart from the second are following the path of disunion and their end is not in holiness—that holiness which does at the issue of all quest behold the Lord in His glory. Of these are our magical potentialities in the literal sense of the term. As regards the second, we are speaking already of our Order on one side of its office; but seeing that it offers an admixture in the external aspects, I want to say that the things of grace in these regions of institution are always conveyed through a vehicle, the correspondence of which with that which it imparts is adequate only according to the measures of symbolism. By the hypothesis of the Eucharist, within the domain of ecclesiastical dogma, the bread and wine convey something to the recipient which is utterly and infinitely unlike the external pretexts; but the imperfect analogy is that the food of souls is like that of the body, while the reality on the external side is that bread and wine are not only our physical nutriment but are the root matter and perfect representatives thereof. In the tradition of alchemical literature there is a vigorous analogy created between the mysteries of the soul and those of metallic transmutation, while in one department thereof—as we have all heard in these days—the deep things of spiritual knowledge were veiled in occult meta-magical nomenclature. The verity of this analogy rested in the knowledge or belief shared by both branches that alchemy was physically a scientific truth, that there was something which corresponded to growth and evolution in metals. So also there is one department in the ceremonial mysteries of initiation which has taken over the terminology of practical magic and has imbedded therein another presentation of the soul's legends, its outreachings and its attainments. This has passed at various times under names which varied, and here in this world of the West the great mystic tradition is carried on under the name of the Order of the Golden Dawn. Behind this institution there are yet other things concealed, for the fraternity holds from Superiors, who to the Neophytes are as yet unknown. They will see, as they pass through the Grades of Magical Art, and the Novices will remember among others that they have pledged not to debase their mystical knowledge in the works of evil magic. If this meant on the reverse side of the shield of our symbolism what it means on the exposed side, I for one should not be addressing you, or taking part in your receptions and advancements. But it is really a covenant on your part to receive the sacraments of the Order worthily, and that which we claim to impart to those who are prepared for reception is a mystery of grace in the soul behind outward forms which are after the theurgic mode. But the verity of the analogy that is thus expressed and formalised resides in the truth that our system is theurgic after another manner than was known to the conventional Magic in days of old. The term theurgy signifies creation of gods, namely; the thaumaturgic processes by which they were caused to manifest: some of you may remember how in a rite of evocation they appeared to the Emperor Julian called the Apostate as pale and exhausted shadows with the weariness of the ages upon them, for the world had ceased to believe in them. But the Order of the Golden Dawn seeks to awaken in its members the essential divine nature and thus in a true sense to create gods which are no shadows and *simulacra* but the powers of the Most High vested in the mystery of His Grace manifested. At the same time the formulae and the processes which are thus pressed into the service of a far higher experiment are not matters of illusion or mere pretexts in their inferior aspects and though our concern is one of dissuasion it is possible that some may be led into a lesser manner of the light, with a substituted certitude—by the actual use of those ceremonial arts which are preserved among us, are interpreted, but not given out to the student as a way of truth or grace. As the members of the Masonic Brotherhood are for the most part speculative Masons, not builders of houses or temples made with hands, but as its vast membership also includes the modern descendants of the old Guild of practical architects, so within the ranks of our more withdrawn and more highly warranted fraternity, it comes about there are some who are attracted by the astral workings, and them we endeavour to guide in the true way, that they also may have part in our terms.

My intention has been only to offer so brief a view of this horizon which is opened by the mystic light of the Golden Dawn that those who are beginners among us may discern even from their beginning the true nature of our preoccupation within this circle of which they also have now entered. There is one thing more, my brethren, concerning the means of grace which are within the secret orders, though it is not to be affirmed that they are exclusive to those orders. You should know that neither ceremonies nor hidden services, nor strange ventures of symbolism, can communicate to you or to any one more than you possess already. It is a doctrine in chief of our philosophy that all things are implied in the mind. You remember that the pact is born and not made, but this notwithstanding his congenital possession of this faculty is without prejudice to this dependent truth that he requires a great deal of making and developing before he can assume the perfect mankind of his art. It is the same with the mystic and adept. The faulters for the attainment and possession in perpetuity of all truth and grace are within you; they are not things which can be infused, but at the beginning they are implied in the mind, and it is the work of the secret orders which are founded for the purpose of raising them into the realm of realisation or the realm of consciousness.

10
THE ALLOCUTION OF THE 5 = 6 GRADE

To the Fratres et Sorores who have entered recently into the Grade of Adeptus Minor, and are Neophytes of the Rosy Cross, the Headship of the Independent Rite offers a loving welcome and certain words of counsel.

In the hush of the mind which follows such a reception, you are asked to put away for a few momnents all images of the outward things; and let us consider by what paths we have entered herein and the place to which we have come. Looking back upon the Grades of the Golden Dawn, you will do well to remember at first only their familiar points, the symbolic consecrations therein, signifying that preparation in all parts of the lower personality whereby that which is capable within is made ready for its proper work under the alliance of redemption. Redemption is in virtue of rebirth, but in the sequence of Rites and Degrees you should understand that the symbolism of regeneration is far away in the series and is in no sense to be regarded as attained in the 5=6 Grade of Adeptus Minor. When the body has been purged, when there has entered into the lower consciousness of mind that sense of the all-ruling importance of higher things which casts out the false sense of permanent interest in the things that are below; when it has been realised that the emotions fixed on earth are errant in the void of the perishable, and of that which is even now as dead; when in fine the will has been turned and directed towards the Divine Will, there opens that inward door which corresponds in symbolism to the Portal of the Rosy Cross. It is the Portal of those who have made clean their whole personality and will abide henceforth in the life of purity for the simple reason that other refuge they have none. We pray of you to realise this state

The Allocution of the 5 = 6 Grade

in your hearts, believing that in many cases it is one that has been already reached in the Order. It is presented by the Order in symbolism, and there is no fraternity in the world, whatsoever the traditional knowledge which it transmits by perpetuation from the past, that can communicate it to you in a direct way. Your work is to take it into your life, that you may truly awake and arise, that you may keep the holy vigil till you are called to rest in God.

Now you have learned in the Portal that the synthesis of holy research in the Order of the Golden Dawn is signified by the letters of Tetragrammaton Yod-He-Vau-He-, and the Celebrant who certified thereto was the messenger of the Second Order, bearing on his breast the Rose Cross of five mystic petals, corresponding to the letters of another Divine Name, Yod-He-Shin-Vau-He, which is the synthesis of Tiphereth and the symbol of the Christ life. The purified life of that Grade, the life which you cannot help leading, if peradventure the message of the Grades has passed within you out of the world of symbolism, is the path to the life that is in Christ and to the life which at some far distance becometh the Christ within you.

Bear in mind however that it is the path only, for the Christ life is not declared in the symbolism of Tiphereth. It is allocated to another Grade; but it may come about, Fratres et Sorores, that some of you may attain it in the world of realisation within before you reach it in symbolism. You must therefore learn that you contain in your spiritual nature all the measures and all the world of symbolism, but you are not contained thereby. Do not think therefore that you can rest from the work of the wise in the Grade of Tiphereth till the Chiefs of the Second Order, at the close of some mystical period, shall call you to a further stage. Go before your initiations and advancements that when you shall hear glad tidings therein you may yourself be the bearer of tidings. So will you come into your own and then will your own receive you.

There is an intimation concerning this kind of progress in the Zohar, when it speaks of those elect who pledge themselves to observe the law before they have heard its proclamation. This is another mystery of the will in its direction, the state of complete readiness, in advance of counsel and ordinance, the realisation that every moment is in a practical and vital manner the accepted time and the day of salvation.

The Zohar opens with a kind of exordium on the mystery which is symbolised by the five petals of the Rose and says that they correspond to the five doors of grace. They are also the five virtues which lead to perfection. These are explained in another Kabalistic book to be the love of God, chastity, charity, humility and the study of the Secret Doctrine, which last is described in the Ritual of the Portal, also on Zoharic authority, as the work of all the works and the prayer of prayers. That which is intended however is the practical and vital study, and it is another sense of the counsel which it has just been sought to convey. It is the realisation of the path of symbolism and the sacramental economy of doctrine so that they shall enter the life and transmute it. It is not the study of texts or the pursuit of the paths of knowledge. The Ritual also says that the five virtues are five manners of wounding, by which the Adept is crucified to himself and to the world for the manifestation of the Divine within him. Now the purified life of Tiphereth is the life of gladness and joy, but it is also a life of the Cross and on that Cross the Adeptus Minor remains for the whole symbolic period of his spiritual subsistence in the Grade. The purpose is that he being so exalted, may draw the parts of his lower personality after him. When he has done this, he can bow his head, saying that it is finished, and can give up the ghost mystically, because it is appointed unto man once to die and after this there is the great and undeclared grace of the Divine judgement in Geburah. This is the sense in which the Adeptus Minor accepts the bonds of suffering and self-sacrifice. The crucifixion which is imposed upon him at the time of his Obligation is a presage of the life of the Grade, even as that which he experiences subsequently in the holy Ceremony of the Rite, foreshadows those Higher Mysteries which follow in the later Degrees of the Order.

According to the explanation of the five virtues which has been given on authority outside the Zohar itself they begin in the love of God, which is the aspiration of the spirit upwards, and they end in God's love towards us made manifest in the state of our election, actuated by which love God has given us the Secret Doctrine, or the knowledge of the door which opens on the path of our return to Him. The intermediate virtues are those of the purified life and they belong to Tiphereth. The Cross of

The Allocution of the 5 = 6 Grade   153

humiliation on which the Candidate is placed at the Ceremony of reception of the Grade, is in this manner the preparation for a Cross of Glory. Think for a moment of that which is signified by the versicles of the Chief Adept when the stigmata are impressed upon him. They refer to the Triad in the Archetype and because of the correspondence between things above and below they refer also to the Triad in humanity; to the Spirit, which is the Divine part; to the Water which is the psychic part; to the Blood, which is the life in Nephesh, the animal part; and in fine to mystical death and resurrection, or the Greater Mysteries which are the crown of the crucified life. So is the Candidate prepared to hear in the historical part concerning the life of research into the Mysteries and concerning attainment therein. It is this which must be repeated in ourselves and it leads in the symbolism to a knowledge of the burial of our Divine part in the Pastos of the body, within the sacramental universe represented by the Vault of the Adepts. In the words of the Portal Ritual, the Candidate hears in a high symbolism the Divine Voice speaking in the universe, the Christ spirit testifying concerning itself and concerning the path of his own attainment. Fratres et Sorores, when the Chief Adept invokes the Divine White Brilliance, may we receive the communication of that Light by the realisation of the mystery of Tiphereth in its inward meaning. It is no mere formula of a Ceremony but a vital act by intention. At the true moment there may and does descend the Great White Light upon the Order in response to the expressed and unexpressed desire of the Celebrant, the other priestly officers and the brethren concurring therein; it depends upon us and upon the dedication of all our earnestness in what sense and to what extent it comes down. The channels are there always, the Light and the graces are there. Some vessels may be closed and can receive nothing; some others in their present estate can by their nature contain little, but they receive according to their proportions and individual measures; some are like expanding vessels, open to all the channels and increasing in capacity as they receive. To them the Light comes, comes grace, and the truth comes. They live, but not in the Light, for it is the Great White Light of all which lives in them. And this is life in the Rose. Give us, O Lord, to know the glorious Rose of Life and to rest in the Life of the Rose.

11
THE SYMBOL OF THE ROSY CROSS

THE relation which subsists between true Ritual and Symbolism should lead us to discern that there are many aspects of both, notwithstanding in either case those which may be offered as the result of initial impressions, by anyone who has come newly within the circle of their influence. As to these, it must be said that there are cases, some of them are known among us, when a real light has been cast out of all expectation—possibly through the utter absence of cognate preoccupations. Those who have followed the paths of Ritual and Symbolism belonging to the Instituted Mysteries will have met with great things—*magnalia Dei et naturae*—and the art of signifying concerning spiritual truths. They will never have met with any now working in the world which compare in importance of root-matter with those of our two Orders. Assuming this statement to represent firsthand experience on the part of practised students, and of presumptive value as such, it may be added and should indeed be affirmed positively, that the Order Rituals may not only be approached in several ways and do offer themselves under various aspects: of these aspects it is natural that the importance should vary, but there is a message in all. The triple division of the 5=6 Grade, as exemplified by its three points, is comparable to bird's eye views of great periods belonging to spiritual life, of which the three points are synthetic and summary-outlines expressed in the pageant of ritual. To speak of initiation and advancement—of Neophyte, Adepts and Epopts—is to speak of progress symbolised, or stages of attainment in the paths of sanctity. From the Portal of the Golden Dawn to that ineffable and concealed point where the glorious Grade of Chesed melts into the light of the Supernals, the two Orders have no other concern or they would end in a blind alley and not, as they do in their symbolism, and as they should and may in conscious realisation, at the threshold, which is an open gate, of the world of union. It seems necessary to state this clearly—though it is scarcely for the first time—because there are sometimes misapprehensions, as if the science of the soul were other than the science of God. The symbolic and summary outlines are, however, broad and general, as the words imply, and there are other particular aspects, with a few of which it is proposed to deal here, on the understanding that the root of all can be only a single root, grounded in the life of Tiphereth. The preliminary consideration shall be one belonging to a palmary point of symbolism—that Rosy Cross which is shewn to the Postulant under what may be called its primitive aspect in the Portal Grade of the Second Order. In the Grade of Adeptus Minor he sees it inscribed with all its attributes and correspondences, but again the root is one. In other and higher Degrees there may be further developments and simplifications, for as the garden rose has many petals and all are developments by culture from the primal wild rose form, so in our Temple symbolism that form is taken and is attributed to the Portal of the Second Order; but beyond this point the culture processes of the High Degrees produce many new flowers of increased beauty and multiplied meanings. There comes a time also when the Rose is seen no longer crucified on the Cross, because the day of sacrifice is over and that of glory is at hand.

As intimated by these words, the symbolism of the Rose and Cross is the threshold of another path of aspects from which we may consider the Grade of Adeptus Minor, and attention should be directed in the first place—though it may be only in passing—to the fact that the Grade in question has a message on the Macrocosmic side as well as on that of the Microcosm. This could not indeed be otherwise, seeing that it is a mystery of the Cross. The modes of initiation and advancement in every secret Order are of necessity personal to the Candidate. It is for his requirements alone that they are called into being. The statement is true of the older Instituted Mysteries—Egyptian, Greek or Roman. It is true of Masonry, in the Craft equally with the High Degrees. Rituals which in any predominant sense are on the Macrocosmic side are not rituals of initiation and advancement.

Great personal Grades have, however, almost always a macrocosmic side, though sometimes it may scarcely pass into verbal expression and although the implication has often to be sought with care, since it does not lie upon the surface. The Third Degree in Freemasonry is an especial case in point. It is a cosmic event which has been brought down into personality rather than arises therefrom. The Grade of Rose-Croix is another instance, but herein the macrocosmic aspect lies on the very surface. It may be regarded for this reason as so far in the perfection of symbolism; and if only its implicits had been developed under a true light of inspiration, it would have carried away the palm entirely from the Holy Order of the Temple, wherein the cosmic aspects are clouded by the *mise-en-scène* of a particular devotional pilgrimage which, on the historical side, must be termed obsolete in all true respects. Indeed the cosmic sense of the Ritual is so utterly overlaid that it seems arbitrary to suggest its presence. It is there, notwithstanding, as a hidden pearl of meaning, little as its presence may have been realised by those who constructed the Rite.

The Grade of Adeptus Minor is of course much greater than anything that is to be found in Masonry, and when we hear that the tomb of Christian Rosy Cross is made in the likeness of the universe—when we see the Vault and its symbolism—we know at once that the cosmic aspects are on the surface and not in concealment. There is no cloud in this respect on the sanctuary of the Grade, as there is so often in Masonry. The question which arises is the true manner of understanding the likeness and seeing that the Vault of the Adepts is (1) an universe of symbolism, but (2) the cosmic world exemplified by symbolism; what is imported by the fact that the Postulant is set upon the Cross of Obligation before he is permitted to enter and behold the wonders of that world? It is for such reasons as will enable those who follow the question seriously to realise that the Grade is an eloquent system of foreshadowed spiritual experience veiled like Masonry in allegory and illuminated on all sides by a glorious pageant of emblems. The subject is, however not less difficult than important and the present place is one in which only prefatory remarks can be offered thereupon.

Taking the symbolism of the Cross itself in the first place, this has two forms which belong more especially to the scheme of

The Symbol of the Rosy Cross

Sephirotic mysticism as it exists in the Order. The first is the Crux Ansata, of which something is said in the Ceremony of Opening the Temple in the 5=6 Grade, and this does not enter into the consideration here in hand. The second is the Calvary Cross, being that of the Obligation. The foot of this Cross is in Malkuth, the head is on Kether and the arms extend to Chokmah and Binah. It follows therefore that when the Postulant is bound thereon, he embraces the whole Sephirotic system with the exception of Kether. The base of the brain is at the point called Daath, which is knowledge in transcendence, and the Divine White Brilliance descends upon him from the Crown, to ratify his dedication in the light. He is suspended therefore in the perfect symbol of adeptship, which alone can encompass the aspiration represented by his pledge.

It should be observed at this point that the Ceremony of imposing the Obligation is of a threefold nature. When the Postulant has been placed upon the Cross in the position just described, the Mighty Adeptus Major, representing Severity and Judgment on the side of holiness, lifts up his own arms so that they are above those of the Postulant, and fixing his eyes upon the apex or Kether point of the Cross, he invokes the Angel Hua, who is the Shekinah in transcendence, or in that world where, according to the Zohar, there is no distinction between her and the Holy One. He implores her to look down upon this work and to ratify it by imposition of hands on the head of the Postulant. This signifies the ordination of the latter to the life of adeptship. It implies also the communication of the efficacious grace which is necessary to that life. Here is the first point of the Ceremony. The Second is the pledge itself, but about this it is unnecessary to speak in the present place. The third is the sealing of the Candidate, representing the crosswise descent of the influences for their operation in all parts of the personality. The formulae include the witness of those who are in heaven, summarised symbolically in Kether and encompassed also symbolically by the wings of Aima Elohim, who again is Shekinah. The triad of Supernals bears testimony to that triad which is below, the Spirit, the water and the blood; the spirit which is the self-knowing part; the water, which is the psychic part; and the blood which is the part of the body of man. Hence the sealing of the Postulant is direct from the head in the place of Daath to the feet in Malkuth. The sealing of the right hand has reference to the Severity side of the Tree and the formula is that of prohibition, through necessity, in respect of the Kingdom of Heaven. That which is understanding in the supernal world is righteousness in that which is beneath, and this operates as justice. It is in particular the severity and judgment by which the elect measure unto themselves. The sealing of the left hand corresponds to the Mercy side and the formula is that of guarantee to those who have accepted the work of the Divine life in the manifest world, as it here and now encompasses us. That which is Wisdom in the supernal world is Mercy in that which is beneath, and this operates as love. It is the compassion and the charity reflected from the infinite good will by which the adept in the Christ-state ministers unto those whom he would lead into the life of redemption. It is written: Let not thy right hand know what thy left hand doeth; and this is the counsel of distinction between ourselves and those who are about us. Out of it comes perfect love. There is finally the sealing on the breast, which corresponds to the Tiphereth part; and the formula has reference, on the one hand, to the sum of spiritual consciousness ascending in the heaven within us and, on the other, to the term of our work in union with the Divine.

Such is an outline in brief of the mystery of the Cross in the Grade of Tiphereth, so far as that of the Obligation is concerned. It is personal to the Postulant, to the life of the Cross during the period of the Grade and therefore to Adepti Minores, all and several. It has other aspects, but these do not concern us here. That Cross which is the Badge of the Grade is, however, a macrocosmic sign, though this also has other aspects, as is known by the Ceremony of Advancement in the Grade of Philosophus. As a macrocosmic sign, its length is between East and West and its breadth between North and South; the triple foliation of its extremities refers to the presence of the triad in the whole creation. It is at the centre of this Cross that the Rose of our Order is emblazoned, and that Rose signifies the Macrocosmic Christ, Who is one aspect of the Divine Immanence. The Key-word of the Grade is inscribed on this great symbol, and its interpretation has reference to the Christ of Palestine, Whom it follows that we regard as the expression in chief of that state which we understand as the Christhood. This is a mystery of that Sanctuary, full of grace and truth which is behind all Christian Churches, all great and holy religions; but the explanation is not in this Grade.

The interweaving of a sacred Name with the mystic Rose is in consonance with Kabalistic tradition, for it is said in *The Faithful Shepherd*, a text embodied in the Zohar, that the names of God are roses, that they are gathered by a Prince of Angels and that they form a crown on the head of the Holy One. Kether is therefore a crown of roses, and these roses which are above are completed, so as to speak, by another rose which is below, for Malkuth is the Rose of Creation. It came forth at the beginning as a perfect flower, but the dragon of symbolism emerged and laid waste the sacred cosmos of its petals. The Rose on the Cross, the Holy Rose which is Christ is, however, a perfect blossom; and when the Adeptus Minor is placed on the Cross of Obligation, he should understand that he is there and so bound to the end of his conversion from the stained and trampled rose of our fallen humanity to another Rose of the Christhood.

The same Zoharic text says that when Adam was located in Paradise to cultivate and watch over the Garden his work was to tend roses, regarded as research into the deep mysteries of grace and wisdom behind the Sacred Names. In a somewhat fantastic sense of symbolism, it might be said that this is also a work of adeptship, for the letters of all sacred books have been put into the hands of the mystics, and it is for them to form them into roses of inward meaning, sacred names of true and deep things in the spiritual life, roses of Hod and Netzach, Shekinah roses, roses of understanding and wisdom and when the Great White Light shall so help the culture which is the practice of the Presence of God, then the one true rose of all comes into manifest being, which is the Rose of Kether.

Having thus drawn something from the great book of Kabalism, it may be added that there is one thing more in the text which has a particular bearing on the present subject. Speaking of the four quarters of heaven, the Zohar says that an angel is set over each—Michael on the right hand, Gabriel on the left, Auriel in front and Raphael behind. In the midst of all is Shekinah, to whom the symbol of the Rose is especially consecrated. The meeting points of lines drawn from each of the four quarters are obviously the centre of the Cross; and the Rose on the Cross of pure untinctured Kabalism—if Kabalism recognised the Cross—would be that of the Shekinah.

There is no such recognition in any place, but the fact signifies nothing, for it remains that the meeting place in Order symbolism at the centre of the cross with equal arms is the point whereat is emblazoned the Rose of the Order and that Rose is Christ, as already said. In like manner, the Zohar recognises an identical middle point from which the four quarters of heaven are equidistant, and that point is the Rose of its own system—that is to say; the Rose of Shekinah. This indwelling spirit of Kabalism has many names, several of which are familiar. Adonai, Elohim, Adonai Ha Aretz and Metatron are all titles representing various aspects of Shekinah. Now the Cohabiting Glory, the Indwelling Spirit, the Abiding Glory are all titles of Christ, and what is therefore the relation between the Shekinah and Christus? Within the limits of the 5=6 Grade there are only slender means of realising the importance of this question to the Second Order as a whole, but it is known that the Chief Adept represents the Christ-spirit specifically embodied, while that which we invoke as Hua has aspects which are not out of correspondence with the conception of the universal Christ-spirit.

The Cross in its union with the Rose is not without a practical lesson to all Adepti Minores. The Postulant on the Cross of Obligation is the Candidate for the Christ-state; when he has become an Adeptus Minor, he wears the Badge of the Grade; it should be a testimony to himself and to his brethren that he is on the way of attaining the state; and he should remember that the Rosicrucian emblem was uplifted into the Paradise of Dante, a living Rose about the Throne of God. This is the term of adeptship—God present in the consciousness and the flower of perfect life, the soul and body of redemption folded as a rose about it.

12
THE TAROT AND THE ROSY CROSS

BEFORE proceeding to a study of the Tarot Symbols in the Paths of the Tree of Life, it seems desirable to state that the attributions with which we are familiar are not found in that transcript of the Cipher MSS on which we depend for our guidance in respect of the Order of the Golden Dawn, and which was transcribed from the originals by our G. H. Frater ARYABHATHA,[1] who has entered into his rest in the Lord. The fact is not surprising in itself as they do not belong to the Outer Order, being communicated in the Portal of the Rosy Cross.

It so happens, however, that Frater F.R.[2] has an indifferent and indeed a very bad copy of the Ciphers; it is one of uncertain origin, but is believed to connect with the Temple which a few brethren once attempted to found in Weston-super-Mare, and failed therein. It contains, after a piecemeal fashion several things of which we do not know otherwise except through the early Rituals. Among these there is the attribution in question, and it forms an integral part of the originals, I do not understand how it came to be omitted by so careful a maker of copies as my late Co-Chief. The miscellanea among which it is found do not carry with them much conviction as to their original integration in the Ciphers; they include the position of Officers and Members in a Temple opened for Neophytes, notes on Hebrew names of Grades and so forth. The attribution with which we are concerned is not itself under suspicion; it is correct on the evidence of the Ciphers up to and including the 4=7 Grade of the First Order, and there is no question that what follows in the

[1] [i.e. the Revd. W. A. Ayton. RAG]
[2] [i.e. Finem Respice = Dr R. W. Felkin. RAG]

ascent of the Tree is in absolute accord with the prevailing numeration of the Tarot cards, save for one substitution or reversal of Strength and Justice, by which the one is allocated to the 19th and the other to the 22nd Path. The actuating reason is obvious, because the attribution of the Zodiacal Signs proceeds downwards, from the 15th path and in their order Leo=Strength belongs to Path 19, while Libra=Justice is referable to Path 22. I should add that for the beginning of the Zodiacal arrangement there is authority in the Cipher Rituals, while the allocations of the Tarot cards throughout the paths of YETZIRAH being founded also on the Ciphers it follows almost certainly that the Fool is at the summit of the Tree, because it has not been placed at the foot according to the usual procedure. Whether there is another arrangement of the Tarot Symbols possible at certain points within the measures of Order symbolism is another question. There are no cards attributed to the World of ASSIAH, and this is of necessity because ASSIAH, the Fourth World, is ascribed to MALKUTH in our symbolism, while the Tarot cards are referred to the Paths only. The SEPHIROTH are degrees or states attained and the Paths are modes of ascent thereto. As the various SEPHIROTIC stages are Grades also in the Order of the ROSY CROSS, we have to determine whether the allocations of certain cards to certain Paths is explicable in an adequate manner by methods of progress through the various Grades, or whether there is a deeper meaning within them which has dictated modes of progress. This is one point of view, and the most comprehensive from which the subject can be approached, but it is a question only concerning the way of the soul's return, as this is delineated in the scheme of the Tree of Life, and there is an alternative question whether the Tarot cards have anything to tell us respecting that outward journey by which the soul entered into manifestation. The relation of the cards to the worlds in which they are placed is a further subject on which we should expect to get light. For this and for other reasons, it is desirable to begin with a brief retrospection concerning the Worlds and the Paths.

The ascent from one World of Kabalism to another is always by a vertical Path; it is the 32nd Path which leads from ASSIAH to YETZIRAH; the 25th Path goes from YETZIRAH to BRIAH, or from the Order of the GOLDEN DAWN to that of the ROSY CROSS; and the 13th Path ascends from BRIAH to ATZILUTH. Now, in three out of the four Worlds, this progression takes the Postulant—understood as the Seeker after Eternal Life—to the lowest SEPHIRA of that World wherein he is called to enter; from MALKUTH, which is ASSIAH, into the YETZIRATIC sphere of YESOD; from YETZIRAH into TIPHERETH of BRIAH. But according to the arrangement of the Tree it would seem that the travelling of the 13th Path should bring the Postulant at once into KETHER, the first and the highest of the Supernal SEPHIROTH, so far as there can be said to be degrees in a Triad which is also an Unity.

We should expect therefore that there is some well-marked break at a certain point in the manner of attaining ATZILUTH according to the ceremonial symbolism of the Order, supposing that ATZILUTH is attained; and though it is impossible to explain its nature—actual or hypothetical—within the limits of the Grade of TIPHERETH, some tentative intimation can be given. There is a Portal of the Golden Dawn, which is the Court of the Temple in MALKUTH, and this Temple has a Holy Place beyond it. They symbolise together the external Church and the literal sense of doctrine in every faith and age. It is the ASSIAH side of religion. Beyond these things the initiate of the Order enters the YETZIRATIC World and the First Grade therein brings him into the Holy of Holies, the creative principle which has developed external religion into the realm below; but it is only in the high YETZIRATIC Grades that the seeker is brought into communication with the first expounded mysteries of the Secret Doctrine and the hidden sense of the Law. There is also a Portal of the Second Order, which is the Court of the Temple in TIPHERETH, and a Gate of Entrance into the Christ-life realised by practice in the personality. It is reasonable, therefore, to infer that there is a Portal of the Third Order. Now, the Portal of the Golden Dawn is not a SEPHIRA, but, as I have said, is the Court of MALKUTH. The Portal of the Rosy Cross is not a SEPHIRA, but the Gate of TIPHERETH.

And again, it is reasonable to infer that the Portal of the Third Order is not a SEPHIRA.

The mode of progress from Order to Order is, however, by a vertical Path, as we have seen, and it is not this rule which can be broken in the way of ascent to ATZILUTH. The reason is that the

Middle Path which is called in the Grade of Zelator 'the straight path' that 'turneth not to the right nor to the left', the 'Path of Equilibrium' is 'the way of return to the height'. From SEPHIRA to SEPHIRA the scheme of the Tree of Life is traversed in various directions, but there is always a going back to its centre, the Path of Benignity concerning which it is said in the ZOHAR that SHEKINAH is above and that SHEKINAH is also below it. The SHEKINAH in transcendence is really referred to BINAH, but we are told that in the Supernals there is no distinction between Her and the Holy One; and in the Altar Diagram belonging to the Grade of Practicus KETHER, CHOKMAH and BINAH are placed within a great circle, where they are covered by the wings of AIMA ELOHIM, that is the wings of SHEKINAH—under which the souls of the just abide in the worlds beneath.

If the Tree of the SEPHIROTH were delineated according to the true spirit of the Rosy Cross, it would appear as the Rose-Tree of SHEKINAH, she being the Rose of all the worlds. In MALKUTH, she is the Rose of manifested things; in the Supernals she is the Mystical Rose of Heaven; in TIPHERETH she is the Rose of Purified Life; and all the remaining SEPHIROTH are states or phases of the archetypal Rose, which is she who is the mystery of womanhood in all her grades and degrees. We shall recur to this intimation presently.

It should be observed in the meantime that in order to reach TIPHERETH the Postulant re-enters YESOD, whence he proceeds upward to the threshold of the Second Order; and so it may be gathered—by the virtue of another inference—that the point of departure for the entrance into the Third Order will seem to be TIPHERETH of necessity. But if the Postulant enters ATZILUTH by the help of a Portal it is not assuredly that of KETHER, which would involve overstepping BINAH and CHOKMAH, as if these were not stages of his progress; and the Portal of the Third Order must be therefore in the Path itself. In certain delineations of the Tree of Life there is the indication of a middle point in the Path of GHIMEL, which point passes under the name of DAATH, or Knowledge, and one reason—though of an exceedinly presumptive kind—why it may be the Portal of the Third Order is that DAATH—like the Portal below—is not a SEPHIRA, but the centre of influence coming from CHOKMAH and BINAH. It is that which they produce between them, and there is a sense in which it stands for them both. That DAATH is or may be the Portal of the Third Order is of course only one further matter of inference, and we have to recognise that there are many interventions which are likely to transform the face of speculations made only in TIPHERETH. Yet the notion is based on materials which have been long in your hands and it seems to explain at once why our system of Grade-progression suggests the number 11 rather that the ten of SEPHIROTH. From one point of view it is, however, a false suggestion. The addition of the alternative numbers ascribed to each Grade in the Order would produce 11 invariably, but they are connected by the sign of equality and the literal meaning is explained in the Grade of Zelator, where it is said that MALKUTH is the 10th SEPHIRA on the way of descent from KETHER but it is the 1st on the way of return. This method of comparison obtains throughout the scheme—at least until the great dividing line is reached upon the threshold of Atziluth. But the numeration is deceptive of set purpose—always suggesting 11 but always producing 10, because of DAATH, which would be an eleventh SEPHIRA, if it were a SEPHIRA properly: it is on the verge of that position but does not attain it in the convention of Kabalism, and so with their mode of numeration—which offers therefore a certain air of subtlety. It has also an important implicit, though it may not have entered previously into the consciousness of the Second Order at large. This is the doctrine of unity through the whole SEPHIROTIC scheme, in virtue of which the things which are below are not only in correspondence with those which are above but are identical as to the roots therewith.

And because the SEPHIRA MALKUTH is outside the three Triads, alone in a place that is lowest, it is mentioned especially concerning it that the vestige of KETHER is therein, so that it is properly and fully incorporated; and all that is above is within it and it is contained by all that is beyond. In particular it is assumed into the Second Reflected Triad by the scheme of ceremonial advancement which obtains in the Outer Order. Of the unity which prevails therein I have no occasion to speak. So also in the Second Order there is an intimate mystical marriage between the Grades and SEPHIROTH, and they are all summarised in TIPHERETH. But in the Supernal Triad there is that quality of union which is transcendent as the world to which it belongs, and all unions below are its reflection or shadow.

If 8=3, 9=2 and 10=1 all this is preliminary within the measures of the Supernal Triad, and it is thence that the Law is projected into the worlds that are below. Wheresoever in the region instituted ceremonial ATZILUTH may be expressed in ritual–if indeed anywhere–we may be very sure that it is under a law of unity with which other pageants of the Rosy Cross can be called scarcely in comparison.

I may seem to have spoken very plainly of the things which lie without the measures of the Grade of TIPHERETH, but I have really preserved the covenants and have not lifted more than a corner of the veil, so that you may understand better where you are in respect of the symbolism of the Tree.

What I have protected from your view at the present stage is the genuine distinction between that which takes place in TIPHERETH before the Path can be opened to the Portal of the Third Order, as compared with that which takes place in YESOD before the Postulant is drawn between the Pillars to the Portal of the Rosy Cross. As another instance of an essential difference or break between the Second and Third Orders, remember always that BRIAH is the First Reflected Triad, but ATZILUTH is not a reflection. In YETZIRAH and BRIAH the mode of progress is indicated naturally by the position of their SEPHIROTH, the inverted apex of each reflected triad being the lowest SEPHIRA of the series—YESOD in the one and TIPHERETH in the other case. But BINAH and CHOKMAH are at the ends of the first horizontal or reciprocal path and the natural entrance to BINAH as lowermost of the Supernal Triad is either from GEBURAH or from TIPHERETH, and is not in the hierarchic Order because the true ascent is only by the Middle Path. On the other hand, no transition is possible from CHESED to BINAH, as there is no path between them.

Now, we have seen that in respect of the Middle Path the SHEKINAH is a Spirit which is above, and in this sense it draws upwards; that it is also a Spirit which is below, and in this sense it leads to the height. If we look at the Tarot cards as they are allocated on the Tree of Life we shall find that in one or other of her aspects she is the guardian of the gates of entrance—actual or speculative—to the several worlds of advancement represented, on the authority of Kabalism, as the various Orders of our Fraternity. As the SHEKINAH in transcendence she manifests in the vestures of a High Priestess keeping the Path of GHIMEL, because she is religion in attainment. The Book of the Secret Doctrine is in her hands, and it lies open on her knees, seeing that she is Divine Law wherein is the process of attainment. She is clothed with the sun, and this signifies that she is the Moon in astronomical symbolism, being also the Queen of Heaven. Her light comes from the Eternal. She is the Guardian of the Gate of DAATH. Below she is pictured as the personified Spirit of the universe. She is Virgin, Bride and Mother, because she is the splendour of purity in all her states and planes. She is *Anima Mundi;* Divine Immanence in MALKUTH, as she is the Spirit which leads to the recognition of these in unity. There is much which might be added to her description in the Grade of Theoreticus, but I will say only that in so much as she is the creation adorned with the perfection of its beginning, it must be said that she is her own builder, or the power behind the manifest. For us, however, and for our concerns, she is the restorer of worlds. It is for this reason that she is the Gate of YETZIRAH, or the Guardian who stands thereat.

Because of her purity the Hegemon, who is her representative in the Order of the Golden Dawn, wears a white robe which represents innocence sanctified. Her picture in the 21st card is naked—on account of the perfection which resides in innocence—save indeed for a scarf that flows over her, as if naturally and undesigned, and this is because there is a mystery of divine possibility which lies behind innocence, being the mystery of nuptials as the completion thereof in nature, sealing it with holiness to the Lord. Earthly womanhood is the type of SHEKINAH, and this is one aspect of the Isis of Nature shewn in her unfallen beauty in the Altar-Diagram of the $3=8$ Degree.

In respect of the 21st card, it should be observed further that the physical centre is intimated after an especial manner, though under an art of concealment for modesty, by the erect position of the figure: it is the only Tarot card which exhibits womanhood in the fulness of her erect stature, the reason is given in Gen. 11, 25: *Erat autem uterque nudus, Adam scilicet et uxor ejus; et non erubescebant.* The position and all that is implied thereby—

including the mystery of the state of wifehood which lies on the surface of the text—should be contrasted with the Diagram of the 4=7 Degree, where the woman of the 3=8 Degree appears in the fallen state and is shewn stooping, so that the physical centre is indrawn by an operation of shame, as it is written: *Cognoviscunt se esse nudos;* and again: *Et timui eo quod nudus essem, et abscondi me.* This emblem is the antithesis of the 21st Tarot card as well as of the Practicus Diagram; it is this which keeps the Portal of earthly life for all who enter therein. Of every son and daughter of man who comes to that Portal, bearing the titles of admission, it prays that the fallen SEPHIRA MALKUTH may be raised up in his or her person, so that once again the figure may stand erect—if only in them.

Here is another aspect of the work indicated by the Portal of the Rosy Cross, when it is said that 'it is in ourselves and so only that the SEPHIROTH which fell in us also are raised'; but the inherent difficulties of exegesis in this most secret field have closed up the mouth of research so far as TIPHERETH is concerned. When the body of imperfection is dissolved in the halls of GEBURAH it shall be possible to speak more plainly, that the true stature of adeptship may be attained in CHESED.

As a conclusion to the 21st card: in the great oval which encompasses it, and in the four external angles, we behold a symbol of that eternal truth which Nature exists to manifest— the indwelling and encompassing powers of the Divine, signified by TETRAGRAMMATON, and by the extended Name which abides in all quarters of the universe. It is in virtue of this knowledge that the Postulant begins the return journey of the soul. Because of these Divine Powers within and without, the Isis of Nature is also the Bride of the Apocalypse, understood as the Church of Christ. For Nature is a great Temple in which GOD is manifested to man, and in proportion as man can read the messages that Temple is assumed, becoming a great sanctuary for the administration of redeeming sacraments. It was said of old by Zoharic writers that all things are in MALKUTH; the Church which is of GOD is not therefore apart from the Temple that is Nature, and the office of man in his election is so to work at his own inward transmutation that he shall manifest the Divine on all planes of the Cosmos, making that new Heaven, that new Earth, wherein the former things have passed away.

The Tarot and the Rosy Cross

This is why the Isis of Nature, the unfallen universe, is shewn to the Postulant as he enters the Gate of YETZIRAH. As the soul returns to GOD, it takes Nature with it, but the archetypal Nature. The restored and redeemed world is also before the soul; the spirit thereof, the Bride and Queen of the Kingdom, stands at the Gate and opens, while, from the furthest point of the Path, the great height, the Spirit and the Bride call it into that region where there are communicated the 'Waters of Life freely'.

We have so far dealt with the SHEKINAH in two aspects—as she stands at the door of YETZIRAH and at the concealed Portal of ATZILUTH. On the threshold of BRIAH, at the Gate of the Second Order, in the Portal of the Rosy Cross, she appears as Temperance, the Keeper of the Middle Way. As it was said by a great master in the theurgic path of crucifixion, we must even be content with what we have, but the symbol as it is presented commonly and under the name which I have mentioned here seems far from our high purpose. I should rather write about another figure such great words of paradox as '*Ego dixi in excessu meo, Omnis Homo Deus*', because in the proper understanding of our symbolism the strait path does not lie exactly between the evil and the good. This is the thesis which has come down to us, but in the higher Degrees we must give the higher meaning, and the complexion of the path upward, as we proceed further in our course, has more of the aspect of ecstacy than that of Temperance. All that is possible, however, within the measures of the Portal of the Rosy Cross, has been done to uplift the symbol, and it is of all truth that it represents the principle of sacramental life, the ascent of human nature. It is said further, and very truly, in respect of the SHEKINAH as she is seen under this aspect, that it is she who brings forth to life. This is in our old records, but the reason in its fulness lies beyond this Grade. The same memorials call her the Daughter of the Reconcilers, and it is assuredly she who leads therein. She is the Guardian of the Gate of BRIAH, calling into perfect reconciliation. The essences, elements or elixirs which she mingles in her chalices and which are called in the Ritual of the Portal the influences of CHESED and GEBURAH, signify the union of the inward and outward states, indrawn and manifest, the mystic life and the life of man in the world, by which alone it is possible to attain the perfect manhood of adeptship. As she stands at the threshold of TIPHERETH she signifies by her symbolic action the true counsel which may be derived from those who are prepared from the higher Grades of the Second Order.

We have now completed our study in summary form of the manifest cards of SHEKINAH on the Tree of Life. It should be noted, however, that each emblem is the synthesis of the world to which it guards the entrance and into which it leads the Postulant. The High Priestess before the door of DAATH, representing at once the Path of Descent from KETHER and of going back thereto, is really in the position of AIMA ELOHIM, covering with her wings the three Supernal SEPHIROTH, as she is shewn in the Diagram of the 3=8 Degree. Above her is that state wherein there is no distinction between SHEKINAH and the Holy One. The Angel of Temperance is termed in the Portal of the Rosy Cross the synthesis of TIPHERETH and TIPHERETH in its turn is the synthesis—as we know otherwise—of the whole Second Order. So also the Divine Presence represented by the 21st card, is typical of that state which is delineated by the work of YETZIRAH in the Order of the Golden Dawn—the re-making of manifested man, male and female, in the likeness of ELOHIM, the restoration of man in the perfect terms of the archetype.

Fratres et Sorores, I have mentioned there and here the Divine Name TETRAGRAMMATON, and this has been allocated after several manners to the Tree of Life in the old theosophy of Kabalism. I give you hereby and herein, for the first time in the history of our Holy Order, the mystery which appertains to its descent through the Four Worlds.

YOD, HE, VAU, HE are KETHER, CHOKMAH, BINAH, the HE final abiding in DAATH, at the centre of the Path of GHIMEL. This is the Daughter of the Voice, who according to the symbolism, is begotten by the Eternal Mother from the Father Eternal and is nourished by the Begotten Son for the maintenance of the Eternal Covenant between all that is Divine and all that comes forth therefrom. Hereof is the world of the Supernals; and this Daughter is the High Priestess. YOD, HE, VAU, HE: CHESED, GEBURAH and TIPHERETH, with the Portal of the Rosy Cross. By CHESED the world was made; by GEBURAH it is re-made in Christ; and TIPHERETH is the working of those forces which lead to the new birth. Hereof is the first Reflected

Triad, and the second HE, or the Daughter, is the Angel whom we call Temperance, standing at the Gate of Adeptship. YOD, HE, VAU, HE, the Second Reflected Triad, or NETZACH, HOD and YESOD, and the Portal of YETZIRAH looking towards the Pillars of MALKUTH. Therein the Daughter—she who is the Second HE—is represented by the Angel of the Presence in things manifest, and this is the 21st Key of the ancient Tarot cards. In ASSIAH, as you know, the four parts of human personality are modes of the utterance of the Divine Name in man—the imperfect and halting expression—and it is the object of our research to uplift it into a true image of the Word. This is so far as regards the Two Orders of the Rosy Cross, but after it is a Divine Silence, wherein the Word reflects upon itself.

In fine, as regards the Four Worlds, the entrance into ASSIAH is through the sacred body of womanhood, as into the Garden of Venus, but is now a ravaged garden, and the SHEKINAH therein is at best a clouded splendour, because she is in exile with the Israel of GOD: while in a certain very deep sense of Zoharic theosophy she has been cast out with him.

But when the Postulant comes to the Portal of the Golden Dawn, desiring in his own person and with his proper personal eyes to gaze upon her unveiled countenance, till the world is restored therein—he in that and that of truth in him—there is opened for him a Gate of Entrance into another mode of ASSIAH, and she who stands thereat, his Guide through all the Paths, is the SHEKINAH manifested as the Hegemon of our Holy Order. She is the Guardian of the Gate of ASSIAH.

We may summarise at this point as follows; on the hypothesis that we came forth from the centre, which centre is also the height, or the world of ATZILUTH in Kabalistic symbolism, there is Zoharic authority for saying that our descent into manifestation was by the central Pillar of Benignity and the paths comprised therein. According to the symbolism of our Order, we came down, therefore, through those doors by which, in the same symbolism, we go up on the return journey. But this is another way of saying that we enter into objective existence by and through her who is SHEKINAH, for there should be no need to affirm that our mystical paths are not distances between two points in space and that our doors are not of this literal understanding.

She who is the Guardian of the Gates is really both Gates and Paths, because she is the Mother of souls, who brings them into individual being in virtue of her divine womanhood, even as the womanhood on earth brings children into the life of flesh.

Lastly, as the wings of AIMA ELOHIM cover the Supernal SEPHIROTH in the world of ATZILUTH, she is the synthesis of that world and is represented as such in the Tarot card of the High Priestess. in her substituted form of Temperance she is called—as we have seen and know otherwise—the synthesis of TIPHERETH, and TIPHERETH is the synthesis of BINAH. As the Isis of Nature in the 21st card, she is the synthesis of YETZIRAH; and in ASSIAH—which is the world of things as they are, the earth and the fulness thereof—she is represented in our Outer Temple by a human being, the Hegemon of the Golden Dawn, who from one point of view should be therefore always a woman, save and except that in the truest and highest sense the male is not without the female nor the female apart from the male, each implied in each and both expressed in either.

I pass now to a brief consideration of the Tarot cards which are allocated to the Paths within the several worlds—but in separation from those which belong to the Pillar of Benignity—and are the modes of progression in the Order from world to world. It is obvious that the Rituals of the Golden Dawn comprise all that can be said as regards the symbols in YETZIRAH. They are memorials of the soul's legend, of her quest and the way of attainment. The Angel of Judgement calls to the risen life in the place of purity in soul; and the Path of SHIN is the path of heart's desire towards all high ends of being. The fire therein is reflected into the Kingdom of this world for the conversion of our material part. Into the Path of RESH is reflected a certain light from the glorious sun of TIPHERETH, and it falls upon the world of mind. The symbol of the Moon is connected with the Path of RESH, as the light of wisdom and of will reflected from the state which is in Christ shining on the earth of our mortality. The spirit of the Great White Star in the Path of TZADDI is SHEKINAH under another aspect, directing the waters of life to the great world of intellection and keeping the ways thereof. But the symbol of the riven Tower in the Path of PE indicates the work of him who enters the Grade of Philosophus and the region of the dedicated will. It is the way of the King in Israel, of him who is earning his titles to reign in BRIAH.

Before the Portal of the Rosy Cross are the symbols of the Path attributed to the letters NUN, SAMECH and AYIN, and here again you are acquainted with their meanings. The Paths lead from YETZIRAH, but one of them alone is traversed because SHEKINAH is the way to the heights. The three symbols comprise the last counsels conveyed on the threshold of Adeptship, so that what is externally a ceremonial title may become an essential and inward gift. That which they teach might be summarised in brief words as follows: (1) Those who escape from the toils of that death which is in sin shall not see death for ever. (2) For those who cast out the evil from within them Satan becomes the emissary Goat, a sacrifice for those who go up the Path of reconciliation, path of purified life and way of redemption. They shall rest under the wings of SHEKINAH.

Beyond these things, my Brethren, are the Grades and the Paths to the Grades beyond the life of TIPHERETH, but these remain in the hiddenness, awaiting that due season when the call shall come to each.

13
DIONYSIUS AND HIEROTHEOS

PART I

FRATRES ET SORORES, I am asking your attention to what on the present occasion is a departure from our accepted procedure. I am going to read to you certain portions of texts which in a technical sense have no connection with the Order, though in the higher understanding they are of its essence and spirit, its quest and the term of this. The first is of pseudo-Dionysius on the subject of mystical philosophy, while the second is referred to his putative master Hierotheos. It is not my intention to discuss the very difficult question whether the tract which passes under the name of Hierotheos really anteceded those other works which pass under the name of Dionysius, and still less shall I attempt to determine the date of the latter—I mean whether it belongs to the first or the fifth century, or to some period between these limits. Both subjects are important within their own limits and after their own manner, but not in the present connection. It is my intention to take the practical and formulated teaching of Dionysius on the question of return to the centre, seeking to ascertain briefly the nature of its message to ourselves. What has this way to God, as it was sought and perhaps found in a specific case very early in the ages of Christendom, to suggest in the specific case of each one of us? The intimations on the method may give us that which we need or they may not. In any case they represent the utterances of a voice raised in testimony as to the reality of a certain path. When we have considered this testimony and the conclusions which arise therefrom I shall refer to that of Hierotheos, drawing from the one source which is alone available readily except to Syriac scholars. There are reasons for thus reversing the usual and on the surface more logical procedure which would take the master or precursor before the disciple, but they are questions of scholarship and criticism which I have set aside expressly because they do not belong to my subject.

The tract of Dionysius dircts those who would devote themselves to that deep contemplation which is understood as the path of the mystic to lay aside the services and operations of the understanding, all that is material and intellectual, the things which are, those also which are not, and by a supernatural flight upward, to unite themselves, as intimately as possible, with Him who is exalted above all essence and all idea. It is by such a sincere, spontaneous and total abandonment of ourselves and of all things, that, delivered from every impediment, it shall become possible to precipitate ourselves into the mysterious brightness of Divine Obscurity.

This is the counsel, while the foundation on which it rests is that 'God manifests Himself in His truth and unveiled to those only who set aside the material and intellectual world, scale the heights of most sublime sanctity and, dispensing henceforward with all light, with every mysterious accent, all word from heaven descending, do plunge into that darkness wherein He dwells Who reigns over the universe.' In respect of the darkness, Dionysius would have us understand that manifest Divine things are an expression in the order of symbolism of that which by its nature exceeds all thought, when it has been delivered from the sensible and intellectual world by paths of contemplation in the highest, 'the soul enters into the mysterious obscurity of holy ignorance and—renouncing all intellectual data—is lost in Him who can neither be seen nor comprehended; is given up unconditionally to this sovereign object, belonging henceforth neither to itself nor to others; is united to the unknown by the noblest part of its nature and in proportion to its surrender of knowledge; and, lastly, derives in this absolute ignorance a knowledge which the understanding is not capable of attaining.'

The terminology of Dionysius is of course a symbolism, and it is this in a high degree. His darkness is not darkness, but transluminous obscurity; in a word, it is excess of light; his blindness is sight exalted; his mystic ignorance is the precision of all Knowledge; and the path of this Knowledge begins apparently in the intellectual realisation of God as nothing whatsoever of all that which exists. In order to attain this state which is denominated ignorance in a transcendental sense we must dare to deny whatsoever can be affirmed of God. That which we know concerning all other beings is a veil in its application to Him. By a splendid extravagance of language, the path of His attainment is therefore one of sublime ignorance and Divine Darkness, while He who is the term of our research is nothing of that which is not, besides—as already stated—nothing of that which is—Himself neither light nor darkness, neither truth nor the opposite thereof, for He surpasses all our negations as well as all that which we affirm.

It is obvious and a mere commonplace to admit that this thesis will produce a very different impression on different minds. Those who are acquainted only with the path of simple faith and its sweet humanities will feel that such a Deity is out of all relation with man, yet there are further texts of Dionysius which—although in language unimaginable for them—tell of the fatherhood of God, the ministry of the Holy Spirit and the incarnation of the Eternal Word. Other persons whose gifts are only from normal source of intellectual light, will challenge the warrants of Dionysius for such an attempted delineation and may say that at the goal of his mystic path no God at all abides, and much less One who 'recompenses those who seek him out.' There are yet others, and I do not know that for such reason they are to be counted among the Elect, who will conclude that the Areopagite is concealing a patent platitude in a language of acrid paradox. To none of the classes enumerated would it serve to point out that his thesis is concerned with a Doctrine and an ordered mode of practice leading to Divine Union. Unfortunately, his tract is addressed to a friend or disciple who, by the hypothesis, was acquainted already with this method and knew something also of its terms, and he says only that concerning it which I have quoted previously; it is an unceasing exercise in mystic contemplation, performed in the casting out of sensible images and those also of the mind.

I should add that his mystic ignorance is said, in an extant letter, to be in no sense a state of privation but one of superiority in science, that God is known in a transcendent manner. But as regards the superiority of science it is said immediately afterwards that the science is eclipsed and in respect of that which has been termed the transcendent Knowledge its Essence

Dionysius and Hierotheos 177

is that He is not Known and that He does not subsist. This is the 'absolute and felicitous ignorance' which 'constitutes precisely the science of Him who surpasses all the objects of human science.'

It will be seen that the last paragraphs at least are an attempt to express the inexpressible by a play upon the alternatives of contradiction, or otherwise to convey an intimation although contradiction is inevitable. For some of us who approach the subject intellectually indeed but with a knowledge as mystics of what is involved therein it will seem an experimental research attempted in the world of non-thought, non-seeing and non-knowing, because thinking has its limits, seeing does not satisfy and the knowledge which comes to us through the accepted channels of experience is not the knowledge that we need. In other words, the paths which are about us are each a *cul de sac* when we are on the quest of God. In a sense this is true enough and in another it is entirely false, because all the paths are open and all the true paths lead. It is only *qua* wayfaring man that the wayfaring man errs in any of them. There is nothing that leads more truly than ordinary life itself when that life is sanctified; but the reason of course is that it ceases then to be ordinary in the common—which is the unclean—meaning of the word. Yet the kind of leading at its best is to the good things of the Lord in the land of the living, the rest of the faithful departed, the sleep in Christ and all that is included in the attainments of the Kingdom of Heaven, understood as the Kingdom of the next world and not of this. It is only in a very secondary, derived and reflected manner that, along these paths, we get any vital intimations of that which God has reserved for those who love Him. The path of Dionysius is *ex hypothesis* for realization in this life, and that is the path which we are all here to seek. But is its delineation in his case an attempt to make capital out of the complete bankruptcy of the mind in the face of the great subjects? Well *Fratres et Sorores*, if the mind is indeed bankrupt when so confronted, it is good to make capital out of that rather than stop the quest: we must even be content with what we have and go on somehow. Like the old adage, our need may be God's opportunity. And there is no doubt that we are bankrupt in respect of Divine things so long as we sit within the form matter of the senses, though material images are a medium of exchange in the world of material vested interests. We know by all holy doctrine that God is immanent in material things, but He is realisable in transcendence only. The mind is a great channel of communication with the Divine, working sacramentally upon us, but in respect of that which is understood as realisation, the High Priest and the other ministers in that Temple must be led outside with great reverence and the offices must be suspended if we are to get experience instead of symbols. Now we all know that the mind is the great maker of image. Thesis and antithesis, opposites and the pairs of these are all part of the pageant of images; and I think, if I speak frankly, that Dionysius was multiplying symbols instead of reducing them when he laboured to exhibit the dark side of his shield of Divine things. We know in all simplicity that the state of consciousness in God is the most remote and unlike of all experiences. We are not gaining anything when we try to talk of it in terms more desperate than an attempt to describe how two straight lines may after all enclose a space.

The counsel is a counsel of emptiness and stillness; whatever we add to these words only clouds the issues. Even the term contemplation is dangerous in this sense because it supposes one object and all objects have to be put away. The thesis is that in the stillness of sense and the emptiness of mind there supervenes a state in which the spirit knows itself and knows that it is one with God. Many and many saints, ascetics and holy men have put on record their ingarnerings into the mind of that which came to them in the deepest state of that mind's suspension. They may have done it to their own satisfaction, but they have not done it to mine, if I speak only under the light of the logical understanding. It is no doubt essentially irreducible into the terms of that understanding, but some are better than others—by which I mean that they are less in conflict with themselves.

The fact remains that whether in the East or the West no mystic has borne testimony to any other root fact than that of which Dionysius is the witness. They also concur by their insistence that there must be a preparation for the indrawn state in the outward and inward life. It is a path of sanctity. We must not go unclean into contemplation except with the firm desire of being cleansed. It is not till we are cleansed that we shall gain anything save the shadows and deceptions of the threshold. It seems to be therefore, that very early in the Christian centuries we get under the Christian aegis a witness concerning the higher way of truth and life which is identical with the other testimonies, is quite distinct and is yet highly individual. As we might expect, it is so far beyond the official field of sacraments and symbols that all doctrinal complexion of Christianity has dissolved; the work indicated is a work between the soul and God, as it is in the *Cloud of Unknowing* and the other great texts. It can serve us only as a brief presentation of philosophical teaching designed, firstly, to gratify and, secondly, to introduce a contemplative practice. But as I have said, this is wanting in the tract.

We come now to the second of our two memorials which passes under the name of Hierotheos, who is spoken of by Dionysius as his Master and two of whose works are by him quoted. Neither of them is the work extant and the attribution is itself dubious, hostile criticism affirming that it belongs to the beginning of the sixth century. The alternative view does not tend to place Hierotheos or Dionysius much earlier than the latter is allocated by scholarship, for whatever scholarship on the subject and its date may be worth at the moment. The *Book of the Hidden Mysteries of the House of God* exists in a Syriac MS, and the nature of its contents is known only by a pamphlet of Mr C. Frothingham published in 1886. This has been made the subject of a study by Mr Mead in the last issue of *The Quest*.[1] He describes it as an 'epic of the soul setting forth the mystical steps of the ascent of the mind or spirit to the Supreme.' The condition of the ascent is the purification of the soul and body, so that broadly speaking it corresponds to the processes which are delineated symbolically in the Grades of our outer Order. After this preparatory stage the aspirant has to pass through the 'opposing' and 'chastening hosts' in 'the purgatorial realms of Hades'. He then undergoes spiritual rebirth and ascends 'beyond the firmament' into 'the heavenly realms'. There are mysteries, however, which are beyond those that are understood by the term heaven and its experiences and their path is the Way of the Cross. 'The crucifixion, however, is not of the mind

---

[1] [i.e. in Vol. III, No. 1, October 1911, pp 100-19. RAG]

alone, it is of the whole human nature; for the mind (or spirit) is crucified in the midst and the soul and body (are) crucified on the right and on the left.' The mind is then laid in the sepulchre to rest for three days, after which it rises from the dead on the third day and 'unites to itself its own properly purified soul and body'. This is, however, in no sense the end of the process, and whether that which follows is still a work in this region or has assumed a cosmic character may seem doubtful to those who do not follow carefully the involved pageant of the symbolism. I may say, however, that it is still individual and inward. The root of evil has to be eradicated; there is a descent into the depths of Sheol, another crucifixion therein, followed by a baptism of the spirit, and it is thereafter that 'the Mind passes into that seat where there is no longer vision to enter on the slopes of (the) mystery of union with the Universal Essence itself. Yet this also is a place of strife and trial rather than of rest. It has also to descend again, even to Sheol and Hell, armed with a Mystic sword. The reward of its victory is the attainment of universal purification when its sole will is 'to be united with the Arch-good above'. In virtue of this will the reascent begin by resurrection and ascension. It is thereafter that the mind is really and fully united with the Universal Essence and 'embraces all in itself'.

At all risk of imperfection and the suppression of important points in critical appreciation, I have endeavoured to reduce this involved system to the simplest part of its Elements. It suffers on the surface from the expression of personal inward experience in cosmic terms and as there is subsequently a cosmic part which I have left over it is a little difficult to decide where the one ends and the other begins. The procession of the imputed experience is exceedingly interesting, its inexplicable confusion notwithstanding, because at so early a period it embodies a recognition of the great principle which characterises Christian mysticism—that the mystery which began at Calvary and ended—so far as the visible plane is concerned—on the Mount of Ascension has to be inacted within each of us before it is of effect in us. This is the path of our redemption and this the scale of our ascent. So much as we know of Hierotheos gives the pageant and not the doctrine; Dionysius furnishes the doctrine, not the pageant. Over the process itself both pass lightly;

contemplation is the keynote of the one, purification of the other, and there are words which stand doubtless for years of preparatory toil. As by the doctrine we are reminded continually of what I have called the universal teaching of mysticism so by the pictorial scheme of the *Book of the Hidden Mysteries* we are reminded more of the sequence of Grades in our Order, especially at the heights thereof and again of another scheme which connects with the name of Saint-Martin, whose New Man offers, amidst great differences, recurring analogies with Hierotheos.

I think therefore that they have a message for us, Fratres et Sorores, for the sense in which our own quest was pursued and described by our precursors cannot be less than important. Sometimes it may be vital.

PART II

FRATRES ET SORORES, I have spoken to you of Dionysius and Hierotheos from the standpoint of their message to us brethren of the Rosy Cross. It is now about 25 years since there was announced our English version of the *Book of the Hidden Mysteries* and I know not who can tell us whether he who promised the gift is still with us in the body. Now, outside the Syriac MS, the text of Hierotheos has no history and I do not think that its influence is traceable in later centuries except through Dionysius. Even this is under all reserves in respect of the unsettled question whether the extant document is to be regarded as the work of him who was precursor and master of him who was called or called himself the Areopagite. Anything therefore which may be deemed desirable in extension of our previous considerations must take shape in the following of Dionysius himself, for the influence is his influence. With the fact of it every one is acquainted, since there is no need to go further than our great counsel of caution, which is Vaughan's *Hours with the Mystics*. He says that the traces of the Aereopagite are found everywhere and that in the writings of the medieval mystics his authority is cited, his words are employed and 'his opinions more or less fully transmitted.' I do not think that it is needful for a purpose so simple as the present one to make any prolonged study of paraphrasts and commentators whose volume is considerable. The Greek paraphrase of Georgius Pachymeres was dedicated to Cyrus Athanasius, Patriarch of Constantinople, and the small tract of Dionysius on mystical theology becomes in his process of expansion, a work of considerable dimensions. He says that the light of this theology is received in the absolute stillness of mind and is unattainable by the mental processes. St Dionysius himself had said that it exceeds all demonstration and surpasses all light, the reason being that mystical theology, as it was understood by him, was not so much a discourse on doctrine as the result of an experiment in realisation of union with Him who is exalted beyond all essence and all notion. In virtue of this hypothesis, it follows that the host itself is a formulated recollection of that which was attained or intimated in the deep interior state. Perhaps, if he had been questioned, he would have said that the written word was a shadowy reflection at best of that which was revealed in the experience. The paraphrast is naturally later than any date to which we may refer his original, but he preceded St Maximus, who belonged to the seventh century. The canon of the New Testament was therefore in front of him and when he read in Dionysius that God was not power, not truth, not wisdom, he remembered that the incarnate Godhood said: I am the truth, and that the author of the Epistle to the Hebrews had defined Christ as the power and wisdom of God, he was thus in a difficulty on the question of texts and he issued thence, by the help of refinements, with the skill of the later schoolmen. God in this view is not truth or wisdom in respect of our measures of these qualities, yet is He truth and wisdom itself in the absolute sense which transcends such measures utterly. So also as his authority denied that God was goodness or divinity, Georgius Pachymeres explained that these other qualities were not of the substance of God but of the glory which encompassed Him. This is excellent as a *tour de force*, which is to say that it is scarcely convincing; and St Dionysius himself in his second letter to Gaius has dealt with the difficulty after another manner—not too convincing either. He says that if by divinity and goodness are to be understood those gifts of grace by which we are ourselves made good and are made divine ourselves, then the source of these must transcend them—*tanquam principium divinitatis et principium bonitatis superior exsistit*. I venture to think that in this instance the author of *Mystical Theology* had written more deeply than he of the epistle to Gaius had a mind to discern at the moment.

If we turn to the Jesuit Corderius, remembering that he is of the sixteenth century, we may look for great adventures. When Dionysius lays down that God is neither soul nor mind, the annotator explains that the term soul describes humanity by the principal part of man, but mind is angelical nature. So also God is not number because He is Himself unity and the sole true unity, from Whom is every number, though essentially He is above all number. Now, Dionysius in the same chapter has categorically distinguished God not only from number but from unity, but from the dilemma Corderius escapes by referring to the treatise concerning Divine Names (c.13), where it is said that the Divine Unity is not part of a whole but the antecedent determinator of all multitude and universality.

We do not get nearer to the real sense of things by researches of this order, and I confess on my own part, that I have dipped very lightly into the memorials of commentary and annotation by which the works of Dionysius are extended to make great proportions. What they bring home to myself is that which I know too well already by the experience of my later years and that is the vanity of the path of research as a means to the extension and much less the illumination of consciousness. It is of all things needful over matters of the historical order and it is the first and one indispensable warrant for those who would speak with authority on the witness of precursors in philosophy. But for our own purpose we need the witness of experience and nothing short of this as our guides on the path and to the term. A study at full length of the Jesuit Corderius may fill us with admiration for the careful subtlety which has brought Dionysius into a perfect right line with later accredited theology, so that he seems almost as if he had entered the life of Christian literature to smooth the way for St Thomas, the Angel of the schools; but it is only within moderate limits that this is a part of our concern. Johannes Scotus, the first who translated Dionysius into the scholastic tongue, found great things in Maximus and is said to have taken him into his very heart. Perhaps and indeed I know that, in the words of Mrs Browning, I have 'brushed with extreme flounce', the circle of the commentary; but I have not found it enlightening to any very high degree and as regards the maker of the Greek paraphrasis, I do not know what were his titles to write out at length that which Dionysius expounds in brevity only.

It is well for those who have time to follow these issues of the holy byways and if I were myself writing a commentary, translating or editing the text, my precursors in the distant centuries would lend me their aid, whatever their measures of light, for the points of erudition would be involved. It so happens, however, that several witnesses of experiences either drew after their own manner from Dionysian theology or followed a similar method in the quest of Divine union and in the formulation of its doctrine. They are those who went before us on the path which we seek to travel and their testimonies concern us in a peculiar manner. Meister Eckart, whom it is usual to rank among mystics of questionable orthodoxy, though the ground is not substantial, mentions Dionysius in one place as his authority for a simple doctrine concerning the Blessed Vision: 'To be separated from God is hell, and the sight of God's countenance is heaven.' But he drew more deeply when he did not quote so openly and a memorable instance is found in his sermon on the self communication of God. Then he speaks of the Godhead, as it were, behind the Trinity, flowing from the eternal height or depth, filling the Father with joy and the Son with wisdom, the Father and the Son flowing into the Holy Spirit and filling Him with goodwill. Hereof is the unknown Deity and of the abysmal Godhead the Father is defined as a revelation—that is to say, to our own human or other created consciousness, while the Son is the Father's image or countenance and the Eternal Spirit is the love which subsists between them. It follows that the Divine Trinity is the mode in which God has communicated to man the knowledge of Itself, but behind this self-expression there is the essential and infinite nature which is outside all communication, in the great darkness and for ever behind the Veil.

Eckart's idea of the Union and the mode of its attainment recalls Dionysius but the sense that one who has attained some knowledge at first hand concerning the hidden mysteries may recall another who has searched the mysteries before him and with whose testimony he is acquainted. The likeness is with due regard to the independence and leaves untouched the individuality of the later mystic. In one state of the soul it enters into comprehension of the Holy Trinity by its capacity of intelligence and with one which it has thus comprehended it becomes one by grace. By the capacity of the will, but this is in another state, it plunges into the Unknown which is God. 'It may arrive at such an intimate union that God at last draws it to Himself altogether, so that there is no distinction left, in the soul's consciousness between itself and God, though God still regards it as a creature.' The path is that of sanctification, which is placed by Eckart even higher than love, but this is a confusion of terms, as it is certain that sanctification is love in its activity approaching God in the way that we can alone approach Him. Sanctification itself he describes in the terms of Dionysius as that race or running which is 'nothing else than a turning away from all creatures and being united to the Creator.' Eckart, adds that when this state is attained by the soul 'it loses its own distinctiveness, and vanishes in God as the crimson of sunrise disappears in the sun.'

According to Ruysbroeck, 'God created man that He might confer beatitude upon him; He created that He might have love distinct from His eternal self; that He might love Himself in us; that we might find ourselves in Him, having first lost ourselves in order to find Him, in Whom is all. After the corrupt nature has been trodden under foot, the path is that of contemplation in perseverance and unity of spirit, or the understanding that the holiest is he who loses the most. When the spirit is transformed in love, it enters into the possession of itself or the sanctuary of its created being. The eternal sun rises therein; beyond reason and beyond even love itself the man is rapt at length into the naked vision and reaches the mystery of unity as it is accomplished in the spirit. The spirit is united by a triple tie to its eternal life, the principle and source of life. We are the beatitude in His Divine Essence.' This is the attainment of the Kingdom of those who love God—*Regnum Deum Amantium;* the fruition therein is likened in Dionysian terminology to a certain perpetual nascience. And this, says the *Book of the Adornment*, is that dark silence wherein all loving spirits do lose themselves after a certain manner.

With the author of *The Divine Cloud*, the great work of making and attaining God is a work of Divine Love for God's own sake and of man for the sake of God. It is a long following of the course of common grace in a cleansed and purified conscience. It is a work also of prayer, which differs however, both in kinds and degree. It is a casting out of knowledge, even as of sensible passion, and a service both of body and soul, in the subjection of things earthly to things ghostly, that the bodily personality may be as if nowhere, while the spirit is in all and everywhere. To this end, however, there is more than one class of hindrance which must be overcome, for the operation of the natural understanding does not lead to God's Knowledge, and here the author of the *Cloud*, quoting Dionysius testifies that 'the goodliest manner of knowing God is to know Him by unknowing'. This is the kind of life and the practice is a passive contemplation, an abstraction of spirit, in which says the Ven. Augustine Baker, a man 'loves the feeling of his own being' and has 'being and living in God'. It is the state of perfect union, removed from soul itself, as well as body, and dwelling on the height by spirit.

Now in fine, *Fratres et Sorores*, as I must make an end of these commentaries, there is the excellent Tauler and there are his *Institutions*, very noble in conception and yet, like the rest of his work, rather a practical guide to men in the way of the world who would keep God in their hearts and live in the law of religion, contented if they can walk in the narrow path but feeling that the great heights are beyond them. Whether he knew Dionysius I cannot say: there is nothing to suggest it in those of his writings which I have met, but he could not discourse of the great things without reflecting him, unawares or otherwise. In the 35th chapter of the work mentioned I find some prudent counsels on the banishment of all mental images and on cleaving to God by an inward act which is apart from the forms of thought. He recommends very naturally that such a course should have been preceded by long contemplation on the purest and most sublime images of Divine things. Yet these are ways only by which we may be led to the simple and naked truth. This is to be attained only in disengagement from everything, by veiling the eyes of the spirit and proceeding by the way of love, holy desire and pure, Divine intention. This is a path of crucifixion in the uttermost sense, for the price of essential truth on its perfect attainment is such an emptying of self on the altar of love that the seeker is deprived even of that which he would attain, being the inward consciousness of God. It is this dark void which God at length fills in the state of ineffable and inseparable union.

I should have spoken at an earlier step of Johannes Scotus, but this is not a chronological discourse and if I mention him now at the close it is because he is now exactly of our subject, his intellectual greatness notwithstanding also the fact that he simulated Dionysius. It seems to me that he was theologian rather than mystic, glorious in the life of debate rather than in annals of attainment. In his work on the Eucharist he identified true religion with philosophy and he was not therefore regarding the former as a way of life and a practice for the attainment of life. His five books on Nature are a monument for their period, but I know scarcely where some of the speculations might have landed unwary minds. As regards the return of man's spirit to God he distinguished seven stages of progression, of which the last was the absorption of all in Deity, and hence, I suppose the charge of pantheism once made against him, though another construction seems possible.

Such, *Fratres et Sorores*, are the testimonies of the Christian centuries on the dark night of Dionysius, the Divine Darkness and the part of man's spirit therein. I have tried in a few words to shew, firstly, the state in its attainment and, secondly, the mode of life by which it was entered. One lesson which is conveyed, I think, to us must be that there are no short cuts, that those who would reach the goal must head the one way and pass through the one gate. It is not that he who enters the sheepfold otherwise is a thief and a robber, for he will not find an entrance nor will he get within sight of the fold. Many pretended paths are offered us at this day, and their temptation is sometimes the greater because they are offered in sincerity by persons who are not intending to substitite consciously an easier way of advancement than that of the purified life and the life of the cross in Tiphereth. I do not propose to particularise on the present occasion: I would say to you only: Remember the last things and the life of all our precursors—the saints and the adepts of old.

For the rest of us, as regards Dionysius, we may approximate to the realisation of its final mystical date by such expressions as the union of nothing with nothing, but this approximation is in virtue of an intellectual excursion, and there is no reason why one side of the pair of opposites should be more efficacious than the other. We should be able to approximate as effectively by seeking to realise that it is the union of all with all. The old ascetic basis is broken up in either case, for its conventional terms are equivalent to a contract instituted between nothing and all. If we are nothing, we have no part in God, supposing that He is all. Conversely, if we are all and He is nothing in the Dionysian sense, in Him we have still no part. These are intellectual distinctions, but if they help to clear the issues, they are at least on the Divine side.

14
ON CEREMONIAL UNION

FROM considerations of the mystic life, or that which is called the Path; from the attempts to express in a language, which shall be common to us all, our understanding of the term of our research and whatsoever is involved therein; it is desirable on certain occasions; and I have chosen this as one—to look at a diverse aspect of things within the Order, and to dwell upon other kinds of duty which belong in a particular manner to the life of Tiphereth. When I speak of other kinds of duty, you must know that I am postulating some duty in chief which is imposed above all and before all by the Grade of Adeptus Minor. Some of us have passed that Grade in the official sense, and in symbolism are no longer on the cross of Tiphereth, but in one of the deeper and further states. They know what those behind them can be told only—that in this life we never leave Tiphereth, but continue to explore it further. The truth of this is implied in the Ritual and procedure of the 5=6 Ceremony, which is a summary of the whole Second Order exhibited in Tiphereth. The Candidate is taken down from the Cross in the First Point of the Ritual only from the necessity of procedure; in the symbolism he is still upon the Cross during the Second and Third Points, and thus he remains, as you have heard so often, during the six years of his life as an Adeptus Minor. These years are the theosophic addition of the 33 years of the Christ of Palestine. You have been told already that this life was a crucifixion from the birth at Bethlehem to the consummation on Calvary. We also, who remain in Tiphereth as I have said, are still upon the Cross of Sacrifice, though in symbolism we may have risen with Christ, and in the Grade of Adeptus Exemptus, some of you may come to know that there are greater crucifixions than those of Calvary, because there is the Cross of Glory, and because the Lamb is slain from the foundation of the world.

Well, Fratres et Sorores, the first and highest duty of the Adeptus Minor is that implied by his Obligation; the offering up of his life in sacrifice 'on the mystical Cross of the Adepts for the divine and declared in the heart and the soul'; the leading of the purified life of Tiphereth; the aspiration after consciousness in the spirit; the following of the rule of Tiphereth, which is that of 'crucifixion in Christ'; and finally that 'neither death nor life' shall separate any of us henceforth from 'the love and the service of God'.

Now the lesser duties about which I am called to speak are only the descent of our general undertaking from universals to particulars, and they arise out of the fact that our bond is a bond in common because we do not stand alone, but are integrated in a living organism; I am not now referring to questions of good fellowship and fraternal feeling. It has always seemed to me that in this respect we are as nearly like a house in union as it is possible to expect in the prevailing nature of things. But there is another aspect of unity which is not less important to the health and welfare of our Order life as a whole, and it may be summarised to begin with as a realisation that the sodality of the Rosy Cross is in each one of us, even as we are all in the Order. There are certain occasions when, more than at other times, it is not only desirable to remember this, and act as those who remember, but when the effect of negligence and forgetfulness becomes manifest immediately, creating a partial suspension in the psychological vitality and activity of the whole.

A notable instance is ready to our hand without seeking. Do you understand, Fratres et Sorores, the bond of sympathy which is so precious between a speaker and his audience at any public meeting? There are occasions when its absence is almost a paralysis to the former and this is felt so intuitively by the common run of spectators that, in the absence of controversial subjects, they are nearly always ready beforehand to give him a fair chance and even a little favour in the field, so that he may make a good beginning. Yet they have no special duty respecting him, except in the sense of humanity. If this is the case with an audience under circumstances of such a general kind, you will recognise, I am sure, that there are other circumstances under which something that is dictated by natural good feeling, as in the example specified, may become a sacred duty. You will recognise further that in the Ceremonies of our Order, and in particular that of the 5=6 Grade, sympathy with the work of the Celebrants is more than a work of kindness; it is something that you owe to the Order as represented in their persons and in the sense that those persons are consecrated by the sacred task which they have undertaken. As you depend on them that it shall be done not only with decency but in an efficient manner, not only efficiently but with reverence, and not only reverently but with a living realisation that they are priests of the Most High God, so they depend on you that your part in the great and most holy pageant shall not be wanting. But what is this part, my brethren? Let us recur for a moment to our position as Adepti Minores on the Cross of Tiphereth. I have said that we remain on that Cross in the symbolism through the whole experience of the Grade and indeed the great and sacred testimony contained in the Second and Third Orders is in reality communicated to us because we are exalted on the Cross. Now, this being the case, I want to bring home to you, in the uttermost simplicity, the question as to what should be your feelings in respect of any other Postulant for exaltation in this initial Grade of the Second Order. He is about to be fastened to that Cross on which you still abide; he is about to make the oblations, to assume the dedications and responsibilities which you have taken into your own hearts. I say unto you, Fratres et Sorores, that such an one is and should be accepted by you as more than a brother. Within the symbolism of the Grade itself he is a sacrifice in common with you which is about to be offered on the Altar which is above the Pastos. In another form of symbolism he is a fellow-pilgrim on the path of the Spirit—one who is taking the great homeward journey so that the story of his manifest life may like yours, be one of redemption. It is not enough therefore that you should concur by the fact of your sympathy in the priestly work of the Celebrants, or that you should be present as simple spectators. If I may put it so clearly, this is of the character of formal and artificial membership and does not signify that which it should mean above all, namely, your integration in a living mystic organism as an essential part of an elect company, or of those who confess by dedication and experience that they are drawn to the eternal centre.

Now there may be a few of us perhaps, who will admit that this fraternal and loving suggestion does awaken something in them to which they would respond by the way of conscious and willing intention but that it does not convey the mode. It is to these more especially that I would suggest the counsel that follows, and I can assure them beforehand that it comes from a heart of sincerity and is a fruit of experience at first hand. The counsel is this simply—that those who are audience as distinguished from those who are Celebrants should regard the ceremonial of the 5=6 Grade as a renewal of that memorable experience when they were themselves brought therein. I can assure them that there is a plenary realisation along this line by those who are acting Officers, and that if experience of my own can be taken as a criterion of that which occurs with others, there should never be an occasion to suggest that the least of the Officers is not doing his or her part. Whether in the Celebrants or in the audience, and in these as much as in those, where the realisation which I have mentioned is not present to the mind, the ceremonies are mechanical, so far as the personalities in question are themselves concerned. As to this there are two points, (1) that it is bad for them, and (2) that it reacts on the Ritual procedure as a whole. It is felt first of all by the Celebrants; it would be difficult for me to convey to you the extent to which it may be realised by them; and next—by a reduction of the grace and efficiency of the sacrament—it reacts on the Candidate. You should understand that he receives only that which we can convey and if we should communicate only the symbol apart from its life, then that which he receives is dead, instead of—as it should be—vital. The ceremonies which are enacted externally within the consecrated walls of this Temple should be also fulfilled within the person of each member—the desirable atmosphere and environment are then created and maintained. It is in this manner, and so only, that you can concur properly and fully in the work of the Celebrants, that what has been made perfect without in the best capacity of the Order, as communicating the instituted mysteries, may be perfect also within by virtue of your living activity.

This is part of the watching with Christ which belongs in a

particular manner to the Grade of Tiphereth. I have intimated that on the Cross of Obligation not one of us is fastened alone. We are there in a common act of sacrifice with all our Brethren; but there is one more than this, and that which remains over is the essential consideration of all. For the Christ also is with us. Shall we not therefore, my Brethren, watch for one hour with Him? But it is a watch of six years, corresponding, as I have said, to the period of the Christ-life in Nazareth. One of our Second Order members who is bringing an unusual gift of discernment to the study of the Tiphereth symbolism, has likened the period of the Grade to the vigil in Gethsemane, referring to the temptations which beset it. The counsel is one of watching and because—on the side of ritual—the Adeptus Minor has attained a point therein beyond which formal progression is denied him for a stated period, so that he is in certain respects thrown back on his inward resources, he is liable to feel that the work of the Order is suspended so far as he is concerned. The truth is the very opposite of this, but the work—by the nature of things—is now on his own part. The great types and symbols have been put into his hands—the preparations have been made for his assistance in a long sequence of Grades; and he has been told in the Portal of the Rosy Cross that the intimations of spiritual consciousness should begin to manifest within him. That is a state which no man—whether Hierophant in the G.D. or Chief Adept in a Temple of the Second Order—can communicate to recipients. The most that can be done is to awaken that which is sleeping, and for this work the concurrence of the Postulant is essential. It is for him so to order the life which he leads in Tiphereth that it shall be in real analogy with that other and Divine life which was begun in Bethlehem and closed for a space of three symbolic days on Calvary. The counsel therefore is—watch; but the counsel is, pray also, lest we enter under that law of temptation which shall make void in our own case the whole spiritual value of the crucified life.

But some of the disciples fled and some of them fell asleep and one of them denied his Master. Hereof are the qualities of our temptation and hereof also is the counsel which I am called to give you. The Spirit bloweth where it listeth, but it rests with those to whom it comes, over whom it moves, to open the doors of the heart; be sure that they receive it inwardly, as the Guest for whom they have waited, that it shall truly have part in them and that they shall abide in it.

It is thus and thus only that the stones which we have prepared for the building in the shaping processes of the Grades of the G.D. can become part of our living Temple. The dead matter of nominal and official membership is of no service to them and of no account to us. The counsel in this form of symbolism is therefore the old Rosicrucian maxim, *Transmutemini, transmutemini, de lapidibus mortuis, in lapides vivos philosophicos*; and the point is Fratres et Sorores, that those stones must transmute themselves. This is the philosophical work, this is the work of our redemption; it is the business to which we are called in our advancement to the Grade of Tiphereth; it is that which we have undertaken to accomplish with our own hands; but they are hands of zeal and desire, of intuition carried out in action and of holy will.

Thereby and therein shall we make that condign preparation by which we shall be qualified ultimately to pass not only in the official and ceremonial sense from Tiphereth to Geburah, but shall proceed by inward realisation to that deeper state which is the mystic death, and shall enter it with a firm hope that thereafter is the glorious resurrection of the Adept.

15
THE INTERIOR LIFE FROM THE STANDPOINT OF THE MYSTICS

[First printed in *Light*, the organ of the London Spiritualist Alliance, Vol. 10, No. 521, 27 December 1890. Reprinted as a pamphlet by the Office of *Light* early in 1891.]

This address was given to the London Spiritualist Alliance on 16 December 1890, Waite having been invited to speak by the Revd W. Stainton Moses. Although Waite looked upon this paper as 'of little or no consequence' (*Shadows of Life and Thought*, p. 127) it is significant in illustrating his thought at that time—consciously rejecting both psychism and occultism and turning decisively to mysticism. Despite a growing scepticism about the phenomena of spiritualism, Waite remained on friendly terms with the Alliance and delivered occasional lectures for a further forty years. He also contributed regularly—usually anonymously—to the columns of *Light* under the successive editorships of Stainton Moses, E. Dawson Rogers, and his close personal friend, David Gow.

IF IT were necessary to divide the science which is called mystical into two chief branches, we might speak of them as phenomenal and transcendental. It is not actually an accurate division, but it will serve a practical purpose by indicating a definite line of demarcation in a dual process. There is that which, under the term 'Magic', comprises most branches of the occult or secret sciences, including the doctrines concerning the nature and power of angels, ghosts, and spirits; the methods of evoking and controlling the shades of the dead, elementary spirits, and demons; the composition of talismans; all forms of divination, including clairvoyance in the crystal; and all the mysterious calculations which made up Kabalistic science. Between the spiritual and psychological phenomena of our present epoch and these experiments of the past there is a strong basis of similarity; they are of the same value, and serve a similar purpose. To those who are in search of a 'sign' they may be evidence of worlds transcending our normal senses, and they are valuable to that extent. But they are not true Mysticism, and those who pursue them are not real Mystics. With the entire world of phenomena, normal or abnormal Mysticism has solely an incidental connection. The object of transcendental science is to get beyond the phenomenal world, to penetrate the veil of appearances, and, outside the spheres of illusion, to enter into the grand realities. It is to this second, more elevated, branch of what is so loosely termed transcendentalism that your attention is invited tonight. It must be admitted at the outset that it is not an easy subject, for it is concerned with the highest aspiration which it is possible for man to entertain, and the highest act which it is possible for man to achieve.

All transcendental philosphy recognises and is based upon one great fact—that the true light is to be sought within, and that the avenues of interior contemplation—the withdrawn state—and the hidden life are not only the way to God, but that they are the way of the soul's peace. Now it has been truly affirmed, by the Quietists, that 'there is no real happiness save that which is the result of a peaceful heart'; so we see that the *summum bonum*, the supreme and permanent felicity, of all human existence is also to be sought within. Those who by the study of the soul have made themselves acquainted with the highest mysteries of being, and, in a certain sense, have spoken to us as from behind the veil, have denied truth and reality, as they have denied joy and contentment, to the merely outward life. On their authority, therefore, we must add to our previous affirmations that the true life, the life which is alone persistent amidst the everlasting flux of apparitions and evanishments, which is alone real amidst the multitude of the things which seem, is also to be found within. Men have sought it in the kingdoms of this world wherein God has not anything, and have failed miserably in the quest. They have sought it amid the splendours and beauties, the consolations and felicities, of exterior nature, but all her attractions and delights have been only the vesture and the threshold of the 'still rest and the unchanging simplicity, which are the conditions of the grand reality.

What is there which can be offered to the mind of man that shall be of higher value and of greater intellectual affluence than is offered us by the interior life when it promises God and truth, light and the undivided permanence and beatitude of real being? It will be said that such amenities are possible at most for only an infinitesimal proportion of our race, and in the existing conditions of our environment that is unfortunately true; but the value of the interior state is not to be estimated by the standard of social disabilities. A thing is not less good, rather is it the more desirable, because it is difficult of attainment, and can, therefore, be attained by few. Let the quest be attempted by those whose surroundings make it possible, and we may profit in a measure by their achievement if we cannot achieve ourselves.

The conditions of the life of contemplation are to be found in the word 'detachment'. The Quietists speak of 'detachment from the things of earth, contempt of riches, and love of God', and these terms of ascetic theology in the West admit of being converted into the language of modern science, into the terminology of that natural law which it has been attempted to follow through a few of its ramifications in the spiritual world. The detachment in question consists in cutting off correspondence with inferior things. The isolation which follows is not to be confounded with that of the cynical philospher who withdraws himself in disgust from a world whose beauty he is unable to discern, and with whose goodness he has ceased to be in affinity. The isolation of the interior life is devoid of pride and jealousy; it abstracts from the humanity around us and nothing which can be given to humanity, and, like the lone inspiration of the Scald, its result in the ultimate to the world may prove better than a long cycle of familiar companionship in our ordinary daily life. The suspension of correspondence with things exterior and phenomenal is the means to a higher operation, and that is the creation of correspondence with the absolute realities which transcend them.

According to Cornelius Agrippa, we must learn how to leave the 'intellectual multitude' if we would come to the 'superintellectual and essential unity,' for that is 'absolute from all multitude, and the very fountain of good and truth'. 'We must ascend,' he assures us, 'to sciences, in which although there be a various multitude, yet there is no contrariety, until at length, we reach to that one inclusive science which supposes all below it, while there is nothing that can be supposed beyond it.' And above even this apex of attainment, and there only, he tells us, is the positive knowledge of a pure intellect. Therefore—it is thus he ends—'let us attain to the first unity from whom there is a union in all things, through that one which is as the flower of our essence; which then at length we attain to, when, avoiding all multitude, we do rise into our very unity, are made one and act uniformly.'

Solitude is essential to such a work, and the education of the superior conditions is best accomplished among the primeval sublimities of Nature, in mountain fastnesses, in the Divine desolation of the wilderness, or, as the Mystics themselves tell us, in the middle of the open sea. For the majesties and splendours of the outside world are the threshold of the unknown grandeurs. The gorgeous incandescence of the sunset is eloquent in Pentecostal tongues of revelation, but not to the exclusion of the all-permeating ministry of Night, which utters a *fiat Lux* to the strong in soul. *Dies diei eructat verbum, et nox nocti indicat scientiam.* 'Day unto day uttereth speech and night unto night showeth knowledge.' It is thus that we are advised by the voice of one of our illuminators, Thomas Vaughan—he that was the most translucid of all the English Mystics, he that was the brother of the Silurist, sweetest and most silver-tongued of all our devotional singers: 'Translate thyself to the fields, where all things are green with the breath of God and fresh with the powers of Heaven . . . Sometimes thou mayst walk in groves, which, being full of majesty, will much advance the soul; and sometimes by clear, active rivers, for by such (say the mystic poets) did Apollo contemplate:

> All things by Phoebus in his musing spake
> The bless'd Eurotas heard.'

So also the most advanced inspirational poet of our own spiritual era, Thomas Lake Harris, has revealed to us the spiritual ministry of night, when thoughts more subtle touch

> The inner mind,
> And all the fettered inner wings unbind.
> When an infinite sight in the spirit is born;
> When we see, as the sun sees, creation below;

The Interior Life

And we thrill, as the earth thrills, with Heaven's warm glow;
And we move, as the light moves, from world unto world;
And we change, as the skies change, when morn is unfurled;
And we breathe the sweet breath of the angel's delight,
Till our thoughts ope, like roses, in fragrance and light;
Till within us, as round us, the Heavens are spread,
And our thoughts to our loves, like twin angels, are wed.

It will be seen, therefore, that the first recompense of the interior life is the 'seeing sense' of the poet, the possession of that strange instrument of interior alchemy, which dissolves the natural world, to discover in it a new and higher order. A life led near to the heart of Nature can be sanctified by such a possession. There can be no doubt of the amenities of such an existence, for then the individual is in harmony with his surroundings, and this initial attainment will be possible to many who may be barred from the higher achievements. On the other hand, the most perfect environment which can be offered by Nature to man is devoid of the softening, sublimating, and glorifying influences ascribed to it when the heart and intelligence of the individual are without any instrument of correspondence with that environment. No one was more intimately and passionately aware of the truth of this principle than Coleridge, and, indeed he has enunciated it in one of the most profound passages of spiritual insight which can be met with in the whole range of English poetry. From Nature, he tells us, we can receive only that which we give:

'And in our life alone does Nature live.'

Unless there be resident within us those undefinable qualities of appreciation, perception, and discernment, which constitute the poetic temperament, there is no utterance from the heart of the external world to the heart of man, there is none of that electric and magnetic contact between the centre without and the centre within, and the local proximity is worthless. The life of contemplation merely in the natural order brings, therefore, its own reward.

In the supernatural order, as it is understood by the orthodox religions, there is an immense literature concerned with the cultivation of the interior condition and with the spiritual pleasures which may be reaped from it. In the supernatural order, as we have seen, the end is God; that, at least, is the supreme, ultimate, and perfect end, and with the Quietists the life of contemplation consists wholly in the soul's surrender without reserve to God, that it may be filled with His own peace. We are told that this state stills all passions, restrains the imagination, steadies the mind, and controls all wavering; it endures alike in the 'time of tribulation and the time of wealth'; in temptation and trial, as when the world shines brightly on us. Martyrs, confessors, and saints have tasted this rest, and 'counted themselves happy in that they endured'. A countless host of God's faithful servants have drunk deeply of it amid the daily burden of a weary life—dull, commonplace, painful, or desolate; and to each one of their disciples the Quietists promise that all which God has been to the most exalted in the hierarchy of the saints He is ready to be to them, if only they will seek no other rest save in Him. But the hidden life of Christian theology is only the threshold of the true interior existence which is the subject of Mysticism. The devotional literature to which we have hitherto referred can at most promise to man that joy and peace in well-being which is the consequence of harmonious correspondence with a certain supernatural standard, which is called the will of God. It is to the Mystics that we must look for more. They are in possession of a science which claims to grasp the Divine essence or ultimate reality of all things, and to enjoy while in this life, and in this body, the blessedness of an immediate communion with the Highest—'free perspicuity of thought in universal consciousness'—an ecstatic immersion of the spiritual substance in man with the pure substance of Deity—all peace, all truth, all light, being seen and known, and enjoyed to an infinite degree by virtue of a community of sensations with an infinite form of subsistence.

The secret processes which constitute the science of the Mystics accomplish the development of the interior life through a series of successive stages, from the New Birth, or Regeneration to the manifestation of the Divine Virgin, Psyche, the vision of Diana Unveiled, the manifestation of what is called the dual flower, being the interblossoming of Pneuma and Psyche, the interior translation, which is the soul's flight towards God, and, lastly, the transcendental union which is known as the Mystic Marriage. Concerning this ecstatic state of nuptial being, which

The Interior Life

is the crown of the process, I will lay before you a short account, translated from an arcane source. The union of God with the soul is the principle of all mystic life. But this union, the fulness and final consummation of which cannot be absolutely experienced till the ordeal of physical death has been withstood, and till eternity has been achieved, can be accomplished even upon earth in a more or less perfect manner, and the literature of entire transcendentalism has no other end than to unveil to us, by a full and profound analysis of the different stages of evolution in the spirit of man, the diverse successive degrees of this Divine union. Seven distinct stages of the soul's ascent towards God have been recognised by Mystics, and they constitute what has been emblematically called the Castle of the Interior Man. They represent the seven positive processes of psychic transfiguration. The first link in this arcane sequence is called the state of Aspiration, which, from the pneumatic standpoint, is the concentration of the intellectual energies upon God as the object of thought; this state is commonly assisted by the ceremonial appeal made by religion to the senses. It has, however, a higher aspect, comprised in the second evolutionary process, which is called the condition of Mental Aspiration. Here the illusory phenomena of the visible world are regarded as informed with an inner pneumatic significance, to divine which is an important end of Mysticism. In order to make progress therein, and so attain the third stage, it is necessary that the aspirant, shaping all practical life in conformity with this theory, should perform no outward act except with a view to its inward meaning, all things which are of time and earth and man being simply figures and symbols of earth and Heaven and God. The postulant, as he advances, will perceive that the inmost thoughts of his own conscious being are only a limited and individual speculation of the speech or Word of God, concealed even in its apparent revelation, itself a veil of the Divine truth, and something which must be removed, or effaced, for the contemplation of the truth absolute which is behind it. When he has reached this point the Mystic will have entered on the third stage of his illumination. This is the most difficult of all. It is termed by the Mystics the Obscure Night, and here it is necessary that the aspirant should become stripped in the interior man, should empty himself completely, should defraud himself of all his normal faculties, renouncing his own predilections, his own thoughts, his own will—in a word, his whole self must be made void. Aridity, weariness, temptation, desolation and darkness are characteristic of this epoch, and they have been experienced by all who have ever made any progress in the mysteries of mystical lore. The fourth condition is denominated the Absorption of Quietism. Complete immolation of self and unreserved surrender into the hands of God have repose as their first result. Such Quietism, however, is not to be confounded with insensibility, for it leads to the sole real activity, to that which has God for its impulse. The fifth degree in the successive spiritualisation of the soul is called the state of Union, in which the will of man and the will of God become substantially identified, and the individual, as a consequence, is energised by the first influx of the Divine intelligence which elaborates the eternal purpose. This is the mystical irrigation which fertilises the garden of the soul. During this portion of his development, the now regenerated being, imbued with a sovereign disdain for all things visible, as well as for himself, accomplishes in peace, serenity, and joy of spirit the will of God, as it is made known to him by the Word of God supernaturally speaking within him. On the extreme further limit of this condition, the Mystic enters the sixth state, which is that of Ecstatic Absorption, or the soul's transport above and outside itself. It constitutes a more perfect union with Divinity by the instrument of positive love. It is a state of sanctification, beatitude, and ineffable torrents of delight flowing over the whole being. It is beyond description, it transcends illustration, and its felicity is not to be conceived. Love, which is a potency of the soul or of that *anima* which vivifies our bodies, has passed into the spirit of the soul, into its superior, divine and universal form, and this process completed comprises the seventh and final stage of pneumatic development, which is that of Ravishment. Renouncing all that is corporeal about it, the soul becomes a pure spirit, capable of being united, in a wholly celestial manner, to the Uncreated Spirit, whom it beholds, loves, serves, and adores above and beyond all created forms. And this is the Mystic Marriage, the perfect union, the entrance of God and Heaven into the interior man.

There is evidence to show that this process has been

The Interior Life

accomplished in all ages and among all nations. With it the Egyptian hierophants would seem to have been acquainted in that 'early dawn and dusk of time' which preceded the first dawn of the Mosaic dispensation. This also was the end of the Mysteries in their primeval and undefiled condition. And when, scaling the 'mountains of our ignorance', we look forth upon the immeasurable antiquity of far Oriental countries, upon India, China, and Japan, there also was the positive philosophy pursued with the same objects and by rigorously parallel processes. In the beginning of Christianity it was known to the Gnostic ascetics and to that wonderful circle of withdrawn *illuminati* and supreme masters in transcendentalism, who comprised the theurgic school of Alexandria. The writings of Hermes Trismegistus are the disguised history of the evolution of the human soul, and the doctrine of reconstruction is developed in the Old and New Testaments. From adepts of Egyptian wisdom and from Jewish keepers of the secret keys of knowledge, from Greek initiates, from Platonic successors, and from the first hierophants of esoteric Christianity, the absolute tradition with all its processes and all its mysteries passed on to the medieval alchemists, to those bizarre writers and profound thinkers who have succeeded in persuading centuries that they were in search of the transmutation of metals, when under the cover of physical experiments they wrote only of the soul's transmutation, and rectified the secret *Sol* and the true *Luna* with the energies of Deific elements.

It is unnecessary, however, to have recourse to the remote Oriental world for instruction upon the highest mysteries of arcane science. There is a fund of wisdom, a fund of light, and a great body of positive and practical doctrine in the Western Mystics, who devoted their retired lives to the attainment of Nirvana in Christ, and even in the order of phenomenal achievement they did not fall behind the East. The history of Christian spiritualism informs us that in the seven stages of transcendental absorption the body of the Mystic was seen to rise from the ground and to poise itself mysteriously in space. Ravished by interior visions, he became insensible to all that was passing around him, and, at the same time, his physical senses, which had suspended correspondence for the moment with normal exterior environment, were ministered to in a manner which we should term magical; he saw, heard, felt, tasted, but on another plane of being, and occasionally his indescribable ecstasy was manifested in the apparition of lights and halos about him, and in the diffusion of an unearthly fragrance.

The processes of Mysticism are, however, arcane processes; the science is a secret science. You have been put in possession of the exact nature of its most transcendental end; it has, however, many ends, many purposes, and many methods, but, indifferently, all of them are esoteric in their character, concealed in a literature which is difficult to understand, and is often purposely misleading. It is, therefore, with real satisfaction that I am permitted to state that there is a practial movement on foot among certain circles of mystic study for a systematic instruction of qualified persons, under due safeguards, and with all proper precautions, in the inner wisdom of the positive knowledge. I am now able at the moment to speak more plainly, and, perhaps, it is a little too early to speak at all, but I know that there is a quickening of mystic zeal in several quarters, and I know also that the zeal is taking shape.

16
A MESSAGE OF SAINT-MARTIN

[Printed in *The Seeker*, 'A Quarterly Magazine devoted to the Study of Christian Philosophy and the Writings of the best Christian Mystics', Vol. 5, No. 17, May 1909, pp. 43–58.]

The Seeker was founded and edited by the Revd G. W. Allen, a friend of Waite's who had contributed frequently to *The Unknown World*. Although an Anglican priest he held somewhat heterodox views and encouraged contributions to his journal on the more obscure mystics who were doctrinally difficult to place. Waite looked upon Saint-Martin—whose own progress from magic to mysticism paralleled that of Waite—as one of the most important of all Christian mystics and was himself recognized as an authority on Saint-Martin's philosophy. His study, *The Life of Louis Claude de Saint-Martin, the Unknown Philosopher* (1901), remains the only critical work in English. It earned for him the unsought distinction of 'Docteur en Hermetisme', awarded by Papus (Dr Gérard Encausse), the then head of the Martinist Order.

SEEING that they are still few, those who love and understand the Christian mystic Louis Claude de Saint-Martin are a little company apart, which might be compared to a secret church, or rather to a hermit's chapel, in a wild withdrawn even from those ways which are trodden in the study of Christian exotic literature. It is my proposal to consider very briefly whether he is fitted only to remain, as one may say, a local devotion, or whether, if better known, he would have a wider appeal—in other words, whether there is anything in his message which is sufficiently catholic to become the common concern of all those whose quest is the attainment of peace in light on earth and of God in the kingdom. When some plenary knowledge, declared and demonstrated among us, has 'made the pile complete' of mystic literature, I suppose that we shall be rich indeed if we find that ten per cent of the vision on the part of each individual seer proves vital in respect of the end; and I am assured in my heart that, as things now stand among us, the most precious gift which could be made, even by a writer with purely intellectual warrants, would be an entire restatement of the root-matter of everything from which quest and attainment depend. Saint-Martin might not suffer more than other sons of the doctrine from the consequences of an expert sifting, but he would share to the full therein; or if there are one or two who would issue with a smaller percentage of residual gold of wisdom, I have no intention to name them, because there are many listeners and the auditorium is sure to represent several keen interests, while—above all—it is no part of my concern. It is for this reason that, also like some others, under the rule even of a relaxed observance, Saint-Martin is almost indubitably better represented to the sympathy of an informed reader—so only that it is by a trusty hand—in the condensation of summary rather than by his collected works. The originals of these are very scarce, but some of them have been reprinted, and those therefore who choose can judge for themselves on the question. I have further done what a sympathetic and, I hope, understanding mystic could do to present his precursor's philosphical portrait, in part *fait par lui-même;* and I mention this because it is necessary to say that I have not entered into the life of letters for the purpose of reproducing in another form, by a shorter or longer recension, that which I have written already. There is something that remains over from my previous study, or this paper would not be passing into existence: what it is I have indicated already—it is a settlement of the question whether he has a message at this day for us and for our salvation, being so much more than arises, by necessity, from the presentation of his life and his doctrine in substance. I leave therefore his life, since it is known or can be known—save only that, for the benefit of those who are in the outer courts of the most noble and compelling of all literature, new or old, it may be desirable to mention that Saint-Martin was a Frenchman of his period, which was that of the Revolution; that he belonged to the noble class; that he worked from this point of vantage, preaching the knowledge of the inward life by word of mouth, by his presence, by personal contact, among his peers in society, but also—and for us above all—by his books, which are fairly numerous. He was devoted utterly to the cause at his heart, and if he was not the Galahad of Gallican mysticism, he was at least the Perceval, a man of blameless life and 'glorious, great intent'.

If I were in search of a key to his character and also to that of his personal influence, I should say that he was one to whom the atmosphere of sanctity was as air to the nostrils of man's body. He was not a saint in the sense of the palm or the aureole, nor perhaps in another sense, because the great heights are above high thinking and most of the high acting; but he was one who loved holiness for its own sake and who, after his proper manner, was an illuminated and Christian philosopher in the best sense of the term. He was also 'high-erected thought, seated in a heart of courtesy'; and when a disposition of this kind is turned towards God and the realism of things divine; when it can and does say that 'in the interior man we shall behold the all', it is about this time that the 'gay, licentious crowd' begins to remember Jerusalem and to look thereat—or almost.

Well—though I have exceeded my intention—here is the key of character, which, for those who choose to go further, opens a very wide door, even into a garden of exotics. Now, Saint-Martin's practical key is contained in that pregnant word—Purification. The knight Galahad was born with 'a fire in the heart and a fire in the brain' of God's love, and we can read in the great, chaotic romance called *Tristram of Lyonesse* how his touch itself purified. Saint-Martin, much as he had realised, could only teach us to search and to pray for purity of heart, addressing ourselves to Him *qui labia Isaiæ prophetæ calculo ignito mundarit*. Like Sir Bors, he had been in the spiritual city and had returned again to Logres; he carried this word in his mouth, and of his commentary thereon I will give, as a decorative specimen, one luminous dictum, which tells us how 'the universe is a great fire lighted from the beginning of things for the purification of all corrupted beings.'

It will be seen that Saint-Martin, within the limits of his literary understanding—all haste and negligence accepted—was an occasinal lover of the phrase, and he must sometimes have paused to take pains, or he could scarcely have produced his results. He is indeed the most literate and finished of the professed mystics—of those to whom, except in momentary flashes, the sense of form and expression never dictated anything, but the spirit and the matter everything. There is evidence that he loved his own books, which is to be counted to him for righteousness. He would have affirmed, I suppose, if questioned, that he came hither to write them, and write them he did, as one who was performing the will of God to the utmost extent of his power. He had indeed a great and holy reverence for all that he accomplished in connection with the business of his mission. We may note as an instance his proud renunciation regarding the necessity of books in the last resource. All his instruction made, and was intended to make, for that direct experience after the attainment of which our ships can be burnt and our ladders cast down, since the soul never goes back. But he knew—in his heart he knew—the remoteness of that millenium to which he deferred his dispensation concerning their necessity. When would mankind understand, for example, the key which he gave to his *L'Homme de Désir*—that key which could be wrought only by the desire of man? I hold, as one who has been called to a work which is not different in paths that are the same or parallel—I hold that of such love there come the sweetness and light which make the path even as the aisles of a church leading to a great chancel, and the way clear, even to a sanctuary within. It is of the accidents only, but I think also that an age which like ours has awakened so vividly to the sense of expression and form should, if other things are equal, be drawn with chains of roses by his *grande manière*, his occasional skill and his curious clouds of enchantment. So also, as they come to know him, they may conceive the kind of detached affection which he ought to inspire. Though he wrote as a man of desire, though that is the categorical description which he would have given at need of himself, I think that the quality of peace which had come into his heart was so utterly apart from all passion that it is a little difficult to regard him as the apostle of love and therefore the master of the last secrets. He is proportionately hard to know well, or, at least, it is hard to realise the fact, even if one is knowing him well. He says indeed that 'love is more than knowledge, which is only the lamp of love'; that it is 'the helm of our vessel'; that it is 'possible to dispense with science, but not with love'; that as love began, and as it now maintains, so it will fulfil all. And yet, as it seems to me, these are the words of one 'who hath watch'd, not shared, the strife'; and though there is evidence in his outward life that he had real, strong, lasting affection, I think that he spoke of love as one who had seen but not entered the Promised Land. Perhaps after all it was with his best friends even as it was with his books; they were part of the cause or the work—they in it and it in them. There is no affection so salutary as this can be, but it is not that for which we are all looking with our whole souls. Again, however, there is no testimony to compare with that of a man of insight concerning the insight which he has put into writing. And it is on the basis of his own appreciation of that which he placed on record that—if I did not know otherwise—I should say that his books were good—and so were his friendships. I think, in fine, that he treated his own personality with the respect which was due to his vocation, and the man who knows how to do this in the true manner has the seals of his own sanctity and moral goodness in his very hands.

These things, however, are titles to consideration, but not the warrants that we are seeking, and though they are part of our subject they are not its marrow and essence. Now, it is necessary to point out in the next place that the question whether Saint-Martin has a real and living appeal to us at this day does not depend upon the source of his message. I am not speaking of the commonplace things; I do not mean that if one should rise from the dead he is not going to convert us at this day—as I hope—to false doctrine. Such a resurrection would be only a question of fact, very interesting of course, as something displacing certain centres of accepted physics; but if the risen spirit testified concerning anything save the great things of which we know otherwise, we should not—as I think—be moved—by him or an angel either. We are on the side of the angels surely, but it is on the assumption that in their turn they are on God's side, like the mule of Perceval. I should demur very strongly regarding any premature first-fruits of resurrection which could not recite *Credo in unum Deum*, and I should reject with no second thought the testimony of one who had searched the universe and returned to advise us that there was no God. But further, the appeal does not depend on whether Saint-

Martin drew his doctrine, in so far as this has new aspects, out of a tradition perpetuated from the past or from his own excogitation. Yet it is more convenient to approach the question from this stand point, because a tradition from the past has been perpetuated through Christian times, which tradition is important, and because there are many who are looking at this day to see it decoded. Finally, Saint-Martin did enter one initiated circle; it is so, on the historical side, that he comes before us. It is certain, therefore, that he did not owe his first lights initiation in any especial sense to books, nor is it traceably from such source that his vocation arose. An old Lutheran tract on the pleasures and advantages of self-knowledge by a writer named Abadie who is practically unknown in England, is said to have influenced him at an early period; but it accounts for as much as nothing; although it may have helped him to think, it could scarcely have opened the path along which he travelled so far in later years of life. So also his familiarity with Jacob Böhme, though he confesses eloquently thereto, and it is as impossible to disregard as it would be unfair to reduce its influence, came much too late to do more than confirm him. He has told us that he would have written *Le Nouvel Homme* differently had he then known the Teutonic philosopher, but he refused either to revise the work or to indicate the modifications which he claimed to have in his mind, while we have fair warrants for deciding in other ways that it would have suffered no change in the root-matter. Böhme helped him to see that there were greater deeps and heights in *L'Homme de Désir* than he knew when he put it into writing, and *Le Ministère de l'Homme Esprit* contains nothing which would not have developed in the natural course out of his own implicits. Indeed his debt to books, since in obscure and secondary ways it is inevitable that he owed something, is comparable along certain lines to the debt which he owed to his initiation, but the latter is in better evidence, because it is much more direct.

The initiation which he received was of the occult order, but Saint-Martin drew nothing therefrom which the unversed mind is likely to connect therewith; he did not issue from its sanctuary as an adept of the secret sciences; he took therein, so far as we can tell, no predisposition towards these. It was a time when there was every variety of overt claim offering and producing all grades and stages of official and simulated adeptship. There were also some masters of the lesser kind in evidence. While Saint-Martin was certainly a Hermetic philosopher in the spiritual and mystical sense, while he used some of the Hermetic terminology, he denied the first principle of metallic alchemy and derided the end thereof. As to all its methods and concealments, his words are the words of scorn. Of astrology one would hardly suppose that he had heard, by which I mean that it had not entered seriously into his consciousness. The curative and psychic science of animal magnetism was at its zenith, under the auspices of that Anton Mesmer who invented or recovered its process. Saint-Martin served a period of apprenticeship therein, and he loathed it ever afterwards in all its ways. From Mesmer he shrank, and, as regards the conventional *illuminati* of his day, it is sufficient to say that he was not to be seen in the same street with the prodigious Count Cagliostro, his shadows or his alternatives.

The question therefore arises as to what he derived from initiation, and the answer is very nearly the whole of our concern regarding him. Again, I do not propose to offer particulars in outline which could not delineate properly, and for delineation there is no opportunity here. The Master of the Lesser Mysteries into which Saint-Martin was brought, when he had not so long passed his majority, was Martines de Pasqually, who, in accordance with the preoccupations of the time, had come forward with yet a new Rite of immemorial and esoteric Freemasonry, he claiming all powers, and carrying all warrants. Under this veil was practised a theurgic system which requires to be set apart from most things that have passed under this name, or are now understood thereby. It is true that the most ready comparison between the Rite of the Elect Cohens—for this, it must be confessed, was the name of the secret order—and any of the occult sciences is that of ceremonial magic, for it made use of processes and accessories which are analogous to the well-known devices of that art. But the Rite was saved by its intention, the term of its activity being communication with the personal Christ Himself, Who, in the belief of the initiates, not only responded to the invoking formulæ but appeared in the arch-natural body, and even gave written instructions. The history of the proceedings is obscure, and imputed extensions of our knowledge under the auspices of French occult interests at this day are not very far removed from the class of *choses suspectes*. I do not propose to recite them. There is every reason to accept the utter sincerity and devotion of all concerned in the order when we first hear concerning it, not excepting the supreme magus and founder of the Rite. But, in the midst of all the astral workings and the wonderful results supposed to be obtained, there comes the message to us and to our posterity in the ways of mystic life. Saint-Martin was in the midst of the prodigies, and the result of it all was that he issued therefrom, once and for ever renouncing the practical ways for the inward path of contemplation. Such was his decision upon Art Magic, the Higher Magic, and all that we should today include under the name of psychic science. This is one message of Saint-Martin, and such lesson, I affirm, is as necessary and eloquent at this day, which has so many points of comparison with the years more immediately preceding the French Revolution. We also are encompassed by all the quakings and upheavals of intellectual dissolution, while the astral workings are more prolific and more in evidence than they were in France of the eighteenth century. It is to be noted, however, and this makes the lesson more valuable, that Saint-Martin did not come out from the Rite of the Elect Cohens as one who denounced or denied. Never thereafter did he speak except with respect concerning the way of his initiation. He believed that Martines de Pasqually had exceptional powers, and when he made reference to these it was always as if there lay behind them the graces which can alone justify their possession. He himself had found a more excellent way, but, having profited by the instruction, he did all honour to its source. He recognised that his early teacher differed from most of the period in respect of the horizon entered by his practical art. He admitted his own debt to him in another sense, for he certainly drew from Pasqually a part of the theosophical instruction which appears in his first work, *Des Erreurs et de la Vérité*. From my point of view it was the least part of his system, which grew in light, grace and the sense of sanctity in so far as it receded from any phase of novelty or variation in doctrine, and treated only of the mysteries of the inward life regarded as the way of Christ in the soul, with all the worlds of thought arising therefrom. The soul in its phenomenal manifestation may sometimes arise in beauty; the soul may arise in power and confuse the doctors in the official temples of knowledge; and these things are well; but in its higher investigation the soul appears only as a world of grace unfolded in holiness, and for ever and ever it opens to be explored further in the light of the Divine Presence. For God is within, and so only we enter the way of reintegration, of union and beatific vision.

Hereof is the echoing counsel which we can bring away from the works of the French mystic, and it is on this ground that I regard him as having a distinct message for us at the present day. He did not have all lights, and some of his lights are clouded. His tacit acceptance of the French Revolution might tend to alienate some; his dubious and contradictory voice upon the mission and importance of the Church can please neither its friends nor enemies; but he was the first to expound in intelligible language of theosophy the whole scheme of Divine Revelation as the symbolic and mystical picture of the great drama which has to be enacted in the soul, and we have all since borrowed therefrom—sometimes without realising from whom we derive. Hereof are also his titles, but many others will be found in his books. Within these measures he has also his appeal. I do not think that he had all the secrets which are conveyed intellectually regarding the Divine Union. But he did dream, and he did in part know, that it is here and now. We can also see that from the beginning he was in search of God—as witnessed by the pregnant question which he addressed to his theurgic instructor: 'Master, can all these things be needed to find God?' With him also the desire of re-union was as much a memory of the past as a pregustation of the future. All honour to him in his aspirations as a man of desire, and with all the strength of our hearts let us hope that he attained his term.

There is one word to add by way of conclusion, lest some should think that there is little consolation in being dissuaded from the so-called practical paths, since these are idle, if there is now no direct teaching concerning the inward way except that which can be gathered by one's own toil from the holy men of old and the memorials which these have left. For the reassurance of all, let me say that there are still some channels open out of the beaten tracks, and those who have ears to hear can learn in these how the mystery of sanctity is not only behind the veils of Christian doctrine but behind the phenomenal veils of the psychic life.

17
ON INTIMATIONS CONCERNING THE INTERIOR CHURCH IN SCHOOLS OF CHRISTIAN MYSTICISM

[Printed as the Introduction to *Some Characteristics of the Interior Church*, by I. V. Lopukhin (1912). Translated from the French by D. H. S. Nicholson.]

Waite had first suggested translating the work of the Russian mystic Lopukhin in 1907, as a project for his ill-fated Hermetic Text Society, for he looked upon him as a natural complement to Eckartshausen, whose *Cloud upon the Sanctuary* had been published in *The Unknown World* in 1895. Nicholson, who was to be a close friend of Charles Williams, was a member of the Independent and Rectified Rite and shared Waite's enthusiasm for little-known mystical writers. (In 1913 he translated Scaramelli's *Handbook of Mystical Theology* and in 1916 co-edited with the Revd A. H. E. Lee the *Oxford Book of English Mystical Verse*.)

The concept of a Hidden or Interior Church was central to Waite's thesis of a continuing Secret Tradition. It is in no sense an instituted body, rather 'the cohort of just men made perfect'. Waite distinguishes this 'Communion of Saints in the Sanctuary of the Secret Church' from 'the union one with another of psychic consciousness'; those who are a part of the Hidden Church have attained 'an union in the highest part of the soul with That Which is unknown by mind, but above the mind is known'. Alternatively, it is 'an union in still consciousness fixed on the abiding God, realised within'. Those who have experienced this state recognize others who have also experienced it when they return to the everyday world; all such, throughout time and space, constitute the members of the Hidden Church (see, e.g., *The Holy Grail*, 1933, pp. 515 and 516). Waite was fully aware of the inadequacy of the language he used to express the nature of experiences for which no descriptive words exist. His essay on Lopukhin is perhaps the best introduction to his ideas for the reader unfamiliar with mystical texts.

THE importance of Lopukhin's text on *Characteristics of the Interior Church* arises from that which it implies as well as that which it expresses. On the surface, it is a devotional treatise which recalls several accidental prototypes and as many undesigned successors. We may take, as examples, the Italian *Anima Amante*, the *Hidden Life of the Soul*, which is of French origin, and the *Soul Contemplating God*, subject, however as we shall see, to one considerable exception. It is transparent on the face of these little books—excellent within their own limits—that they have been produced under the specific obedience of the Latin Rite, but the work of Lopukhin is so catholic in matter, as it is also in form of expression, that it would be difficult by its content to say whether the Official Church of its author was Roman or Greek, if he had not in one place practically confessed to the latter obedience, Here, as I think, is the first, though a very casual, indication that there is possibly more in the tract than may appear on a first acquaintance to those who are readers exercising ordinary care only. They should be able to see that, even on the surface, there is a suggestion of deeps which are not found in popular devotional handbooks. The title, of course, strikes a note of expectation, and brackets it immediately with Eckartshausen's *Cloud upon the Sanctuary*, to the third English edition of which my introduction, covering such a field as was possible within the limits of the opportunity, has established some of the analogies subsisting between the two texts. We have to carry the inquiry further in the present place.

The translator of Lopukhin has told us in his prefatory remarks more about the author than was known in England previously, but it was not to be expected that the biographical and literary facts, so collected, should throw any real light upon his inner life and much less upon the claims implied by his references to a Hidden or Interior Church. Whatsoever has been ascertained by myself, or may be afterwards found by others, concerning Councillor von Eckartshausen leaves us in the same position precisely. In the latter case, an unusually large number of writings from the same hand do not assist us to understand the *Cloud upon the Sanctuary*, while those of Lopukhin, in addition to the *Quelques Traits*, are unfortunately available in the Russian language only. It is probable that these, too, would give us no key—whether in the guise of personal or other circumstances—

to account for his important, although implied, claim—the essence of which seems to be that he is himself a voice speaking from an Inner Sanctuary. I remember that the present text was reprinted at Paris in the year 1901, and since then a few occult *littérateurs* in France believed themselves to have discovered the influenceof Martinism therein. The presence of Saint-Martin in Russia during the life of Lopukhin, the belief that he made an intellectual mark therein and left his traces behind him, may be taken to account for the suggestion rather than any obvious similarity between the minds of the Unknown Philosopher and the Russian mystic. Like Eckartshausen, the latter was obviously integrated in the external Christian Church, and, especially as he saw deep things within it which pass into no official expression, it would be impossible, in the presence of his very clear statements, to suppose that he deserted it at any point of his career. The sheaf of church devotions under the title of *God is the Purest Love*, offers proof palpable to the same effect in the case of the German theosopher; and if there is nothing so unmistakeable to quote in that of Lopukhin, I am not less certain that it is implied by every page of his memorial on the life of the soul in God. For the rest, it seems safe to affirm that the Martinistic elements in Lopukhin are not so much elusive as non-existent. The Official Church communicated nothing officially in the opinion of the French mystic, though individuals might be and were channels of grace and awakening. For the other, there was the Outward Church as a visible sign of salvation; and, however much in separation, it was the path to the Hidden Assembly abiding within. The one drew life from the other, and there is little or no suggestion that it was inhibited as a channel of grace. In the presence of this fundamental distinction there is scarcely any need to enter into the question of less essential analogies. These are inevitable in the normal dedications of the mystic life, and examples are numerous enough, if it were worth while to recite them. one can put aside for the same reason the question of personal communication between Saint-Martin and Lopukhin during the very brief period when both may have been resident in Russia. There is no trace of their meeting or that they influenced one another, if meet accidentally they did. There is as little reason to suppose that the grace of his fugitive presence which Saint-Martin left behind him came within the horizon of the Russian mystic; the fluidic correspondences between them can be accounted for in a more direct way.

On this subject it remains only to say that the notion of a Hidden Church never entered into the consciousness of Saint-Martin. What he learned of Eckartshausen, through his correspondent Baron de Liebestorf, impressed him in a particular manner, and from this quarter a considerable treatise on Numbers, the work of Eckartshausen, came into his hands; but although the correspondence with the Swiss mystic continued for about five years, when it was closed by the death of the latter, it contains no reference to the *Cloud on the Sanctuary*, which had been in existence already for a considerable period. There is little reason to suppose that it was ever seen by Saint-Martin, nor is there any safe means of judging how it would have appealed to his mind, or in what sense it might have been interpreted therein. Perhaps he would have identified the Holy Assembly with that mystical abode of the soul which was known to 'men of desire,' and out of which those who come are said to speak the same language, as a sign of the communion which still subsists between them. I think, however, that he would have found Lopukhin and his intimations nearer to his own heart than the more express teaching of the *Cloud*. The former's suggestion that external worship has deviated from its source, and that the spirit of light—apart, as I understand it, from the normal apprehension of grace—has been withdrawn therefrom, would have represented his own consciousness as to the body politic of official religion. Eckartshausen has similar intimations, but he was much more obviously integrated in the External Church of his childhood; and though he assures us continually that his Holy Assembly is no corporate institution, it is like a shadow of an organized society projected on the spiritual plane. Now, I think that this shadow, for Saint-Martin, would have been too much in the likeness of the Latin Church.

Enough has been said here on what is in part a matter of speculation, partly a question of facts in life and, for the rest, a study of correspondences. If we turn to the evidence that Lopukhin offers on his own part, in respect of that which has entered into his own spiritual consciousness, we must begin by observing that—in the mind of our mystic—Adam, by the act of his implied repentance, became the first stone on which the Interior Church was built. The patriarchs, and all just souls under the obedience of the Old Alliance, constituted apparently the superstructure thereof. A new spirit entered into the building with Christ, and more indeed thereafter, though still in a sense from the beginning, it was that Spiritual Temple in and by which God accomplishes the work of regeneration in each of us. It is to be understood, therefore, as a great agent at work everywhere. The elect who have been born again constitute the Invisible Church, and the cry of the regenerative process is the old Rosicrucian cry: *Transmutemini, transmutemini, de lapidus mortuis, in lapides vivos philosophicos*. The word 'Ἐκκλησία has reference to people who are assembled by an act of calling, and I suppose that we must distinguish two offices in the Church, as it is regarded outwardly or inwardly. The official and ecclesiastical institution comprises those who are called together for the purpose of attaining regeneration; the interior, hidden, and super-excellent Holy Assembly is composed of those who have attained, and the experience of regeneration is the opening of consciousness in that Church. It is, however, the beginning of a process, which process is a life, and, indeed, the life that is eternal. Those who are born of Christ in Christ also must grow.

That which began in a sense as the Church of Adam—the first who was called into the state of restitution—but which seems to have been more especially the Church of Abel, in contradistinction to the Cainite Church of Antichrist, became in the fulness of time the Inward and Outward Temple of the Redeemer; and at first, or in the days of what is called Apostolic Christianity, that which was without was even as that which was within. The Church was manifested, for the first time, as a corporate assembly, and the Hidden Church was its spirit. Those who had entered into that spirit were integrated mystically therein, and their place—understood more especially, and perhaps only, as a state—was the Holy of Holies, the centre of the heavenly springs of redemption. This, in my apprehension, is the centre where those abide who have perfected the Christ-life within them: they are hidden with Christ in God. It may even be that Christ has given up the kingdom to His Father in their respect. The next state, which is also described by Lopukhin as belonging to the Holy of Holies, is of those who have accomplished their regeneration, and Lopukhin in the present connection gives expression to the great secret of this new birth: their consciousness is in Christ and not in what he calls *la propriété*. It is defined by him as being the attainment in grace of that which Jesus Christ was by nature.

It is very important to notice at this point the succession of events in the redeemed life of the spirit, and some omissions in the sequence of the symbolism which are noticeable in the text. The Holy of Holies is in contiguity to the Holy Place, and the dwellers therein are (*a*) those who have been crucified with Christ; (*b*) who have yielded up the spirit to the Father; and (*c*) who—this being done, *consummatum est*—cannot now turn back or fall away. The dwellers in the Holy of Holies are in the Resurrection-state of Easter, or they are in the state of glory which corresponds to the Ascension. Those who are in the Holy Place, or in the path that leads thereto, are before the veil of the Hidden Sanctuary; they have passed through mystical dying but have not attained that rebirth which is synonymous with resurrection in the symbolism of the Christ-life. Lopukhin might have told us that they are in the state which intervened between the night of Calvary and the morning of Easter—the state of being dead to the things of earth but not reborn into a new life and a sense of the ends therein.

After these holy men and women come those who are leading the life of the Cross, who are following the path of regeneration, who are carrying their cross daily, looking for that time when it shall carry them, which is the state of being lifted on the cross. At the threshold, or in the Courts of the Temple, are those who have been called by the Father, and within the Porch are those who are so far stirred that they are seeking their salvation.

It seems to me that as the symbolism of the Christ-life has been adopted, it should be carried on consistently throughout. Those who are dwelling in the Outer Courts are those in whom, by the hypothesis, Christ has been born, as if in the stable at Bethlehem, by the conception of desire; and those who are in the first degrees of the Holy Place are those who are leading the external life of Jesus Christ. Some are in Egypt, as if they also were seeking after hidden knowledge in holy places of old. Some are with the doctors in the Temple, asking the questions which no man can answer unless he has light from God. Some are in the life of Nazareth; and some again are in the public ministry. It will be thought, if Christ is born within us after this manner, that regeneration is already accomplished; but it is the man of sorrows who so is born and so works in us, by a grace of imitation, and it is we who have subsequently to be reborn or rise again in the Christ of Glory. The suggestion is (*a*) that there is a transfiguration of the psychic vehicles, symbolised as the spiritualised body of Jesus Christ being reborn in us, and (*b*) that the personal physical body also enters into the state of redemption. I regard these indications as important for Lopukhin's point of view and otherwise, because of their connection with certain mystic schools; but I have no opportunity to consider them in this place.

The whole work is accomplished in that central sphere of the spirit where the Kingdom of God manifests in its true power. The key of entrance thereto is a gift of understanding which comes from Jesus Christ. In connection with this gift, we may remember the words of the Psalmist in a hymn which can be construed throughout as referable to the Interior Church: 'I was glad when they said unto me, We will go up to the House of the Lord.'[1] Outside this region is all the realm of astral allusion, wherein the false spirits bear witness. It is no part of my concern to maintain that the emblematic programme of Lopukhin is in perfect logical harmony with itself, and, as a fact, his pageant of symbolism is defective in several respects, though it is always possible to distinguish the real intention. His remarks on the way of Christ in the soul offer certain difficulties, but they can be taken in the sense of the explanation which I have tried already to give. There is, firstly, the conception of desire, and next there is the birth which signifies a certain grade of opening in consciousness. What follows is called broadly the Imitation of Christ, on which we have many theses in mystic literature; it is the path of 'daily identification with the life and virtue' of Christ. As such, it is simply 'the beginning of interior life'; it is the lesser mysteries of initiation in eternal wisdom; it is that preparing of the matter which is necessary before the Great Work can be performed thereon; it is the business of every man who is working actively at his own regeneration. The rebirth which

[1] Ps. cxii., or cxxi. in the Latin Psalter.

follows imitation cannot, however, be accomplished on a man's own part; it must be done for him and in him. The path is one of prayer, meditation and external good works, until the time comes when that is awakened within us which prays independently of our lesser selves, but for us and with us, which offers also a pure sacrifice on the altar of the heart. It is, further, a work of conformity in the abnegation of the will, of abstinence by renunciation of all that diverts from the path, of love fulfilling itself in the spirit of Christ.

It must be confessed that these intimations, as they stand expressed in the text, do not exceed the familiar horizon of devotional books, though they have assuredly another atmosphere, while the observations there and here on external Nature, and the profit to be found in its study, are but a shadowy presentation of the doctrine of Divine Immanence in the key of Hermetic terminology. But a more distinct note is sounded in the teaching concerning self-knowledge and the stripping off the false veils for the manifestation of that which is within, so that the divine *ego* may be known in its essential splendour. There is a certain debt at this point to the *Mystery of the Cross*, which offers, like Lopukhin himself, great occasional lights amidst much that is clouded, negligible and belonging to the conventional order of pietistic considerations.

Now it is at the point which is here reached, in summary and interpretative form, that the text proper comes abruptly enough to its conclusion, or, in other words, where it may seem to have begun only; in the exposition which follows, by way of questions and answers, there are, however, certain lights, as, for example, that the Spirit of God dwells in the temple within us when the will is offered in sacrifice. But it is in the consideration of Lopukhin's allegorical picture that we begin to speculate whether the whole tract is not written around this curious Diagram, about which much more might be said than the author chooses to unfold in the few and rather veiled words devoted thereto.

The correspondence—not only on the surface but integrally—is with the Temple built of old at Jerusalem, and it will be seen later on that there is a possible reason why, though this has not passed into expression. There is no need to add that the material edifice has suffered a great transfiguration. We should observe, in the first place, that which may be termed the porchway or entrance of this spiritual temple of Solomon, on which is written the legend of expulsion from Eden. On the hither side of it is the outer world and the sentence passed thereon: (*a*) the anathema which followed the trespass; (*b*) the law of natural bondage in respect of humanity; (*c*) the penalty attaching to the most sacred work of Nature in the generation of children; and (*d*) the judgment of death. But at an extreme point on the outward side there is erected a cubic altar, around which is inscribed a testimony concerning light shining in the darkness, though the darkness comprehendeth it not. Between this altar and the Porchway of the Temple there is a straight and narrow path strewn with crosses: it indicates the one way back. The altar is that of faith, of spiritual intent, of desire for the House of the Lord, above all of love; but in another sense I understand it to signify the External Churches. Those who would enter the Secret Church of the Spirit—in which the Christ-substance of all things hoped for is manifested by visible glory, and is also as a Tree of Life for the feeding of the nations—must make their sacrifice on that altar before they can pass behind, must receive the Eucharistic communion in elements of bread and wine before the Divine Substance can be partaken of by their souls. The path is through the place of the trespass; on the one side there is the toil, the sorrow and the sweat which provide the matter of our daily life, and this is for transmutation by us; on the other side are the laws of generation and of death, which have to be overcome in fulfilment after another manner before we can enter that mystical Garden of Pausanias which—in another form of symbolism—is dedicated to the higher Venus. The text of Lopukhin tells us that the title to the passage of the Porch depends on (*a*) repentance, to be understood as the undoing of the Fall within us; (*b*) holy abhorrence of the ways belonging to the love of self, in order that Christ may live within us, instead of the self-centred personality; and (*c*) turning of the spiritual axis towards the real goodness. The qualification for the Vestibule of the Temple is to be born again of the spirit, and this work is begun therein. The Holy Place is that of the Wine of the Kingdom, but this is the Wine of Nature transmuted by the word of the Lord and by the Lord's presence. The Holy Place is also the abode and seat of Wisdom. It is to be observed that the passage from the vestibule to the Holy Place is without inscription, but that which leads on from the latter to the Holy of Holies is full of intimations. They concern length of days, entrance thereto through the door of Christ, the clothing of mortal man in the vesture of wisdom, as with a robe of immortal glory, and the death in Christ which is the path unto life in Him. The Holy of Holies is also the place of a new heaven and a new earth, the place wherein the world is overcome with Christ, as also by Him and in Him, and the place of the Gifts of the Spirit for the healing of the nations, because those who dwell in the Holy of Holies have become tingeing stones. Beyond this sacred place is the abode of God unmanifest.

I have spoken so far of the Diagram as explained by the passages of Scripture allocated to its several points. The entrance to the Temple is by an ascent of seven steps, inscribed with the symbols of the planets, as if those who go up thereby are passing from the lights and glories of the visible world. The interior is a curious blending of alchemical and Rosicrucian symbolism in addition to that of the Old Testament, the Christian Scriptures and the Apocalypse especially. There should be no need to say that these intermingled typologies are dificult to interpret, and it is only in virtue of acquaintance with the secret tradition in Christian times that the meaning emerges clearly. The Diagram as a whole represents the stages of spiritual birth, life, death and resurrection. On the threshold of the Temple is an emblem apparently Masonic but here signifying the sword that turned every way to keep the way of the Tree of Life. The reason is that integration in the Temple is actually a return to Paradise. In the court or vestibule there is a cross, and on this cross is placed the triangle of water apex downward. The figure of a child is within it, representing in one aspect him who is in the course of being born again of water and of spirit. The lower limbs are folded, as if still in the womb, but the arms are raised as if striving to come forth. It is really the birth of the Christ consciousness or the man of sorrows within us. The spirit is descending on the child in the form of a dove. Above the cross is a sacrificial cup, and beyond this a seven-branched candlestick, which is in analogy with the seven planets on the steps of entrance, they representing the lights of Nature and this the seven creative spirits, 'the sevenfold light', the divine gifts by which man is led onward and upward. This candlestick shines into the straight way which leads to the Holy Place, and here is the place of illumination. Therein is 'the adolescent of divine light', bearing the cross, behind which shines the light of wisdom, and it is therefore the cross of life. Whereas the child below is immersed, the youth is standing upon the globe of terrestrial things, and on this world is written the word VITRIOL, composed of the initial letters of the Latin Hermetic injunction: *Visita interiora terrae, rectificando invenies occultum lapidem*. In the path leading to the Holy of Holies the sacrifice is consummated on the cross, and in the Holy of Holies he who has died upon the cross mystically rises as a priest for ever according to the order of Melchisedek. It is the place of unity, the place of the healing of nations, and therein is the triple Christ symbolism—the Lamb, the sign of the Logos and the Rose. The crown over the Logos symbol shows that Christ is here in the supernal state. The black void of heaven above signifies that which is termed by Jacob Boehme God in the Abyss. Into this great darkness the Holy of Holies extends, whereas the other parts of the temple stretch down among the lights of the natural world.

Now, there is nothing in the life of Lopukhin, and—apart from this Diagram—there is nothing in his thesis itself, to suggest that he was acquainted with Zoharic Kabalism, though a certain part of it was available to Latin-reading students at his period; but it is impossible to overlook the striking analogies between the formalised plan of his Temple and the four Kabalistic worlds. The Holy of Holies corresponds to the world of *Atziluth*, or that of Deity, understood as comprising *Kether, Chokmah*, and *Binah* in the *Sephiroth* of the Tree of Life. Above them is *Ain Soph Aour*, the limitless, Divine Light, or concealment of all Concealment, even as the unmanifest God is said by Lopukhin to be beyond the Holy of Holies. The second Kabbalistic world is called *Briah*, or Creation, understood in the absolute sense, as if something were produced out of nothing—as, for example, *materia prima*. It is also the archangelic world, the world of loftiest intelligence in the state of distinction from Godhead. This world is suggested by the Holy Place of Lopukhin, for as his Holy of Holies is a state of Divine Union, and is the abode of those who have not only been born again but have made their regeneration perfect, so herein is the highest condition of sanctity outside that of hiddenness in God. The third world is that of *Yetzirah*, meaning Formation, as if first matter were being adapted therein. It is also the world of angels, and is in analogy with the Vestibule of Lopukhin, otherwise, the Courts of the Temple, wherein are those who have died to themselves—so that Christ may dwell within them. They are properly described as in an intermediate state, and in this world they may be messengers of salvation to others, but they do not communicate on their own part and by their own warrant from above. *Assiah* is the fourth world, and in very broad language it may be called things as they are, with all their succession of consequences, their good and evil. In the scheme of Lopukhin, it is in analogy with the great, indiscriminate region outside the Porch of the Temple.

The limits of my comparison must, however, be understood clearly. I have offered only one aspect of Kabbalism, and have put it quite inadequately; there are several other aspects. Moreover, the Four Worlds are especially cosmic, and the Diagram with which I am dealing represents states of humanity, particularly on the spiritual side. It represents also the process of working back towards the Centre, while the other is a plan formalised of coming out. The comparison, I think, helps us to understand the mystic, whether ot not it had entered into his own consciousness; both systems are concerned with actualities—the development of an universe and the return of a great cohort of humanity whence it came. It remains to be said (*a*) that the dwellers in the Holy of Holies, their attainment notwithstanding, are designed for the apostolate on earth; and (*b*) that here also is established in all its parts the Secret Church of God. It is in the world, but the world does not know it, for it is inaccessible to flesh and blood.

These are words from the mystic's own explanation concerning his Diagram, and notwithstanding my feeling expressed concerning this part of the text, we may look at it a little more closely. The True Church of Christ is a temple of Nature and Grace. It is entered by the study of Nature for the discovery of the Christ-light in the state of love, and a moment comes when the glory of understanding descends suddenly into the soul. This is the birth of a new man, who can enter the kingdom. It is entered by the way of the cross, to attain the grace of the temple and the sevenfold gift of illuminated life therein. The seeker has been previously a student of the Divine Immanence in the gospel according to Nature, and this is the practice of the Presence of God in the manifest world. He has now to realise that Presence, or the Divine Immanence, within him; and the work is expressed in the terms of Hermetic philosophy. The first counsel is *Visita interiora terræ*; it is a work of mining beneath the crust of our earthly personality, the reduction of its elements to their principles, thus conjoining the sun and moon, the Divine Spirit and the psychic part, so attaining the state of inward health and becoming qualified to enter the Holy of Holies in the centre of the spiritual temple. It is done by dying on the cross with Christ, and if this is rather a confusion of images, a defect of the kind is to be expected in witnesses like Lopukhin: we must deal with it as we best can. The sanctuary is the paradisical region of light and the renewed Eden. The adept lives henceforth in the union of the sun and moon, which is the great mystery of renovation, and its principle is the Blood of the Lamb. All things are made new therein and thereby; regeneration is completed, and the Rose of Paradise is beheld in bloom everywhere. So does the tract end in Rosicrucian symbolism and suggests the possible connection of the witness with instituted mysteries which were certainly alive at his period, though almost in a *status inanimatus*, as they are alive now and beginning to awaken from their sleep, under many misleading veils. The symbolism is a little difficult to deal with in an intelligible manner without unfolding a system which cannot be explained in public. I must be content, therefore, to leave it, saying only that Lopukhin may, after all, be indebted merely to his personal reflection upon an exotic department of Christian picture-symbolism, assisted by the scattered lights found in the *Mystery of the Cross*. Douzetemps, the accredited author of this text, has many references to the chief Rosicrucian emblem, though his connection with any sodality passing under such name is unlikely. He said that the story of the Fraternity was an invention, but one devised in good faith.

The question which now arises is how the hypothesis of an Interior Church is left by Lopukhin after we have thus collated (*a*) the intimations comprised by his discourse in chief; (*b*) those of the catechism which may be called supplementary thereto; and (*c*) those of his Diagram, which is a key to the whole subject? It must be allowed that the result is little more than a vestige, but it is interesting as such. The communion of saints, on which Eckartshausen dwelt frequently, is not, I think, mentioned in the text, but it is postulated by implication in the symbolism of a secret assembly gathered together in a Holy of Holies, where the Christ-Spirit abides in the midst thereof as the 'celestial springs of redemption'. It is suggested further that the personal Divine Presence may manifest there unfailingly, as God walked with Adam in the cool of the evening. The entrance to this Sanctuary is (*a*) through the life of crucifixion; (*b*) mystical death on the cross; (*c*) descent into Hades, which is the state of being dead in Christ; and (*d*) resurrection into the glory of Christ. These things are not plainly in the text, but I do not think that it is through intentional obscurity; it is rather the result of confused method and the mixture of several emblematic systems. They form, however, an outline in brief of a secret doctrine of Christian mysticism, fragments of which are scattered abroad everywhere, but it is to be found as a system only in one place, and this place is hidden from the world at large.

We have, however, to understand all the stages of progression in a sense which is vital, by which I mean one of inward realisation. It is not the work of discursive meditation; it is not a result obtained by the process of being good, speaking generally, or of trying to do the best that we can, on the whole and reasonably, in that state into which it has pleased God to call us. It is a question of conquering the Kingdom of God by violence—that is to say, by laying hands on oneself, taking up one's life and making it that which it must become so that all holiness shall be our province. In other words, it is an unremitting work in conscious purpose, following the counsels which are revealed by Christ in God. But the words 'conscious purpose' mean that the work is in consciousness, and the quest is for the attainment of a state therein when that which I have called the *propriété*, following the French, has been stripped of the true self, till we are quickened in the inward man and separated from the man without, so far as interest, concern, and priority of claim go. By the imagery of Lopukhin's Spiritual Temple, we are then integrated in a collective living body of higher consciousness in common. Once more, if the eternal necessity of repetition may be overlooked here, it is a state and not a place; the Temple is not built with hands; no one has travelled in search of it in the four manifested quarters. And the body is not a body; it is not a secret ecclesiatical polity; it is not a system of rites in the transcendence; there are no ceremonies, no observances: it is still rest in Christ. It is yet a work of this life, for it seems clear that those who attain are in the body of their mortality.[1] There is no trace of a suggestion that they are apart from this veil; it is not said, for example, that they are in the psychic body; on the contrary, it is hinted that the sanctified consciousness reacts on both the envelopes or vehicles; and people who wish to follow this line of indication will do well to consult Jane Lead, John Pordage, and a few others of that school of mystic thought in England. Finally, the divine mode of this life constitutes the spirit behind the Christian churches; once it was near to these; now it is withdrawn; but there are still the means of entrance. We must respect the official institutions and the authorised ceremonies; we must do more than respect, we must profit by them; and the Eucharist in this connection is mentioned in a particular manner.

The next question which arises is whether we are here in the presence of something that can be called new in Christian teaching on the state of union with Christ. As I have rendered it in my own form of language, the imagery is, I suppose, new to the orthodox circles. Outside these I must not say that it has been set out so plainly in the sequence of the symbolism; but those

---

[1] My friend, Mr W. L. Wilmshurst suggests that there are two instances in the course of practical organised religious forms which seem to him palpable shadows or projections on the physical plan of the Interior Church. 'These are : (1) In the official Latin Church, the College of Cardinals, of whom the Holy Father is the Centre, as equivalent of Christ, the Centre of the withdrawn Church. The Cardinals themselves are subdivided into three divisions corresponding to the three grades of priesthood spoken of by Aletheus, namely, Cardinal-bishops, Cardinal-priests and Cardinal-deacons. (2) In Masonry, the Grand Lodge is the equivalent of the Secret Church, as the ordinary Lodge is the equivalent of the outer Church. Provincial Grand Lodge officers are drawn from the Masters of ordinary Lodges; and Grand Lodge of England officers are in turn drawn from the Provincial Grand Lodge members, whose centre is the Grand Master of England—again a complete analogy to the Pope and the three order of Cardinals.' He remarks further that 'the Freemason who is promoted to office in the Grand Lodge of his province or country still retains his membership in the Craft Lodge in which Masonically he was born.'

who are acquainted with the English mystics of the seventeenth century, already mentioned, and with *Le Nouvel Homme* of Saint-Martin, will be reminded of many things, while the literature of the life of Christ in the spirit begins—if, indeed it begins then, because it may well be earlier—with the Syriac text of Hierotheos, and by the fragmentary knowledge which remains to us of Joachim's *Evangelio Eterno*, one can see that it must have been formulated therein.

To sum up on the subject of Lopukhin: his presentation of the Interior Church is actually and really the theological conception of a Church glorious in heaven, projected on the plane of earth, because (*a*) it seems possible by the hypothesis to enter it in this life, and it is therefore (*b*) an extension of the postulates concerning the communion of saints, so that the life of sanctity brings about a common integration in Christ, which is much more express than we meet with in the authorised texts of Christian mysticism, by which I mean those bearing the *imprimatur* of Latin orthodoxy.

It would seem unlikely that Lopukhin and Eckartshausen came into personal communication; their ways were cast in quite distinct places; the *Cloud on the Sanctuary* appeared in 1791, and though the French translation calls it his swan-song, a good many years elapsed before the death of the writer; the *Characteristics of the Interior Church* is referable to the year 1801, bring a period when the *Cloud* was utterly unknown in France and had not apparently attracted much, if any, attention in its own country. It would be interesting to hear that the two mystics had met; it would be interesting and perhaps more important if we could be certain that the memorial of the one had been at least looked over by the other; it is much more significant, however, if they were at work independently and reached what is so largely a mutual point of view apart from the aid which they could have lent one to another. Let us briefly review the *Cloud*, so that we may realise the points of correspondence, of difference if any, and of amplification which may not signify difference.

Eckartshausen, like Lopukhin, is dealing with experience of a transcendental order in that field of consciousness which is the ground of all experience, and it matters very little if the imagery of his language differs, so only that he reaches the same end.

The mystery of this experience is one of regeneration and of vital union between God and man. The mode of its attainment is by removing the outer veils of material humanity for the manifestation of our inward being. The experience and the science of its fulfilment have been entrusted from the beginning of things to a Hidden School of the saints, to an invisible, interior and celestial Church. This was the remedy necessitated by the Fall; it arose to undo the Fall; and at its inception, as now, the school was illuminated by Him Who is our Saviour.

Obviously this is the thesis of the Russian mystic, and though Eckartshausen is more express as to the circumstances under which an External Church rose up as a witness in the world; he is at one with Lopukhin in affirming (a) its original integration in the Higher Church of the Spirit; (b) the fact that the one became divided from the other; and (c) the necessity for those who would graduate in the more advanced school to maintain their relation with the corporate institution which signifies without. He defends the sanctity and efficacy of external ceremonials, as we have found that his co-heir defends them. The text of Eckartshausen is available, and will be in the hands of many or most of the readers of the present supplement thereto, and, as I wish to avoid self-repetition, I think that this bare outline may be held to suffice for the analogies subsisting between the two works. It remains now to ascertain whether there are important differences or extensions.

Those who will be at the pains to collate the two texts, with some discrimination and care, will not fail to see for themselves that there are no points of difference between them, unless it be on a single point of government; there is no statement otherwise in the one which is opposed to the other, and it would be quite possible, on account of their eminent harmony, to combine them in a single document. But this notwithstanding, there is at least one very important point of distinction, because the *Cloud on the Sanctuary* is much more definite in the presentation of its views concerning the Secret Church. For Lopukhin it is the empire of Heaven's own king, and those who abide in that empire are in the state of beatitude which is connected by Latin theology with the idea of the Blessed Vision. It is otherwise the operation of the life of Christ in the individual soul, but there is no suggestion that the influence of those who dwell in the Holy of

Holies is exercised collectively in a conscious manner on those who are without that pale—as, for example, located in one of the External Churches. They constitute the Spirit of the Church dwelling in separation, and though it may be regarded as implied that this spirit is not without its influence, we have no suggestion concerning its nature or extent. The work is by individual apostolate. For Eckartshausen, on the other hand, the Interior Church is affirmed to rule in all. It is therefore in the collective sense a headship, though it works also individually. It is scattered over the whole world and is in immediate communication with the Divine Master, Who alone initiates into all mysteries belonging to the Kingdom of God as well as that of Nature. It is described further as a school, and from this school all truth flows into the world. The External Church is the letter of the Holy Law, but the Church Within is its meaning and its spirit. If the External Church be sacramental, that which is posited as behind it is the grace behind the sacraments and the virtue behind the form. The Hidden Sanctuary has been the same from the beginning, the Presence therein has been always the Spirit of Christ, and as it projected external religion on the plane of time and space, we can understand after a more direct manner the meaning of St Augustine when he said that Christianity had been always in the world but had not been called always by that name. The shool of the Law and the Prophets under the obedience of the Old Alliance was merged in the New Law and the hierarchy of the Christian Apostolate, but that which was within underwent no change or shadow of vicissitude, for the one High Priest always administered therein. The state of integration in this Church corresponds to what external creeds have formulated as the communion of saints, but it is more expressly a 'school of wisdom', and, as such, 'it has its chair, its doctor, it possesses a rule for students, it has forms and objects for study and, in short, a method by which they study.' As regards the objects, they are described, with extraordinary suggestiveness, as the conversion of faith in Christ into experimental knowledge. The foundation is that Christ has come in the flesh. Before the incarnation in time, He dwelt with the brethren of the Secret Sanctuary in the spirit of the Sanctuary, and I make no question that in the mind of Eckartshausen (a) the manifestation to come was regarded as foreknown from the beginning therein, since this would follow from the integration of its members in the Christ-consciousness; (*b*) that the guidance exercised by the Sanctuary in respect of the world without had, also from the beginning, this 'far off, divine event' in view; (*c*) that it was by the active intervention of the Sanctuary that the world was prepared thereto; (*d*) that as, in virtue of the entire hypothesis, the scheme of redemption was the first, immediate and pre-conceived, consequence of the Fall, so (*e*) the Sanctuary was instituted as part of the scheme, and (*f*) that hence the work accomplished therein was a preparation throughout thereto. Eckartshausen says categorically that 'the Interior Church was formed immediately after the Fall of man, and received from God at first hand the revelation of those means by which fallen humanity could be again raised to its rights and delivered from its misery. It received the primitive charge of all revelation and mystery; it received the key of true science, both divine and natural.'

There is no need to say that, as shewn by the summary which I have given and as shewn by the text itself, which may be compared throughout, there is nothing in the thesis of Lopukhin that approaches this in expressness; his Interior Church seems for a moment to be a shadow of the German mystic's Holy Assembly and 'illuminated community of God', which began, in what perhaps must be called the author's extravagance of theosophical language, at 'the first day of the world's creation', will continue till the end of time and is a school 'in which all who thirst for knowledge are instructed by the Spirit of Wisdom itself.' We have, however, to remember that Lopukhin's plan of the mystic temple is also formal after its own method; it is Solomon's Temple, spiritualised after a manner of which it has not entered into the heart of Freemasonry to conceive, much as it has symbolised thereon; and the question is whether it does not imply in its imagery all that has been formulated by Eckartshausen. It might follow, then, that in both, as certainly in one, there is a clear affirmation of guidance, though the methods of expression are distinct. It would seem further, and in both cases, that those who put off mortality, being members of the Invisible Sanctuary, are not by this fact translated therefrom, like 'sunbeams lifted higher'. However and again in both cases, the Holy Assembly is composed in the main of persons who are still in the body. It is said, however, by the *Cloud* (*a*) that the chief himself does not know all the members, and as this statement on leadership does not refer to the Central Spirit of Christ, which is the all in all of the Sanctuary, so it must be assumed that some kind of informal headship in time is here intended; (*b*) that he who is chosen by God presents himself without presumption and is received without jealousy; (*c*) that if there is occasion for members to meet together, they find and recognise each other with perfect certainty; (*d*) that those who are within can set some who are without on the path of quest for entrance; (*e*) that, all this notwithstanding, only such as are prepared can obtain admission; but, finally, (*f*), that there are methods of preparation. It does not appear in respect of these last that sufficient indication is provided by either mystic to justify their differentiation from the counsels of Christian life which are imposed by the external schools.

The necessary materials for a judgment on the whole subject have now been classified, so far as these texts are concerned, and the next matter which concerns us is to see whether there are any similar claims put forward in mystic literature. My Introduction to the *Cloud on the Sanctuary* mentions certain books belonging to the eighteenth century as shewing correspondences with Eckartshausen; but one of them was the work of Lopukhin, and to the others I do not feel that it is desirable to make further reference. There is, however, the mystic theosophy of Jewry, and it is right that we should question this as to its possible testimonies within the measure of the Old Alliance, because of the antiquity ascribed by both witnesses to the Interior School.

Zoharic Kabalism recognises the existence of a Holy Assembly, or Celestial School, and of a Sacred School below. Between them there is a bond of union, and the prophet Elias seems to have been a kind of mediator. They are described otherwise as the Israel which is above, ascending in the superior regions, and the Israel which is below, which is, of course, the chosen people understood generically as a nation, but more especially that part of it, like a head or crown of all, which is dedicated to the study of the Law and has entered into some part of the deeper knowledge concerning it. The two schools are in a certain separation one from another, and for this reason the

Sacred Name—which is their bond of union—stands incomplete. The Higher School is like a Hidden Church which is joined from time to time to the Holy One, and then the Israel below is also in union with the Divine. The community which constitutes the Heavenly School is also said to be the Shekinah, which is described otherwise as a spiritual communion; but as this Indwelling Glory was driven into exile with the Israel below, it must be understood that there is some confusion in terms and symbolism. The Israel in transcendence is above all the celestial legions, and constitutes a glory of all. It receives the food of souls direct from the king, and it nourishes them therewith in sanctity. It is identified mystically with the moon, because, I suppose, it shines in a light reflected from God and because the moon is a Shekinah attribution. The place of the community is in Paradise, and it is joined with the Holy One therein at midnight, at which time the Sacred School below unites with that which is above. The bond of union is love in the study of the Law, and the Higher School is identified continually with the beloved Bride of the Canticle of Canticles. But it is also called the Mother, which is again a title of Shekinah. It is the hart which pants after the waters. The Israel below is the fruit of union between the Holy One and that Mother which is the Israel above. It is perhaps in this sense, and through an implied law of solidarity, that the Israel which is above suffers or rejoices with the Israel which is below. The same is postulated concerning Shekinah. Those who study the Law on earth are those who receive their nourishment, already mentioned, from the House of the Celestial Community, which is also called Salem, in the sense of completeness, or otherwise the Secret of the Lord and the Mystery of Unity. The community of that which is above never leaves that which is below, and this alone constitutes a striking analogy with our two Christian mystics, who regard the Outward Church as the path to that which is within, whatever separation in spirit they may have held to exist between them.

It would have been easy to amplify this summary but I question whether it would extend our acquaintance with the inward mind of theosophical Israel on the matter in hand; and the broad purpose in view seems therefore to have been served sufficiently. That which remains is to express in a few words the gist of the whole. To myself it appeals simply as an expanded and analogical form of the profession with which we are all familiar: 'I believe ... in the Holy Catholic Church; the Communion of Saints'—it being understood that these clauses of the Christian symbol have been re-expressed in the terms of the Ancient Alliance. In other words, the root of all the intimations is that there was a Church of Israel exalted into the joys of Paradise; that there was a Militant Church on earth; that they were not in separation from each other. It signifies little if the bond of union is the Holy Spirit in the case of Christendom but Elias in that of Kabalistic Jewry. Rabbi Simeon, the prophet of the Zohar, was so uplifted by understanding and illumination in the mysteries of secret doctrine that not only was he permitted to enter Paradise and there take part in the debates of the Celestial School, where the Holy Assembly heard him with grateful hearts, but the Holy One, blessed be He, as the text says, listened in the Garden of Eden when the just man, already made perfect in knowledge, spoke on his own part. Hereof is the enthusiasm of hero-worship, and I have suppressed some things which would be disconcerting at the present day. The bare fact of Rabbi Simeon's freedom of the Blessed Company is in analogy with St Paul's visit to the third heaven. In fine, the Invisible Church of the Zohar is made sufficiently after the likeness of the corresponding Church of Lopukhin and Eckartshausen for the resemblance to be appreciated unequivocally; but they are independent conceptions, and that which was dreamed of in Israel—though exceedingly valuable for purposes of comparison—is much too vague to assist us in understanding better the testimony of the Christian witnesses.

I pass, therefore, to the prototypes and antecedents of these in mystic literature, and I have mentioned already that they are to be sought in England of the seventeenth century. The Philadelphian Society was an incorporation of mystics in London which seems to have begun about the year 1695 and was disbanded in 1705, or a little earlier the period of its private operations being regarded as at an end. An alternative title seems to have been that of Angelical Brethren, and the membership included Jane Lead, John Pordage, Francis Lee, Robert Roach, with some few others. The records of the Society are comprised in (*a*) *Theosophical Transactions of the Philadelphian*

Society, published in 1697, and extending apparently to five issues only; (*b*) the *State of the Philadelphian Society, and the ground of their proceedings considered;* (*c*) *Three Messages to the Philadelphian Society*, by Jane Lead, 1696–98; and, apart from the Society itself but concerned with its dedications, (*d*) *Revelation of Revelations*, by Jane Lead;[1] (*e*) The *Imperial Standard of Messiah Triumphant*, by Robert Roach, *circa* 1725.[2] In a very broad sense it may be said that the Society was founded in expectation of the Second Advent. The coming of Christ was not, however, understood as 'a visible appearance in the clouds' but as in spirit, or in 'powerful demonstrations of the Holy Ghost.' Through unhappy methods of expression, this interior and spiritual return must have been understood otherwise by those who listened from without to the nature and quality of the testimonies.

It should, I think, be made plain that the Philadelphian Society did not on its own part claim to be a Secret Church working, privately or otherwise, within the corporate manifested bodies; its members were seeking an answer on their proper deserts to the question whether the gifts and graces of the spirit are not attainable in this life; and the counsel of their quest was to proceed as if that problem had been solved already in a favourable sense. The official description of themselves is less express even than this. They were a religious society (*a*) for the reformation of manners, (*b*) for the advancement of Christian devotion to the heroic degree, in (*c*) peace and love towards all. Even as Lopukhin and Eckartshausen in their later day, they advised all to remain in the 'community or church in which they had before lived according to the best of their light and understanding.' They regarded their own meetings as a

---

[1] There is also *Enochian Walks with God*, by the same writer, published in 1694, and described in the title as paths discovered 'by a spiritual traveller', whose face was set towards Mount Zion. This work has many corroborative references to the Secret Church; but the standpoint of Jane Lead on this subject is perhaps represented sufficiently by *Revelation of Revelations*.

[2] *The Imperial Standard* is the extension of another book by the same writer published anonymously, two or three years before, under the title of *The Impending Crisis*. It has some interesting material, but is characterised by much irrelevant and virulent denunciation of the Roman Church. To the Interior Church there is no reference whatever.

proclamation of unity with the catholic church and with the communion of saints, affirming that such communion was experienced among them in a spiritual sense. Recognising much that was deplorable in existing churches and sects, they sought 'to re-establish catholic unity in the bond of the spirit'. The society, however, was only a shadow or vestige of that which its name implies. Corporate as in a sense it might be, it stood as an outward sign of a great, invisible, and unincorporate spiritual assembly of people who (*a*) expected the first resurrection, (*b*) prayed and worked for better times, and (*c*) bore testimony of Jesus. Of such people, there might be some who had never heard the name of Philadelphia, and still less of their own association.

Amidst much negligible matter, including casual tales of wonder current at the period, the *Transactions of the Philadelphian Society* contained certain tracts in the form of letters, under the pseudonym of Aletheus, the author being impossible to identify. Aletheus appears as the instructor of one Crito in matters appertaining to the deeper aspects of religious belief, and in the course of his expositions he mentions (*a*) communications established by him with the Hierophants of a certain Secret Temple; (*b*) the knowledge reserved therein to the High Priest, who dwelt in the midst of them; (*c*) being invisible so far as strangers were concerned; though (*d*) he walked manifestly with the *mystæ* and gave them light on all deep and sublime truths. The Temple was 'hidden from the world and impossible to discover'; indeed, the terms in which it is described are substantially and almost literally identical with the claim concerning the House of the Holy Spirit in the Rosicrucian *Fama Fraternitatis*—as regards, I mean, the alleged facts of both. Those who remember the discovery of the Vault where were interred the remains of Brother Christian Rosy Cross, may compare it with the alternative description as follows:—'The fabric is circular, supported by seven pillars, as of massy gold; in the midst of the Temple is a throne ascended by six steps; it is continually filled with the glory of a great king and priest. Around this priestly throne are twenty-four arch-priests or royal presbyters, bearing the sacred *Mishpat* on their breats and called the Sovereign Order of the *Hierophantæ*, of the line of Melchizedek; also a numerous company of subordinate priests perpetually ministering in their courses, clothed in white and crowned with gold crowns, who cease not to worship Him Who lives in their midst. Daily some priests are admitted to the Temple, but there are also certain solemn seasons and convocations when there are particular calls of those who are to be initiated and anointed into this priesthood. There are also priestesses as well as priests, the disparity between male and female ceasing as they come to bathe themselves in a certain miraculous fountain which runs from under the threshold of the Temple.'

So far as this description has proceeded, I must leave my readers to determine whether it should be interpreted in any literal manner, as of a temple built with hands on the plane of space and time, or whether it is to be treated as we should understand the Apocalypse of St John the Divine, with the style of which it may be said, I think, not to compare unreasonably. If they decide in the former sense, they must deal as they choose with the inevitable suggestion that the canonical text will suffer the same treatment; but if in the latter, it will be for them to determine how we shall regard the testimony of Aletheus when he says that he was promised the visible sight of the priest and king invisible, if he confessed to the doctrine of the Hierophants.

The explanation may be that these doctrines were married to a practice by which the prepared novices could be intromitted to a spiritual state, in which such experiences were vouchsafed. It is otherwise made apparent that 'natural dissolution' is the path to permanent integration in the Temple. It is therefore to all intents and purposes a Celestial Church; its members are of 'all languages, nations and tribes of religion'; its priests lay aside their earthly names; St John of the Cross and Jacob Boehme are mentioned among its members. These, and those who are with them, 'having put on their priestly bodies,' persevere in their former qualities of ministration, awaiting the great 'day of the manifestation of the Temple'. Aletheus, in fine, states that 'there are also some subordinate priests, known to me, waiting without the veil'—that is to say, in this manifest life—who have 'liberty of access by the High Priest granted them at certain seasons'— much after the manner of Rabbi Simeon, the light of the Hidden Law in Israel.

It will be seen that the testimony of the *Transactions* differs from that in the tract on the *State of the Philadelphian Society*, the first being concerned with a spiritually located Church, occupying a place in the same way that heaven is supposed to pass into experience, under the terms of localisation in transcendence; while the second mentions only a union in the spirit of all believers scattered through the whole world. It seems obvious that if the latter represented the entire compass of the hypothesis, it would not be worth discussing as there is no question at issue concerning it. To sum up, therefore, in respect of the alternative testimony, it is quite clear that Aletheus means us to understand that he communicated in the flesh with the Hierophants of his Secret Temple, with whom he had long debates; in particular, he received from them a very full explanation concerning the twelve foundation-stones of the Holy City, which, indeed, is the subject at large of his first letter, and the result—also at large—of the debate mentioned. It is difficult to detach the account from the idea of a secret sodality or company of wise men, bound together by a knowledge in common and by transcendental experience, also held in common.

We have now dealt with the record concerning the Secret Church, as this was understood by the Philadelphian Society, and as it entered into record in the *Transactions* which were, so to speak its official organ. The first message addressed to the Society by Jane Lead antedates the *Transactions* by a year, but in order to understand the intimations contained therein and in the sequels, we must go back a considerable distance in her literary history, or to the year 1683, when she published the *Revelation of Revelations*. This work was addressed to the living stones, wheresoever hidden and dispersed, who are elected in God for the New Jerusalem and to be fitly compacted together into a glorious Church of Mount Zion. These living stones are described as persons who have come out of the throng and encumbrance of worldly multiplicity and who have left the rational sense. They are a scattered flock, who shift their pastures continually and can yet find no place of rest until the day of resurrection. The book is written on the assumption that this day is already dawning faintly, the morning star being discernible behind the eastern clouds, from which it is inferred that the Lord is about to restore the kingdom in His saints. His reign will not be immediately universal, as if by an appearance at once and everywhere, but will come about by a gradual preparation. The elect, regarded as stones, are otherwise described as at present lying among the rubbish of confusion; but after what manner they are to be linked together into a strong city of defence may perhaps be understood better in the light of an intimation received by the seeress in one of her visions, when she was told that the city was in process of formation within herself. That which applied in her case obtained presumably for everyone who was designed to form part of the building.[1] The counsel accordingly is that none shall look afar off, 'or run out from themselves and neglect their own vintage at home, but regard how near the grape is to ripeness which contains the wine that is to be drunk at the Marriage-Supper of the Lamb.' I should mention here, though it will be obvious otherwise to the reader, that a bizarre confusion of images is one prevailing defect of the writer; fortunately, it does not interfere seriously with the understanding of her meaning. It is said also that if we would know the nearness of the Kingdom, we must not look outside us but in the unsealed Book of Life within us. Another counsel is: 'Learn to live God, and God shall live thee.' The state herein depicted is compared to a hypostatic union. Temple or city, it again follows that the building is in the heart, and that the Christ Whose advent is expected will first come to those who travail to bring Him forth spiritually, although at the period of His declared reign, its manifestation will be in the renewed centre of Nature.

These labourers in the vineyard, or whichever of the mixed similitudes we may choose to select, are described as an everlasting priesthood of Christ, a kingdom of priests elected

[1] Compare the medieval hymn of St Hildebert, entitled *Extra Portam*. I think that he also must have been conscious in his own day that living 'stones' were the foundation of the Mystic City:

> *Quantum tui gratulentur,*
> *Quam Festive conviventur!*
> *Quis affectus eos stringat,*
> *Et quæ gemma muros pingat,*
> *Quis chalcedon, quis jacintus,*
> *Norunt isti qui sunt intus.*

and set apart, being drawn from their consecrated tabernacles for minstration to the mighty Jehovah. The entrance into this priesthood is in virtue of a special ordination, and its result is permanent fixation within the Temple-Body of the Holy Ghost. There is a long description of the Heavenly Tabernacle in which this priesthood abides; but, notwithstanding the use of these words, it is no formal temple and contains no altar; God in His virtual power, light and purity fills the priestly company. There are degrees recognised in the fellowship, and they are analogous to the grades of ministration in the external church. There, it will be remembered, are (1) Deacons, (2) Priests, (3) Bishops, or in the terminology of Dionysius (1) Leitourgoi, (2) Presbyters, (3) the Divine Rank of the Hierarchs; the first or lowest rank consisting of those who have not passed beyond the ministration of the Son and are still conscious of sin; the second of those who have been separated by the fact of ordination and are set apart for God's sanctuary. The third grade of the priesthood seems to be formed of authorised leaders and teachers, actively concerned in the restoration of man to an estate which preceded this present visible creation. Their work is to make intercession, to atone, to sacrifice. Being themselves in a sinless condition, they have also the power of absolution. For the rest, they have experienced translation like Enoch, and are designed for the company of God. Apparently they have passed beyond the dispensation of the Divine Son, and for them is God all in all. It is obvious that, except in those cases where the Tabernacle has been built within the individual, and subject to one qualification which will be made shortly, this Church or company of the elect may be only a vision of things expected in the future, and would not in such case correspond either with the testimony of Aletheus as to things heard and seen, or with that of Eckartshausen and Lopukhin. The later messages of Jane Lead take up the previous story. The new Temple is now in course of building; it is that of the Holy Ghost; but it is in the wilderness, or alternatively in the womb of the Morning Sun. The seven angels from before the Throne are going forth to all parts of the earth, calling into the House of Wisdom those who will come under her discipline. The manifestation of Christ in the heavens is delayed till the Temple is completed. The communications are not unnaturally full of contradictory statements; the Church which I have just described as in course of building is said a little later on to be as yet unborn; the birth of it will be by means of virgin spirits joined in perfect unity and 'working in the power of Jehovah to bring forth the man-child from whom shall proceed subsequently an innumerable host of the redeemed.' These spirits will apparently be two personalities at the beginning, corresponding to the original Adam and Eve. It would seem further that these two will be one in the mystical sense, for at another stage it is said that a virgin shall bring forth and will herself become the 'spirit and temple-glory of the Lamb of God.' All this notwithstanding, it is certified that Christ in each age has gathered to Himself some who were perfected as the foundation and beginning of this Blessed Church; of these He has taken care, both before and after death, so that they may be completed and joined to Himself. It is difficult to draw anything satisfactory out of such reveries, but probably Jane Lead is trying to suggest that in one sense there has always been an Invisible Church of the elect, but that, as a result of the spiritual quickenings in the midst of which she and others of her period were dwelling, this Church might be expected to enter shortly into a new and wider phase, and that it was likely also to become manifest.

The last witness is Robert Roach in the *Imperial Standard of Messiah Triumphant*. He has no tales of wonder concerning strange metings with adepts, who, on the taking of certain pledges or by the subscription to certain articles of belief, can reveal the Lord of Glory, dwelling with them in a Temple, *non manu factum* or otherwise, and yet he goes much further than what may be called the Advertisement or Prospectus of the Philadelphian Society. It is possible to reduce what he says into a moderate compass, as he writes with considerable clearness. We have to remember that he had seen the rise of the Society; that he had seen also its dissolution; that at the appearance of his book, Jane Lead and John Pordage were both, I believe, among the faithful departed; that he was himself of mature age; and that he is likely to have survived the common kinds of extravagance and illusion. His report is as follows:—

(1) The body of the Christian religion relates to the outward part, and may be termed the history of Christ in the flesh. (2) The soul or spirit of religion is the whole process of Christ

translated and transacted within us, or the life of the Master in Palestine enacted in the soul. (3) The outward part is history and that which is inward is mystery. (4) The object of the gospel is the formation of Christ in the soul of each individual believer. (5) Besides 'the outward and visible church or churches, in their several outward forms and professions, there is scattered through the Christian world an Invisible Church, in her wilderness state, there fed with manna and possessing in privacy the Living Powers of God, and worshipping Him as in an Inner Court, in spirit and in truth.' (6) Some of this company are disjoined from all official forms; some take St Paul as their pattern and, becoming all things to all men, may apparently be living under monastic vocation; though they are 'reserving themselves chiefly for the worship of God in His own way in the secret temple of their hearts.' (7) In common with all other who are united vitally in Christ, albeit under various external forms and professions, these will come forth at the advent of Christ, to the amazement and confusion of nominal Christendom. (8) There shall be then a general submission of all kingdoms to their rightful Sovereign; there shall be a communication between the Church Triumphant in heaven and that Church which will have attained victory on earth; God also will abide with men. (9) There will be a visible and personal appearance of Christ in the restored Paradise of regenerated Nature. (10) The rise of this kingdom will be gradual, and at first among chosen and prepared instruments. (11) There is already 'a liberty of spiritual union to children of the Bride-chamber', being those who, by an extraordinary gift of the Holy Spirit, 'are taken into a degree of participation of His eternal act of love in the true and real marriage of the Lamb.' (12) Those who are thus united to God by His Spirit are united also to one another in the same Spirit, according to a true communion of saints; they are 'priests of the Inward Court, Adepts of the White Stone or Secret Pearl of Union, one in Christ, joined in the risen life, according to the resurrection of the inward man, though subject in their lower degrees to infirmities and defects.' They contribute as such to the regeneration of souls, communicating their own spiritual life.

Such are the twelve stones of this mystic city and temple; but it will be seen that for Robert Roach (*a*) the Second Advent was more than a spiritual return; (*b*) that what he terms the Inward Court, by a certain confusion of expression, is identical with the Holy of Holies, according to Lopukhin; and (*c*) is not wanting in harmony with Eckartshausen's chair of transcendental theology. But, at the same time, it would be difficult to say whether it attains a fuller or more defined state of presentation than is implied in the prevailing conception regarding believers who, remote as they may be in their personalities, are united in spirit and in truth, looking for the coming of the kingdom. If it were possible to follow Roach much further than I purpose here to do, and to consider his attempted developments of the spiritual mystery of sex, its union and fruition in Christ, we should find that, in virtue thereof, there are strange marriages possible *ex hypothesi*, but again they do not actually carry us much further, because it is not suggested that the state is reached except by those who have entered into mystical bonds within the measures of the personality. It is obvious, in conclusion, that, with much greater gifts in respect of force and clearness, the author of the *Imperial Standard* is a reflection of Jane Lead.

Our next task is the collation of the whole testimony, and it is unavoidable that at this point there should be a certain air of repetition. A continual and manifest communication between the Inner and Outer Church through the intervention of authorised messengers is postulated by Lopukhin. That which is external is 'infinitely necessary' as a means of entrance into that which is within, and that which is within is as much on this earth of ours as that which is without. As the Church General of Christendom is subdivided into many communions and represented by multitudes of material temples, so the Invisible Church has various degrees and temples without number, which in this case are all built in the hearts of its members. Such being the connections between the two systems, after what manner is it meant that the spirit of the Inner Church has been withdrawn so that the Church Visible is in a state of separation? The reference can be only to a certain mode of consciousness in which those who attain it know the King whom they serve, as should be the case by the hypothesis with all believers, but it is not—owing to the spirit of the world. As we have seen, Lopukhin terms this higher mode of consciousness a centre, and it is indeed that centre from which it is said that a Master Mason cannot err.

There the Kingdom of God manifests and nothing unclean can enter; there is 'the interior, supernatural and celestial life'. It is attained by a gift of the Spirit of Jesus Christ, and this gift is rebirth. For Eckhartshausen, in like manner, the path to the height or the centre lies through the External Church, but if that which is within is in a state of separation therefrom, it is still the ruling head. It can only be described as consisting of those who have attained the higher consciousness in Christ. The two witnesses in chief are hereby harmonised. The testimony of Aletheus comes to the same thing, except that his Secret Temple is more expressly 'built in the unapparent', because, albeit those who can attain a certain sanctified mode of consciousness in this life have so far the liberties of the Temple that they can go in and out, to be taught of the Christ-Spirit; all permanent integration therein will be after the death of the body. I suppose that the later witnesses would have said likewise, had the point come into their minds. Amidst the confusions of Jane Lead, one thing that stands forth clearly is that she beheld in her visions the same Holy of Holies of which we hear in Lopukhin, and she recognised, like him, that teachers came forth therefrom. Robert Roach is so much in consonance with the rest that there is no need to summarise him a second time. There is variety enough over the details but there is unity at the heart of all. Is it possible on the basis of their agreement to carry our understanding of the claim some few steps further?

If the question of the existence of a Secret Church behind the great pageant of ceremonial and official procedure in official religion had originated as have most claims regarding secret association, it would be easy to dismiss, as one dismissed without difficulty the claims of occult science, of which it is always a part. This would not be in virtue of simple prejudice, for the reasons which might be advanced by a mere sceptic, or for any consideration put forward on grounds of physical science. One is perfectly aware that behind the false-seeming of occult claims there is the root-fact of psychic manifestations, and that these are in rough correspondence with the divisions of occult science. Psychic prevision, clairvoyance with the multitudinous analogies and derivatives of these, can account for all that is veridic in astrology and the whole circle of artificial divinations. Auto-hypnosis, complicated by the exteriorisation of the astral body so-called, and by the phenomena of thought-forms, is the explanation at large of all magical evocations, and the catalogue could be continued henceforward through many pages. It is on the basis of these phenomena that the claim of occultism has risen up, and this is to be judged by its history through the centuries. We know on these warrants that it is a false claim, which has been maintained by every device of imposture. If, therefore, any person representing a link in that golden chain of chicanery which began with Pharaoh's magicians, or wherever one may like to start it, and is continued without any sign of completion in America at this day, should have come forward and have said that there is a Church behind the Church, we should have proceeded on our path of devotion as those who do not hear. But it so happens that the testimony has come to us from far different quarters, and the first suggestion concerning it will awaken in the Christian mystic some things which before may have been outside his consciousness, while it will present many memories of old things as if in another light. Those who have been students of the Secret Tradition in Christian and anterior times, and who possibly regard the fact of the Tradition as explicable only on the hypothesis of secret schools perpetuated from an immemorial period, may be disposed to decide out of hand that it is an old thesis, and, indeed, their own thesis, presented in another form of language. We have, however, to remember that the sodalities of the present and the past, which may be regarded as custodians of such tradition, are not only recruited by initiation but are largely existent for recruiting purposes. Their ceremonials are those of initiation and advancement, *plus* any devotional and sacramental rites which may exist otherwise among them. In the ranks of those which are concerned with realisation in God, there may be some who have attained that state among them, and this, indeed, is the hypothesis of the whole subject, for if the Secret Tradition were only a dream of God, it might indeed be beautiful and moving, but it would still be a path of reverie, whereas it comes before us in the guise of a path of certitude. The Secret Church is, however, a state of attainment, and it is such only, though, according to Lopukhin and others, there are degrees in the state. The Invisible Church, as such, can have no ceremonials corresponding to the Instituted Mysteries, and as, by the evidence concerning it, there is neither a house built with hands nor any formal assembly to be understood thereby, it is not possible that it should have ceremonies at all. It is a brotherhood established under a common realisation in consciousness. Unless the members are brought together in the flesh, it is not suggested that they know one another, otherwise than in a mystic state of co-consciousness, which does perhaps seem to be postulated, for it is certain that there are meetings in the Holy Assembly. They are otherwise friends in God, and when they meet in the flesh, it is said that they recognise one another, as Englishman recognises Englishman, all the wide world over.

This is how I have understood the matter, but one natural and unpremeditated comparison is liable to promote a second, and, as we are dealing with a problem of consciousness, it may be that an approximate illustration of the state is to be sought in that quality of inward being which is defined as the nature of the poet. There is no question here whether the gift passes or not into expression; it is at least an inalienable endowment, which, as such, is a state of consciousness. It cannot be communicated to those who do not possess it, but it can be awakened in those in whom it lies latent. They who have the gift will recognise each other up to a certain point whensoever they shall meet, and up to this point they share a consciousness in common. They are not otherwise united, nor is their consciousness interfused, though we may remember in this connection that wise pleasantry of the Greeks, according to which all poets and poetic souls gather together on Parnassus, the mystical Mount of the Muses, which—in the Greek worship of Ideal Beauty—was an equivalent to Mount Zion, 'where the souls of just men made perfect meet'. The question is whether we can give a satisfactory definition of the quality, and I do not know that this has been done, though I am certain that the attempts are many. It is the state in which a 'light that never was on land or sea' abides in the soul, so that sea and land are beheld in that light. I speak as one who has dwelt in this Arcady, even if I am sure that the essence of my subject has escaped in the present attempt to define. But I want to consider whether the nearness between persons who have entered into the higher consciousness, or Kingdom in the centre of Lopukhin, is like unto that between poets, as to their state and not their personality,—so that their union is really in a common centre of both—or whether it is more intimate. There is very little to help among the memorials of mystics in the West, for the possibility of unions in consciousmess is not within their horizon. The consensus of sanctity among Latins understood the state of beatitude in Divine Vision, and the communion of the blessed therein would be in respect of the common centre—as it is in the case of poets, with due regard to the distinct aspects of the centre. Eckhart may be held to have exceeded this, but it is not certain, because his language wavers. The testimony of the *Divine Cloud* leaves the question open, at least, in my view. Jane Lead and her school had no notion on the subject. It is very difficult to speak of Lopukhin and Eckartshausen in this connection, though I have suggested a state of co-consciousness as perhaps implied by their testimony. If it be this, then the experience at first hand which one is disposed to assume concerning them did not—as perhaps it could not—pass into adequate intellectual expression. Hence Eckartshausen and to some extent his successor while dissuading readers from supposing that the Secret Church was an instituted assembly, use language which suggests that it is. Their centre is in every man, and so is the mystic Kingdom—City or Church or Temple. Their rebirth is the awakening therein, and I do not see how this can be regarded otherwise than as an awakening at a common centre, which centre is also Christ.

The translation of such an experience into the terms of intellect is so beset with difficulties that at the highest it is inadequate and contradictory, while at the lowest the result is sometimes an outrage on the understanding—shall I say?—even of the man in the streets. The explanation is easy; our normal consciousness within the sphere of the senses can only postulate all that it reflects upon as manifested within time and space. By training in the life of thought, we may descry the possibility that these modes are limitations, from which consciousness can look to be liberated outside the life of sense. In support of this view there is no subtlety of the material mind which can help us to conceive of consciousness as itself dimensional. Yet when we try to realise the state of pure being apart from space and time, the mind is baffled, and the most that can be done seems a species of intellectual jugglery. It may be that in seeking to escape from illusions, understood as phenomena, we are entering into another illusion. In any case, those who would attain some shadow of this speculative mode must set aside all excognition and even pure thought itself; if in the emptying of the mind they can reach a state of simple consciousness, an abiding in their own being, there may follow such a realisation as the activity of the reasoning faculty will never communicate. If we postulate that in this state, as the consequence of all external and all inward preparation made antecedently, corresponding to the life of sanctity, the consciousness becomes awakened in Christ, we have the key at once to much that is put forward by Lopukhin and Eckartshausen, whether their use of the word *ecclesia* can be tolerated or not. It follows that the spirit of man is itself the Secret Church, and as it is a question of realisation there can be no other conclusion, seeing that realisation is absolute within its own measures. This is another aspect of the great thesis that all great things are within, meaning within consciousness. And this absolute realisation is shared in common with all who enter therein. It is not identity but union, and that union is at the centre. Herein is the glory of God in the highest and peace on earth to those who have proceeded so far that they contain within them the capacity of becoming peace.

In conclusion, therefore, respecting a Hidden Assembly of sanctity and adeptship corresponding to the idea of a Church behind the Church, the testimony of Eckartshausen and Lopukhin indicates a state of attainment in consciousness by which a multitude of individuals have attained realisation in Christ, so that it can be said, as St Paul said of himself, that their life is hidden with Christ in God, and that in this state there is such an interchange between them as is shadowed forth by the doctrine concerning the communion of saints. The testimony says further that they come out from the centre for the Divine Work in the world. In the case of those who are still in the flesh, and are not therefore permanently integrated at the centre, they are obviously with us and of us. Those who are no longer in the world may come forth too—God knoweth. They may constitute no instituted assembly, no corporate body, but they are here in space and time, carrying the Sanctuary in their hearts. And seeing that we can trace, too vaguely, indeed, for the white heat of our yearning, yet not all inadequately, the presence of certain masters through all the centuries of Christendom, I conclude, on the faith of the testimonies, that those are with us who have seen the presence of the Leader of Salvation for all the peoples of the West. It is like saying that there is a Sanctuary in time even as there is an attainment in state, because these are the men of the Sanctuary, who are here that they may draw others within. Speaking as a pilgrim on the quest, I look with all my heart to that day in a due season, which shall be God's most holy time, when the Cloud upon that Sanctuary shall be lifted in my respect, so that I may see the King in his beauty and the most holy choir which He has drawn within the circle of His attainment. Like the others, I shall then know, in the fulness of conscious realisation, after what manner my Redeemer liveth, and perchance in that company of the blessed may salute my peers and co-heirs who once in time and somewhere in the world here were Karl von Eckartshausen and the author of *Some Characteristics of the Interior Church*.

18
THE VIATICUM OF DAILY LIFE ON THE WAY OF THE HOMEWARD QUEST

[Unpublished typescript, c.1910]

This was a private ritual devised by Waite for the use of himself, Frater Ex Dono (Michael Oswe Illingworth), and Soror Vigilate (Mrs Helen Rand). Illingworth lived in Derbyshire and evidently came to London only on rare occasions; the rite is consequently designed to be worked alone if necessary, the other two participants being present in spirit. It is doubtful that the rite was used frequently—if at all—for Illingworth was not active in the Order and did not carry on into the Fellowship of the Rosy Cross that Waite formed in 1915. The ritual does, however, serve to demonstrate Waite's perception of himself as a priest.

This little Ceremony of Divine Love and one mode of refreshment therein is the gift of Frater Sacramentum Regis to Frater Ex Dono, for his consolation in exile.

Ordo Sanctissima Rosae Rubeae et Aureae Crucis

Viaticum

The following simple Ceremonial Observance, intended as a provision for some who have undertaken the great journey has no official authority in respect of the Order. It has been prepared for the private use in Temple and otherwise of the Frater Sacramentum Regis, Frater Ex Dono and Soror Vigilate. Of these three, there is no one especially designated to act as priest, and when they are at a distance one from another, they may agree upon any day and hour when each of them shall perform the Ceremony, officiating as priest unto him or herself and realising the immediate presence of the other two. It is believed in this way a perfect act of inward spiritual communion with the preservation of some outward signs may be attained. Any private room will answer for the purpose of retirement and any vessels to contain the Bread and Wine. The white robe need not be worn in such cases, but a Rose-Cross or Cross of gold should preserve the link with the Order. When used in Temple, the door of the vault is closed and the Pastos remains inside, but the circular Altar is placed in the centre of the Temple as in the Ceremony of Corpus Christi. The Cup of Wine and the Paten of Bread over it are placed on the Altar. Each member assumes the white robe and Rose-Cross of the 5=6 Grade. Their chairs are set to the East of the Altar but facing West for the seat of the priest and to the West of the Altar but facing East for the other members. When all is ready they sit down in silence.

Priest: The Little Office of the Most Holy and Blessed Sacrament of Union, that we, being joined to the Divine, may be one spirit therein.

A pause

Priest: For a space of recollection in the heart, let us dwell upon the mystery of daily growth in the grace of purified life.

This being ended the Priest rises with clasped hands and says:

Priest: O Lord, I am not worthy that Thou shouldst enter under my roof: but speak the word only and my soul shall be healed.

He approaches the Altar and still faces Westward.

Priest: I beseech you, my brethren, to put away the thoughts of earth and to cast out all its images.

They kneel down and a short pause follows. They have put away the thought of material things. They remain kneeling.

Priest: I beseech you, my Brethren to put away activity of mind and the work of thought therein.

Another pause follows. They have put away the images of mind.

Priest: He shewed me a pure river, which is water of Life. The words of the Lord are pure and pure is all His commandment. Restore unto us a clean heart and renew Thy spirit within us.

They rise up and are seated excepting the Priest. He is still at the Altar looking Westward.

Priest: Being emptied of our own selves, do Thou in Thy good pleasure replenish us.

He takes the Paten in his hands.

Priest: I will make a peace offering, an oblation, that God may be with us.

He raises the Paten a little from the Chalice.

Priest: They said one to another: it is manna. Give unto us, O Lord, to eat of Thy Hidden Manna.

He places the Paten on the Altar.

Priest: Satisfy us with Thy Divine Food.

He extends his hands over the Paten.

Priest: Take up our bread and bless it. On thy part as a minister at need, in the sense of Thy service and the grace of Thy Holy Sacraments, consecrate this creature of earthly matter that it may become unto us a sign of the meat that does not perish, the manna of grace and the bread of angels—+ —. May this be our portion in Thee.

He extends his Hands over the Chalice.

Priest: A vineyard of new wine and the wine is sweet. Be Thou with us in the quickening of wine that we may know that our part is in Thee. The fulness of the wine-press is in Thee and the grapes of Lebanon swelling in the glow of the South. Furnish us out of Thy Wine-press. Come unto us in the Consciousness of the Spirit, which was with Thee, O Lord, in the beginning. The end is like the beginning. Grant that it may end in Thee. Take up our wine and bless it. On Thy part as a servant at the Altar of Thy servants, I consecrate this creature of earthly wine that it may become unto us a sign of the Waters of Life in Thee—+ —. Give unto us of that fountain: shew unto us its pure river.

He raises the Paten in his hands.

Priest: O Lord, give Thy bread to the hungry and Thy wine to those who are athirst. With the Bread of Understanding do Thou feed us.

Pause.

He communicates in the Element of bread and administers it to one of the Brethren saying:

Priest: Shew unto us Thy Great Mystery in the breaking of bread.

The Frater vel Soror who has received it in this manner takes the Paten from the Priest and administers the bread to the third of the Brethren, saying:

Frater vel Soror: Rain upon us the bread of Heaven

The Paten is replaced on the Altar by the last recipient. The Priest remains in his place; he uplifts the Chalice, and says:

Priest: The Chalice of Salvation, the Wine of Bliss, the communion of saints at the Centre. Bring us to the Union that is in Thee.

He administers the Chalice to one of the Brethren, saying:

Priest: May we know Him in the drinking of wine.

The Frater vel Soror who has received it in this manner takes the Chalice from the Priest and administers to the third of the Brethren saying:

Frater vel Soror: May the veils of separation divide that all spirits may know the oneness which is in God.

The last recipient administers the Chalice to the Priest, saying:

Frater vel Soror: In God I am thou, my Brother.

The Priest completes the libation, saying:

Priest: There is no separation henceforward: in Him I am He.

The Priest replaces the Chalice.

Priest: We have known Him in the breaking of bread, in the wine which shews forth our longing. My Brethren, let the sense of Divine Union be poured into our hearts.

The Brethren rest in contemplation, and thereafter:

Priest: The Peace of God which passeth understanding abide for ever in the hearts and minds of the faithful who have departed from the world and the ways thereof.

*Here ends the Little Office
of the Viaticum*